IT DOESN'T END WITH US

THE STORY OF THE *DAILY CARDINAL*

HOW A COLLEGE NEWSPAPER'S FIGHT FOR FREEDOM
CHANGED ITS UNIVERSITY, CHALLENGED JOURNALISM,
AND INFLUENCED HUNDREDS OF LIVES

ALLISON HANTSCHEL

FOREWORD BY RICHARD SCHICKEL

HERITAGE BOOKS
2007

HERITAGE BOOKS
AN IMPRINT OF HERITAGE BOOKS, INC.

Books, CDs, and more—Worldwide

For our listing of thousands of titles see our website
at
www.HeritageBooks.com

Published 2007 by
HERITAGE BOOKS, INC.
Publishing Division
65 East Main Street
Westminster, Maryland 21157-5026

Copyright © 2007 Allison Hantschel

Illustrations and photographs are the property of the *Daily Cardinal* Media Corporation, reprinted with permission from the *Daily Cardinal* Archives. Copyright © 2007 by the *Daily Cardinal* Media Corporation.

All rights reserved. No part of this book may be reproduced or transmitted in any form or by any means, electronic or mechanical, including photocopying, recording or by any information storage and retrieval system without written permission from the author, except for the inclusion of brief quotations in a review.

International Standard Book Number: 978-0-7884-4447-0

For the Shadow Cabinet

> If you came this way,
> Taking any route, starting from anywhere,
> At any time or at any season,
> It would always be the same: you would have to put off
> Sense and notion. You are not here to verify,
> Instruct yourself, or inform curiosity
> Or carry report. You are here to kneel
> Where prayer has been valid.
> — T.S. Eliot, *Four Quartets*

TABLE OF CONTENTS

Foreword	vii
Preface	xi
Acknowledgements	xiii
Introduction	xv
1. Beginnings	1
2. The Cardinal and Its Campus	7
3. Freedom and Fairness	13
4. Frat Boys and Jewish Kids	19
5. We Are At War	29
6. Prosperity, Generosity, Challenges	39
7. Upheaval	51
8. Breakdown	61
9. Bombing	95
10. Revolutionaries	109
11. Competitors	123
12. Typographical Error	139
13. Shutdown	149
14. Cardinal Journalism	167
15. Distinguished Graduates	183
16. Life Lessons	193
17. The Cost	201
18. What's Next	209
Afterword	217
Appendix: Notable Alumni	219

Foreword: Hell-For-Leather Idealism

"The prattlings of boy journalists." Thus spoke Alfred Lunt upon receiving a bad notice from the *Daily Cardinal*'s reviewer when he and his wife, Lynn Fontanne, brought one of their brittle "sophisticated" comedies to Madison sometime during the post-war years. Lunt was a Wisconsin native and he and his wife had a sort of imitation English country house in Genesee Depot, where the likes of Noel Coward and Helen Hayes often visited (it is now an interestingly restored tourist attraction), so he was not expecting a snotty notice from a source so close to home. Indeed, the Lunts rarely got bad notices anywhere, so besotted were critics and the public with their comic-romantic badinage.

Their kind of theater — the prattling of tired hams you might call it — is no more, which is a good thing, and its reception by the *Cardinal*'s reviewer was probably a good thing, too. Culturally, no less than politically, we felt compelled to dissent—or at least to be impolite—to all the official enthusiasms of public life. Among my entirely self-imposed duties when I worked on the paper, was drama criticism. I remember giving a supercilious review to Katherine Cornell, another of Broadway's great unexamined premises, when she brought her production of Somerset Maugham's *The Constant Wife* to the Union Theater sometime in the early 1950s.

Worse, I was always giving dubious notices to the Wisconsin Players, which in retrospect seems to me quite unfair. I should have had more of a fellow feeling for them, in that many of the Players, like us at the *Cardinal*, were attempting to hone their skills at one of the few campus institutions that offered something like practical, nearly professional, experience in a demanding occupation (the football team was another such institution and we were not especially kind to it, either).

Obviously, this premature cantankerousness worked out just fine for me, in that I did go on to become a critic and even gained a certain national prominence in that peculiar occupation. On the other hand, I pray that *my* boyish prattlings are safely buried in the crumbling *Cardinal* archives. I'm utterly certain that if I read one of those effusions today it would make my ears burn. At its pretentiousness. At its lack of knowledgeable grounding. At the sheer effrontery of the thing.

If I have a modest quarrel with Allison Hantschel's excellent history of the *Daily Cardinal*, it is that it does not quite acknowledge the patience — better make that the simmering, but usually controlled impatience — with which some perfectly decent elements of the community we were supposed to be serving bore our wise guytaunts and misunderstandings. They put up with a lot from us — those ridiculous reviews of mine, our air of superiority to a lot of stuff that many of our readers took seriously, whether it was intramural softball or student government. We were, on the whole, much more opinion- mongers than we were reporters of ordinary campus life, much more in thrall to our self-impor-

FOREWORD

tance than we were to the idea of "Complete Campus Coverage," which was, as I recall, one of our stated goals.

On the other hand, I'm still proud of our opposition to Joe McCarthy and his ilk during my era on the paper. I don't know what good we did in that fight, but at least we stood at the side of what was best in American journalism (the *New York Times*, the *Washington Post*, the *Milwaukee Journal*) when much of the press was hiding behind the pretense of "objectivity" in its coverage of McCarthyism. In fact, we stood at the side of what is best in the American spirit in those days. Or any days.

Looking back with such perspective as — ye gods — a half-century provides, I can see that we boy (and girl) journalists had little choice when it came to striking the poses of dissidence. To begin with, we were kids and balance, judiciousness, is rarely natural to the under-aged. Beyond that, as acolytes to journalism we inevitably had to speak for all sorts of minorities, because it was a minority we hoped to join. Journalism is not an elite profession; it is low-paying and very often despised both by the famous figures it covers and by the public at large. But it is a small and self-selecting group. By which I mean that a particular type of personality is drawn to journalism — to writing in general, individuals who have some mysterious need to define themselves by the controversies into which they happily insert themselves. but who don't necessarily want to make public displays of themselves when so doing.

Doubtless there's something profoundly wrong with us, but so be it. And thank God there's journalism to absorb our bumptiousness. Or, to put it another way, offer us malcontents a place to make a fuss, to do a little sneaky preening. All newsrooms roil with contempt for management, no book writer thinks his publisher knows what he's doing, and all of us who constitute America's writerly minority distrust our society's received wisdom. We require, many of us, something — some person or institution — that, at a tender age, safely permits us to focus our dismay, exercise our contempt and sharpen our cynicism about the status quo.

The ever-embattled *Cardinal* was such a place. Yes, you could learn to write coherently against a deadline there. But much more significantly it allowed you to externalize your natural impulse to distrust institutions and their blow-hard apologists, to harden inchoate suspicion into lifelong skepticism about whatever official view is being bandied about.

Like all *Cardinal*ites, before and since, we were young and enthusiastic romantics, all rosy-eyed and hot-blooded about journalistic ideals. We would argue late into the night about the ethics of taking a job at Time Inc. (The consensus was no, no, a thousand times no.) Or about hitching on with something like *The New Republic* or *The Nation*, which we read with innocent avidity. (Yes, but with some dubious asterisks.) Or about qualifying for the good, gray *New York Times* and boring from within to enliven it (OK, but geez — little us, apparently impregnable them). Opportunities — or so we imagined — were everywhere. Threats — to our precious "integrity" — were equally widespread.

FOREWORD

Soon enough reality would intervene. Inevitably there would be families to support, compromises to be made, the virtue of discretion to be reluctantly embraced. For now, though, it was enough simply to outrage our readers on a fairly regular basis. And since we didn't know enough to know what we didn't know, we sailed blithely along on the notion that we were somehow smarter than everyone else. We were lucky — as the *Cardinal* was throughout its history — to be functioning at what was — what doubtless still is — one of the two or three most liberal large universities in the country, a place that took its obligations to free speech and academic freedom very seriously. We might question this or that university policy fiercely, and its administrators might do what they could to soften our views, but they never questioned our right to be wearisome pests.

The *Cardinal*'s staff has for over a century fought for its independence and you have to give it enormous credit for its gumption in a wide variety of contexts and crises. But still I doubt that it would have survived in its traditional anti-establishment form at any other institution of higher learning. The proof of that statement lies in the indisputable fact that no other campus newspaper can claim its unique and quite unbroken history of dissidence.

There is, frankly, one part of that history that I deplore — the *Cardinal's* behavior during the radicalized 1960s and 1970s. Hantschel's account of those years appalls me and, to a degree surprises me. I really did not know things got this bad. As long as the paper defended the right of self-styled revolutionaries to proclaim their views in print or from the soapbox it was acting well within its proud liberal tradition, though a larger measure of skepticism in its attitude might have been in order. It may well have been correct in challenging the University complicity in the creation of weaponry for the Pentagon. But in the matter of the infamous Sterling Hall bombing, which claimed the life of an innocent researcher, it was tragically wrong. Bombing is not a form of free speech. It is a form of terrorism. And the idea of a newspaper contributing to the defense fund of for one of the bombers sickens me. It does not quite cast a cloud over this book, and I think Hantschel handles the incident with admirable finesse, but still ...

Radical speech is one thing, radical action is another. And it is the obligation of a liberal publication to insist on the not-so-fine distinction between the two—no matter how hot its youthful blood is running. There is a point where the totalitarian impulses of the left becomes indistinguishable from those of the right, and you have to stand against both of them.

But enough of that. This book is, in its essence, a celebration of the *Daily Cardinal*'s good and often desperate fight to survive in the very odd political climate of a state in which a strong liberal tradition (prairie populist subset) has ever been in conflict with a particularly knot-headed Republican know-nothingism. At one end of State Street stands our noble alma mater, that great bastion of liberal tolerance and idealism. At the other end of it stands the state capitol, which, at least in my day, was brimming with people who instinctively hated everything the university stood for — and, not incidentally, controlled its

FOREWORD

budget. I imagine the university could often have done without our support, which must frequently have been inimical to its efforts to find workable compromises with the Yahoos up the street. But we were part of its identity, a good example of what it believed in, and so we were allowed our breathing room.

And our fun. Which we abundantly had. It was fun to be perpetually embattled. It was fun to neglect our classes in order to practice our obsessive devotion to the newspaper which, for many of us, was the greatest educational tool on offer on campus. We did learn to accept the often embarrassing consequences of our enthusiasms. And the pleasure of venting our anger at the many stupidities that surrounded us. Most important — certainly to me — was the very occasional, generally unpremeditated, pleasure of turning the odd phrase that nailed a good point firmly, with enough spunk that people might mention it to you the next morning in the Rathskeller.

Nearing the end of a long career in journalism, I don't think very often about my days at the *Cardinal.* I don't think much about anything I did in the past. I don't re-read my books. Or revisit the television documentaries I've written and directed and I'm always surprised when someone says complimentary things to me about something I wrote in the ever-lengthening past. In the end, if you're a real writer, you're always looking ahead — to the next piece, the next book, the next whatever, hoping always to achieve endlessly elusive perfection. And you're always writing for an audience of one — yourself — in full knowledge that whatever effect it has on anyone else is no more than a lucky (or unlucky) accident.

That said, this too must be said: Print journalism could use an influx of the kind of hell-for-leather idealism that has always animated the *Cardinal.* To take just one example, the press's supine behavior in the face of the Bush administration's phony rationales for the war in Iraq is a permanent shame on the profession. If that kind of lying (about some much less significant matter) had been emanating from Bascom Hall we would have been all over it — joyfully, sleeplessly, possibly, in this detail or that, erroneously.

Error, of course, is endemic in journalism. But embarrassing as it always is, fear of it is more so. So let us spare an indulgent, possibly even an admiring, thought for the *Cardinal* of our various youths — that self-important, self-indulgent, self-congratulating avatar of those doomed-to-disappointment journalistic dreams that have nevertheless shaped a large part of our best selves.

We needed it then. We need it now. And we will always need it.

— Richard Schickel
Author, Historian, Documentary Film Maker
Time Magazine Film Critic
Daily Cardinal Class of 1955

Preface: Notes On Sourcing

The first and best source for this story about the *Daily Cardinal* was, of course, the *Cardinal* itself. This book quotes extensively from *Cardinal* articles from 1892 to 2007, most especially from the paper's anniversary stories, in which most of the information about the *Cardinal's* earliest days was found. I reviewed more than 1,000 pages of microfilm records of the paper.

I have also made liberal use of the *Cardinal's* archives, which I organized while a student at the paper: letters, memos, notes from one editor to another, university records obtained by the *Cardinal*, and other detritus of 115 years of publishing. They are identified within the text.

The *Cardinal* alumni quoted in this book were interviewed beginning in 1999, when at the Daily Cardinal Alumni Association's alumni reunion, past *Cardinal* staff members were asked to contribute histories to the *Cardinal's* archive project. The majority of the interviews were conducted between 2005 and 2007, by phone, e-mail, letter and in person.

Madison's two major daily newspapers, the *Wisconsin State Journal* and the *Capital Times*, were also of immense help in recounting the *Cardinal's* story. Their stories are identified in the text and credited where appropriate.

The tales of the *Cardinal's* staff in the Introduction stem from a three-day visit I made to the *Cardinal* offices in March 2004.

Acknowledgments

My deepest thanks go out to all the *Daily Cardinal* alumni who consented to share their stories with me over the past ten years. It is not always easy to look back on the most difficult and joyous days of your life, but they did so, generously and without bitterness.

I am especially grateful to Richard Davis and Stan Zuckerman, who deserved far better from the *Cardinal* than they got.

The late Robert Taylor donated his papers to the *Cardinal's* archives, and his memos and records proved vital. His lengthy service to the *Cardinal* was selfless, and he is very much missed.

Emily Winter conducted the interviews for the shutdown chapter and reviewed the transcripts with me. Her compassionate, skilled reporting was invaluable. The *Daily Cardinal* staff, including Laura-Claire Corson and Christopher Guess, was helpful and welcoming in every way. Heritage Books supported this project and their staff shepherded it from half-finished story to what you see before you today.

Professor Owen V. Johnson at the University of Indiana generously provided me with sources for student press scholarship, without which I would not have been able to place the *Cardinal* in its proper context.

Jennifer Armstrong and Amy Filak were readers on key portions of this manuscript, and their encouragement shaped much of the later work. Jean Sue Johnson Libkind, Douglas Gomery, Dave Newman, Paige Fumo Fox, Steve Begley, Meghan Paton, Lois Dunn, Stacie Fehr, Ruth, and Antonia read endless versions of this book and were my best bounces for ideas. My family — Bernice, James, Barbara, Paul, Kristin, Mike, and Kathy — listened, supported, and loved.

This book is dedicated to the Shadow Cabinet, the shutdown staff of 1995:

Anthony T. Sansone, organizational and technical genius, who later became my husband, and whose belief in this book never wavered no matter what the bank account or the rejection notices said.

Vincent F. Filak, who settled the *Cardinal's* printing debt and shepherded it through those difficult first months of publication, and who remains my dear friend.

Jason Heiser and Mark Wegner, brilliant artist and courageous reporter, two of the best and kindest men I know.

Holly Shoemaker, who first showed me the Unorientation Issue, and Ben Spillman, who made us laugh during the worst of times.

Amy Zarlenga, who rescued William Wesley Young's first newspaper from behind a filing cabinet and gave it a place of honor on the wall.

Amy Eisenman, who stayed up all night sweeping floors and editing copy, who on the day of the *Cardinal's* comeback ran down University Avenue with me, turning cartwheels and shouting with joy in the early morning light.

I cannot thank them enough.

Introduction: The Slinky, the Smell and the System

"We are the people who have appointed themselves opinion leaders on this campus and it is our job to wade through the bullshit and lay the rest down on paper."
— Daily Cardinal editorial, 1986

ଔ

At the *Daily Cardinal*, the 115-year-old student newspaper of the University of Wisconsin-Madison, there is a system.

At about 4 p.m., Sunday through Thursday, after the paper's advertising staff leaves for the day and the business offices are closed, the editorial staff takes over the paper's small space. Reporters arrive, one by one, with notebooks and binders stuffed with information collected over the course of the day. They sort through press releases and fliers, notes from interviews, phone numbers. They sit down at computers and type, leaning close in to the screens. Some mutter to themselves. Some just stare at their work.

The editors read the stories during the writing and after, correcting errors of fact and advising on matters of style. They coax the reporters into rewriting a paragraph, a section, an entire story. They encourage, cajole, occasionally threaten.

Across the room, around a semi-circular desk, a crew of quiet young men and women sit. They read mock-ups of pages that will make up tomorrow's newspaper. One copy editor makes corrections, and passes it to the next, and so on down the line until it has been read by at least five people. When they are done, the page is marked with a black check and placed in a stack on the desk's end, ready for its final printing.

This has been the system, with remarkably little variation, at the *Daily Cardinal* since 1892. Since English major William Wesley Young founded the *Cardinal* as the sixth student daily paper in the nation, the *Cardinal* has worked

INTRODUCTION

more or less just like this: Reporters write, editors edit, and the paper goes to press. The next night it all begins again.

"You have got to be kidding me!"

At 9 p.m. on a recent Sunday, the *Cardinal's* system was under a bit of a strain.

A University of Wisconsin basketball star, who had been suspended after being accused of beating up a fellow student, was granted permission to rejoin the university's team. It was the kind of campus story on which the *Cardinal* thrived. Tomorrow's readers would want to know why the student had been given his team spot back, the status of his case, the reaction of his teammates to the developments. Copy Editor Michael Worringer held up the pages he had painstakingly designed several hours ago, pages that were now, as he put it, "total crap."

"Tell me what we're going to do now," he sighed, crumpling his work.

"We need to get this on the front page," Campus Editor Emily Winter said, waving the athletic department's fax at Worringer and making pretty-please face at him. "So can you ... can you ... make a new newspaper?"

Maureen Backman, who ran the *Cardinal's* city desk, sat with a phone receiver pressed to her left ear while she groped with her right hand for her beeping mobile phone, somewhere in her backpack.

"Jesus," she said, slamming down one phone and picking up the other. "My best writer has mono," she called out to Winter, interrupting Winter's argument with the copy desk. "Can you cover something at 10 a.m. tomorrow?"

"I have a date with my bed at that time," Winter replied. It would be her third straight day without sleep. "But if he has mono ..."

"Maybe he can go anyway," Backman muttered while furiously text-messaging someone on the mobile.

"Has he been to the doctor?" Winter asked.

"I hope so. I really need that story."

A rented velvet cape and vinyl crown lay in crumpled clear plastic bags on the floor. The *Cardinal's* sports staff was trying to get a group of the university's student athletes into costumes for a joke photo shoot. They considered Superman outfits, sports columnist Courtney Smith reported, but had come to a sticking point with the young sportsmen. Leotards.

Editor-in-Chief Evan Rytlewski pulled his ski cap on over his wild curly hair and announced that he was off to a nearby McDonald's. The fast-food restaurant had shorted him a dollar and 25 cents on a soda purchase. "I'm going back there," he declared, "and I'm getting some satisfaction."

And there was some kind of smell in the darkroom.

"Walk into my office," Photo Editor A.J. MacLean pleaded with his fellow student editors, "and then walk back out again, and tell me you don't smell something strange."

The *Daily Cardinal* is housed in a windowless basement room with poor ventilation and even poorer décor. The dirt is caked so thick on the floor from

INTRODUCTION

the slushy treads of students' boots that staffers' footfalls crunch. The desks are an arsonist's dream come true: paper scraps and stacks and bundles everywhere. While the computers at which the editors work are all in good repair, there is not a single chair in the place that is not broken.

There are Skittles on the floor. There is Silly Putty on the walls.

There is a Slinky in the ceiling.

"I torqued the Slinky," Rytlewski admitted, returning victorious from his McDonald's errand, the top of his hat dusted with snow. "There didn't seem to be anything I could do to 'un-torque' it, so we figured we'd use it for decoration."

The two dozen twentysomethings who run the *Cardinal* – including Worringer, Rytlewski, Backman and Winter – are there every night without fail, without pay, without supervision of any kind save that of one another. They are the smartest kids on campus: the ones who can recite the university presidents and their years in office backwards through the decades, who can argue over the rules of the Senate filibuster and joke about Jane Austen.

They are the most eccentric kids on campus, too: MacLean walks around with a hockey stick in the hand not holding his camera, and Sports Editor Josh Salm takes out frustrations by throwing a green tennis ball at the ceiling.

"I get the weirdest e-mail," Rytlewski said, motioning to Worringer. "Listen to this: 'I'm a student at UW-Madison. Attached is a poem I've written about women, with whom I've had lots of experience but little luck. Please consider publishing it in your newspaper.'"

"Is it any good?" Worringer asked.

Rytlewski rolled his eyes. "The subject of the e-mail was 'Fuck women.'"

Backman, overhearing them, yawned. "You should hear the Shakespearean soliloquy somebody left on my voice mail the other day. It was 13 minutes long."

"What was it about?" Worringer asked.

"Concealed carry laws," Backman replied. "What else?"

Every night they sit and talk word counts, whether stories should jump off the front page, if a photo is too big or a graphic is too small, in the pattering news jargon that turns "brief" into a verb and uses profanity as punctuation. They talk about what other local papers are doing, what they had for lunch, what they overheard at parties, and how they might turn all of it into stories. They talk and talk and talk, excited about the most mundane events: a speech, a burglary, a group of children flying kites.

Hearing that lineup for the next day's paper, Arts Editor Joe Uchill frowned. "What's going on with the cheese truck? Do we not like the cheese truck accident? Smell of burning cheese all over the highway?"

"I like life-affirming stories," Uchill said. "Like that priest arrested over the weekend for growing pot in the rectory. Stuff like that."

Of all the stories it has covered in its 115 years, it is the *Cardinal*'s own story that is perhaps the most life-affirming. The *Daily Cardinal* survived two staff strikes, a hostile takeover attempt, a printing press shutdown, a CIA probe, six

INTRODUCTION

offices, six dozen leaders, bombs, bullets, tear gas, and death threats. Between coverage of the Spanish American War and the second war in Iraq, between the rise of the counterculture movement and the fall of the Berlin Wall, it is easier to count the nights when nobody had to be bandaged or bailed out of jail than it is to count the nights when somebody did.

Through all those tumultuous times, the *Cardinal* never operated under faculty control. Its student editors were its only leaders; its student readers its only owners.

No university advisor taught its staff how to write stories. Its staffers taught each other. No university professor corrected students' mistakes. They corrected their own. No deep university pockets paid for the paper. It earned its own money through advertising, and — when times were tight — rescued itself from financial ruin.

Such independence and freedom is rare among college newspapers. Most of the more than 2,000 student newspapers in America submit to some form of review or oversight by their "parent" institutions, public and private. The *Minnesota Daily* receives $500,000 in student fees from the University of Minnesota. The *Daily Californian* leases its own name from the University of California-Berkeley.

For most of its 100-plus years of existence, the *Daily Emerald* was run by the University of Oregon's Publications Board, which oversaw every aspect of production. At Ball State University in Indiana, the journalism department provides 13 percent of the newspaper's funding and a faculty advisor oversees finances.

The *Cardinal's* freedom was hard-fought and hard-won. Politicians, shocked by the *Cardinal's* stance on student sex, denounced the paper on the floor of the state Senate. Radio hosts assailed the newspaper over the airwaves, accusing the *Cardinal* of harboring communists. Most damaging, advertisers mounted boycotts over editorials about everything from curtailing athletics to supporting anti-war violence.

In adversity and prosperity, the *Cardinal's* staff fended off these attacks. Their reliance on each other was the only assurance that the opportunities they enjoyed would be provided to students after them. Time and again, when faced with the *Cardinal's* "inevitable" demise, staffers looked at the newspaper in front of them and said, "This doesn't end with us."

This battle, this century-plus of fighting with checkbook and notebook, ensured that the only limitations any *Cardinal* staff member ever faced was the limitation of his or her own ability. That kind of environment made the *Cardinal* a journalistic powerhouse, a fertile training ground, and a place where young people learned — most for the first time in their lives — just how much strength they truly possessed.

That challenging milieu existed from the day of the *Cardinal's* founding, which was itself an act in defiance of reasoned skepticism. Tempted in 1888 by the promise of a "Course in English Literature and Journalism" in the univer-

INTRODUCTION

sity's catalogue, student William Wesley Young left his hometown of upstate Monroe and decided to study newspapering at the University of Wisconsin.

After arriving at Wisconsin, he regretted his decision. His first college choice, Cornell, had a daily student newspaper at which Young might have trained for his newsman's ambition. Wisconsin had no such paper. Nor did the university have a journalism department. Young was forced to cobble together courses from a dozen disciplines and design his own curriculum. Young felt this lack diminished his school's reputation, especially when compared to the schools of the East like Harvard and Yale. He determined to change that.

But when he asked the opinions of students and professors he trusted, "Does the University of Wisconsin need a daily student newspaper?" they all answered, "No."

Those early skeptics would be shocked at the state of journalism education on the Wisconsin campus today. Two daily student newspapers — the only two independent daily and directly competing papers in the nation — now make the university one of the most exciting places to practice newspaper reporting in the country. The *Daily Cardinal* — the organization those early university leaders deemed unnecessary — shaped the founding of the University of Wisconsin's School of Journalism itself, after a *Cardinal* founding editor returned to campus to teach the first journalism classes there.

Throughout the past century, the *Daily Cardinal* greatly influenced the university it covered. From chronicling security in student elections in the 1930s to decrying McCarthyism in the 1950s, from university corruption in the 1960s to diversity efforts in the 2000s, the *Cardinal's* reporters broke stories that steered the course of history at this institution.

Legendary football coach Harry Stuhldreher was thought to be untouchable in 1948. The former Notre Dame quarterback led a team of national-award-winning players and was worshiped by fans. Beneath the public adulation, discontent with Stuhldreher lurked. *Cardinal* reporter Bob Teague, who once played for Stuhldreher, published articles about the football team from the players' point of view, and *Cardinal* editor Mort Levine followed up with editorials calling for Stuhldreher's removal. After two months of unrelenting coverage criticizing the coach's competence, Stuhldreher resigned in disgrace.

When *Cardinal* reporter Jim Rowen wrote, in 1969, about secret research at the university which directly impacted the course of the Vietnam War, his revelations echoed across the country, inflaming an anti-war movement already engulfing college campuses.

His stories were accounts of greedy university regents using public money for personal gain, funnelling thousands of dollars in business into their banks and secretly backing military research. Profit Motive 101's tales of abuse of power became the shame of the campus. The year after Rowen's stories were published, a group of radical young men — some of them members of the *Cardinal* staff — bombed the building where the Army research took place, killing a university researcher.

INTRODUCTION

No university authority reviewed or authorized the publication of these types of stories. Many university officials would have liked to prevent them. *Cardinal* staffers, judging for themselves what kind of news coverage the campus warranted, pushed those topics to the fore.

The *Cardinal's* shadow stretches far beyond its university. Many of the nation's foremost journalists — the men and women whose reporting and commentary shape our most vital public discourse — received their training in the same windowless basement rooms in which *Cardinal* editors labor today.

CBS's Jeff Greenfield got his start at the *Daily Cardinal*, becoming the only editor in chief in the paper's history elected to two full consecutive terms. Legendary NBC broadcaster Edwin Newman was the paper's foremost news reporter. Nine Pulitzer Prize winners met some of their first deadlines at the *Cardinal*, including former Associated Press photographer Neal Ulevich, *Washington Post* foreign correspondent Anthony Shadid, and *Los Angeles Times* writer Abigail Goldman. *New York Times* editorial board member Karl Meyer, authors Jerrold and Leona Schecter, *Milwaukee Journal* editor Dick Leonard, all recall their *Cardinal* years as their first and best experiences in journalism. Dwight Pelkin, sports columnist for the *Sheboygan [Wis.] Press* for more than 40 years, put it best when he said of the love for journalism the *Cardinal* inspired: "We briefly made sorties into other work like public relations or advertising, but something always told us to forget it. It wasn't us."

These journalists learned lessons at the *Cardinal* — to question those in power, to publish without fear, and to never take no for an answer. Their achievements validate the way the *Cardinal* trains its young people in the journalism craft.

The *Daily Cardinal* also changed its staff members' lives in ways that had nothing to do with journalism. Among *Cardinal* alumni exists a bond like that of old soldiers and childhood sweethearts, forged over too many cups of coffee on too many sleepless nights. At a 1999 alumni reunion, the editors of the rocky years of World War II sat so long talking over their old copyediting mistakes and deadline disasters that event staff turned out the lights on them.

The power of their *Cardinal* experience influences those who left newspapers and never looked back. Dr. Jack Geiger, a **a founding member and Past President of Physicians for Social Responsibility, the U.S. affiliate of International Physicians for the Prevention of Nuclear War, which received the Nobel Prize for Peace in 1985**, credits the newspaper with teaching him to ask the unasked question and examine the underlying cause of a problem, whether societal or physical.

Professor Douglas Gomery, an author and film scholar, says his days at the *Cardinal* were those when he "became an adult."

More than three dozen marriages started as romances at the *Cardinal*. Staffers decided after months of working side-by-side that they wanted to remain that way for the rest of their lives. The madness of the newspaper's late nights and early mornings forges friendships that last a lifetime.

INTRODUCTION

All this because the newspaper comes out, or does not come out, dependent only on students like those who sit, every night, around the *Cardinal's* copy desk. The same desk — green-topped and wobbly-legged — appears in photographs of the *Cardinal* office as early as 1921.

Then it held typewriters and stacks of yellow copy paper. Today it holds up a massive computer monitor, tomorrow's paper flickering before Worringer as he worked to shoehorn the story about the basketball player onto a crowded front page.

His copy staff chattered around him, about Milwaukee strip clubs, bad movies, and why white singers should not cover reggae songs. MacLean whacked a hackey sack past a new copy editor's head; the young man shouted and ducked.

"Yeah!" MacLean cheered as the little knitted ball rolled out into the hallway. When he followed it out, intending to hit it back in, Salm slammed the door behind him and locked it. Over and over, the slap of MacLean's Koho stick made the door shake. Nobody even looked up.

"This idiot thinks the Bill of Rights is ranked in order of importance," Worringer called out, reading a story about a potential recall of Wisconsin's governor.

"What if it actually is?" Uchill asked.

Worringer thought a moment. "Then the quartering of soldiers shouldn't be in the top ten."

"I don't know," Uchill countered. "I think it's a real problem that more people need to know about."

No salary holds these students inside the drafty newsroom on a cold winter's night. No contract compels their work. No boss regulates their hours. They stay for the experience and the excitement. They stay for each other, for their sense of obligation to the paper their predecessors bequeathed them. They stay *because* no one forces them to, because for the first time in many of their lives, here, staying is their decision alone.

They stay and work because it doesn't end with them.

Backman neatly sidestepped her reporter Alex Balistreri, looping the phone cord over his head so she could keep talking while he used her desk, a regular dance step performed in these cramped quarters. For Backman, the quiet Sunday night before the onslaught of the week was the best time to reflect on the question: What makes this place, these people, so special?

As a college student, there is so much you could be doing. Why this?

She swept her arm out, encompassing the new copy editor eagerly jumping into a discussion about proper work attire for strippers, the loaf of bread and peanut butter on a desk for cheap eats later, the student critic going over his story with Uchill, the reporters telling jokes about Jesus and a vodka martini.

"I got a phone message announcing that sororities are supporting the lifestyle of Scanner Dan," Winter said, referring to an iconic local panhandler who carries a police scanner everywhere. "Anybody else want to hear it?"

INTRODUCTION

"This," Backman said of all of it, past and present and tomorrow's pasted-up future on the computer screen in front of her. "I love this."

IT DOESN'T END WITH US

1.

Beginnings

We believe the University is in need of a daily paper, and to do without it longer would be an irreparable injury.
– The Daily Cardinal, April 4, 1892

○₃

William Wesley Young chafed at the limitations of the University of Wisconsin from the moment he set foot on campus in 1888.

During the first two years of his college career Young, son of a Monroe businessman, signed up for the staff of what was later called the *Badger* yearbook, various monthly campus publications, and then served as literary editor of the weekly *Aegis*, a student-run magazine. He felt a college newspaper should mimic, as closely as was possible at the time, the conditions an editor would encounter at a professional paper. The *Aegis*, which specialized in lengthy essays and poetry, didn't come close.

A student daily was an ambitious undertaking. At the turn of the century, student journalism most often took the form of monthly magazines or weekly university bulletins, especially at schools as relatively young as Wisconsin, just forty-two years old, was then. The *Yale Daily News*, America's first student daily, was founded in 1878, followed two years later by the Cornell *Daily Sun*. Advertiser-supported student papers were even rarer. Most student journalism took place under the auspices of advisors and professors. They ran papers as lab exercises for their students, and controlled every aspect of publication to ensure it was favorable to the institution.

IT DOESN'T END WITH US

The *Daily Sun* provided the model for what Young's paper would be: founded by an editor at the then-weekly *Cornell Era*, an official university publication, the *Sun* supported itself with advertising, news-stand sales, and 400 yearly subscriptions. Young's plan was not without successful precedent, but when he raised the idea of establishing a daily at Wisconsin, friends were skeptical.

It would be too much work. It won't pay anything. Good idea, Bill, but that's all it is, his classmates told him, thinking of their busy social calendars and pocketbooks.

It will "distract student editors from their studies," his professors told him, thinking of their attendance rolls. It will be "an intolerable annoyance."

All of which served only to encourage him.

He got a canvassing group together. Two young men from his hometown, William Saucerman and Malcolm Douglass, walked the campus with petitions, asking students if they would subscribe to a daily student newspaper should someone begin one.

Within a week, nearly 300 students — one-fourth of the student body at the time — had put down their names.

Young was on a roll now. He went to the offices of the *Madison Democrat*, a 24-year-old party broadsheet on South Carroll Street near the state capitol building, and asked for help creating dummy papers to show prospective advertisers.

Young got a quick tutorial in typography from the *Democrat*'s owner, George Raymer, a fellow Monroe man, and its editor, O.D. Brandenburg. Then he sat in the composing room, trying to come up with a name for the paper that, still, existed only in his hopes and imagination.

"After trying various names for the proposed paper, such as the *Daily U. of W.*, the *U. of W. Daily*, etc., the name the *Daily Cardinal* was finally put on one of the dummies and it appeared to meet the approval of everyone to whom it was shown," Young wrote twelve years later, in a retrospective for the paper. He named his paper not after the bird, but after the official color of the university: *Cardinal* red, like Harvard *Crimson*.

Now, with pages in hand, he would conquer and woo the Madison business community.

"I ... remember distinctly of working over them all at one night, ruling them off into columns and printing with pen and ink in half of the columns of highly decorative prospective advertisements," he later wrote.

> They were (to me) such striking advertisements that I pictured in my mind the wild scene that would ensue when the munificent Madison merchants scrambled over each other to secure every inch of space which the future Business Manager would condescend to give them.

One trip around Madison's downtown and a dozen matter-of-fact rejections later, Young's generosity had taken a beating.

IT DOESN'T END WITH US

"I would rather not talk about it even now," he wrote in his *Cardinal* remembrance. "I recall that the most frequent response was, 'Well, if you do get your Daily started and anybody else takes space in it, come around next Fall and we may put an Ad in your Friday editions.'"

Young gritted his teeth and decided that if the Madison merchants wanted to squander this opportunity, perhaps business owners in Milwaukee and Chicago would not be so foolish. He borrowed money from his parents and spent his next weekend break from classes beating on doors in the two big cities, selling as many subscriptions as he did ads.

The *Democrat* had already offered to print the *Cardinal*, and lend its typefaces to the new publication, but a semester's worth of issues would cost $750 to print — about $26,000 in today's costs. Young estimated his subscriptions and ad contracts would bring in about $550.

Young had taken note of the fate which befell early campus publications at Wisconsin and elsewhere, publications which purported to exist for students but were privately owned and operated for profit. The very first publication on campus, the weekly *University Press* which debuted in 1870, had been owned by one man with no connection to the university save seeing it as lucrative market. When the student-owned *Aegis* appeared on campus in 1886 it was embraced by students because it was theirs.

"Offers from men with capital to make it a private enterprise were refused," Young wrote, "it being the determination of the founders to make it a purely students' enterprise or let it drop."

Young, Saucerman and another ally, student E.R. MacDonald, scrambled and scraped but eventually had to put up $50 apiece themselves, which they did without any hope or intention of parlaying that cash contribution into control.

The University of Wisconsin's students would control the paper, would own it as a collective, and the paper would run as a non-profit corporation. Every dollar would go back into improving the business, rather than into Young's or other investors' pockets. Young posted a notice in old Main Hall, now the university's science building, calling all interested students to a meeting to "ratify the *Daily Cardinal* project and to elect its staff."

About 75 students assembled in Science Hall, at the foot of the campus, to decide if Young's research would produce any result. Young remembered opposition speeches, but the students voted and "by an overwhelming majority" in favor of a daily paper.

Young had his speech folded up in his pocket, prepared to accept the editorship the students readily granted him.

Some of this early work continued to mirror the development of student newspapers nationwide. By the time Young began his editorship at the *Cardinal*, there were more than two hundred publications at American colleges and universities that called themselves "student newspapers," though that definition covered what might now be more properly called yearbooks and specialty publications.[1]

IT DOESN'T END WITH US

Most of those elected their editors from various literary societies or according to the student classes: one representative for each. In some cases, especially at private colleges, faculty appointed the editors or approved staff selections.

At the University of Michigan in the early 1900s, for example, "there are eight editors, four from the 'secret societies' and four from the independents; these are elected annually by the literary students." At Iowa State University, during the same era, the faculty themselves appointed a committee to found a newspaper in 1868, though the venture was short-lived.[2]

Young, however, pursued a decidedly independent course. Though the paper's name might connect it to the university, and its masthead proclaimed as much, officially the *Cardinal* sought no university funds nor sanction of the paper by Wisconsin's board of regents or any of the faculty.

It was the University of Wisconsin's newspaper because it served that community, not because the university paid for it.

On the night of April 3, 1892, in the dark and noisy press room of the *Madison Democrat*, composing room foreman Henry Casserly pulled a four-page tabloid proof off the *Democrat's* press. Young looked at it, approved it with a flourish, and signed it across the top, giving the final go-ahead for the *Cardinal's* first issue. Four hundred copies, at three cents each, were delivered to newsstands the next day.

On that front page Young announced not only the *Cardinal's* presence to the university, but his own and his staff's as well, laying his long-felt convictions and hard work on the line with a simple declaration:

> We assume the editorial chair with a decided consciousness of our inability to properly conduct such a publication. The time, labor and worry necessary to procure the material for a daily paper in connection with other college duties can hardly be imagined by one who has not had the experience; yet we promise that no pains will be spared to make the *Daily Cardinal* what it should be – a first class exponent of college affairs and a paper worthy of the liberal support of the students, professors and friends of the University. This, the first number, is necessarily far from perfect, but we expect to make each succeeding number more valuable and useful.

The university he intended to cover had changed rapidly in the years immediately preceding his arrival. In 1886 the University of Wisconsin served 539 students; by 1892 that number had more than doubled.[3] The College of Letters and Science, in which Young was enrolled and in which Wisconsin's Journalism School would later be founded, had by far the largest number of students, and of women. Young's staff was co-educational: Two of his reporters and several of his advertising salespeople were female.

IT DOESN'T END WITH US

The University of Wisconsin was only four decades old when he enrolled, in contrast to elite schools like Harvard, which already had more than 200 years behind it. A land-grant university, Wisconsin's students were primarily middle-class, nearly half of them children of farmers or merchants.[4] The rich still preferred the schools of the East.

Nonetheless, the attitude of the campus at that time benefited Young's enterprise. Literary societies ruled the social life of the campus before fraternities multiplied to the point of dominance. Membership in publications like the yearbook or the *Aegis* was counted as a sign of refinement on campus.

Young only served one semester at the *Cardinal's* helm. He graduated straight to a reporting job with the *Cardinal's* printer, the *Madison Democrat*. He would not stay in Madison for long. New York, and Joseph Pulitzer's legendary newspaper the *World*, awaited him.

He wrote no maudlin farewell editorial, no fond goodbye to the infant thing he'd created. He simply passed over the editor's reins to Managing Editor Willard G. Bleyer, his subordinate, and left.

William Wesley Young would not return to campus for 50 years, but when he came back for the *Cardinal's* golden anniversary, he found the newspaper he left young and weak to be strong and proud. Begun a dark room a mile off campus in the building of the *Madison Democrat* at 114 S. Carroll Street, the paper's operation then filled its own building at 823 University Avenue in the heart of the university. Begun printing on the *Democrat*'s presses, with the *Democrat*'s identical typefaces, the *Cardinal's* machinery included its own press, which much like the *Democrat*'s printing company, served other campus publications as well and for profit.

The paper had by then faced challenges to its independence and authority, from within the paper's own staff and from outside it, from the university, the state, and the nation. It had endured lean years when staffers struggled to pay the bills, but it was standing, independent and free to publish what its editors wished without fear or favor.

"Far beyond any vision we had then," Young wrote in a guest editorial celebrating the *Cardinal's* 50th anniversary, "has been the paper's success.

> Every purpose for which it was founded has been vastly more than realized. It is a living school of journalism, a laboratory in which every phase of practical newspaper making may be learned ...
>
> Journalism in America has been influenced and enriched by the talents of hundreds of men and women who got their start on the *Daily Cardinal*. We have watched the careers of many of its graduates who have reached positions of power and responsibility on newspapers, magazines and other periodicals of various kinds. Publishers in cities throughout the

IT DOESN'T END WITH US

country have told us about brilliant work of our graduates who are reporters, feature writers or editors on their staffs.

That is a tribute not only to the skill they acquired in their formative years by working on the staff of the *Daily Cardinal*, but to our university and the famous brand of education it gives ...

We can only guess at the magnitude of the problems of the post-war world, but we know that the wisdom that comes through education will lead the way in their solution.

The press is the force that will shape the course of national and international events. It is doing that now to an extent not generally recognized, and its power is growing, not only in this country, but throughout the world. This "we the editor" knows a little about that, having critically observed newspapers and newspaper influence in 65 countries during numerous voyages up and down and around the world in recent years ...

We envy the young men and women now preparing for this profession.

---

[1] Samuel S. McClure, *A History of College Journalism* (Chicago: O. Brewer & Co., 1882), 2-3.
[2] Ibid, 36-39.
[3] Merle Curti and Vernon Carstensen, *The University of Wisconsin, A History: 1848-1925, Vol. 1* (Madison: University of Wisconsin Press, 1949), 659.
[4] Curti and Carstensen, *University of Wisconsin*, 661.

IT DOESN'T END WITH US

2.

The Cardinal and Its Campus

Student opinion must be free to be attacked ... Student writers must be allowed to be wrong, and take the punishment for it. Heaven knows they always get it, right, wrong or indifferent.
– The Daily Cardinal, April 23, 1933

ଔ

From the *Daily Cardinal*'s infancy to the present day, nothing has aroused more tension inside and outside the paper's pages than coverage of the campus it serves: How much space to spend on football, how much on campus social life, and how much on academics. Whether to side with students whose opinions were mostly progressive, or more conservative professors who used their classrooms to pressure the paper. How to criticize university leaders' decisions without losing that all-important "school spirit."

Throughout its early history, the *Cardinal* was pulled back and forth between its two readerships: students, who occasionally felt the *Cardinal* was a mouthpiece for the university, and university officials like faculty and the board of regents, who often resented their lack of control over the paper's content.

The *Cardinal* from the earliest was a democratic organization, its name chosen by student consensus and its editors elected by an association of students formed once Young left his post. When the *Cardinal* began to turn a profit in the early nineteen hundreds and moved out of the *Madison Democrat* offices, it incorporated as a non-profit organization and established its own board of directors. Several university faculty members sat on that board, at the *Cardinal*'s

IT DOESN'T END WITH US

request and the chancellor's appointment, which dealt primarily with income and expenditures. The students of the university were listed as the paper's owners and each spring elected several representatives to the board.

Young's paper, dependent on the university for crucial advertising and subscription revenue in its early days, nevertheless took its beloved school to task for perceived shortcomings. Just a month after the *Cardinal*'s founding, Young himself chastised the university's leaders for never holding a college-wide event that included all students:

> At commencement time the graduating classes and a few lower classmen represent the University. It is not a University Day, some orator from afar gives the address, the University is not mentioned ... Somebody ought to take hold of this thing and no one can do it better than the faculty. The *Cardinal*, that vigorous breath of the new life in our University, has not yet awakened enough enthusiasm in the students to cause a college meeting called by the students to be anything other than the failures they have been all the year.

Young wanted Wisconsin's small college to become the campus that exists in Madison, Wisconsin today: stretching across the city's isthmus, from one lake to another, with huge buildings training students in every possible field of study. The *Daily Cardinal* asked for a new library. A memorial to Wisconsin veterans. Greater turnout at athletic events. A school song. Even leniency toward freshman during fraternity rushes. Young saw the paper as a way to influence the institution. With a hometown boy's pride, he wanted to spur his teachers on to do greater things, and the *Cardinal* tradition of challenging the status quo began in his columns.

At the turn of the century Young's deputies took over the paper and its influence began to grow. The *Cardinal*'s advocacy had begun to concentrate on a single topic: a school of journalism. Its lobbying for such a school would become the *Cardinal*'s greatest and most lasting contribution to the university it covered.

Cardinal editor "C.C. Case had a paper on the possibility of a school of journalism," a *Cardinal* reporter wrote in 1893, covering a lecture series the *Cardinal* was sponsoring.

> He said it was difficult in the first place for one contemplating journalism to select the field he was best fitted for. Newspaper work requires a certain class of talent, magazine work another, and both of these lines of work are complex in character. The journalist finds that he must spend a great many years before he can gain the experience necessary to discover what best suits his particular talent.

IT DOESN'T END WITH US

The *Cardinal* staff, along with the staffs of the *Aegis*, the *Octopus* campus humor magazine and the yearbook, organized a press club which served primarily to highlight other universities' journalism prowess and plump for a journalism school. "There are a considerable number of students interested in journalism in one form or another as was shown by attendance at the club last year," the *Cardinal* reported in 1894. "The organization is intended to form a nucleus of a school of journalism which will probably be organized at no very distant time in connection with the university."

Deputy editors W.T. Arndt and Amanda Johnson wrote editorials. They invited journalism professors from other schools to speak, announcing the lectures in huge block headlines on the front page. When all that failed to move the college's governing body, *Cardinal* Editor-in-Chief Willard G. Bleyer joined the university faculty and founded the journalism school himself.

Hired as an assistant professor in the Department of English in 1904, after several years as a writer and scholar, Bleyer called for volunteers to sign up for a non-credit course in libel law. When twenty-five students signed up, Bleyer used that attendance to lobby for permanent, accredited journalism courses.

The *Daily Cardinal*, with all its imperfections, was the best model for a method of training journalists, Bleyer argued. The scion of a legendary Milwaukee newspapering family, Bleyer "grew up surrounded by people who revered journalism."[1] In an editorial in the *Cardinal*, Bleyer stated that a school of journalism at Wisconsin would "attract students of the best class, and that prestige of formal training might entice those who otherwise would be drawn to other competitive fields such as law and medicine."

Shortly after the turn of the century, schools of journalism were either founded with funds from newspaper magnates like Joseph Pulitzer or visionary college presidents like Charles Eliot of Harvard. Those that existed had organized around two distinct schools: the practical and the theoretical. Bleyer saw the study of journalism at Wisconsin in the *Cardinal* model, a combination of both ideas. Journalism was not, as Pulitzer would have it, a scholarly study of languages, history, arbitration, statistics, law and ethics. Nor was it, as Eliot opined, purely a vocational program.[2]

Bleyer saw the program as a social study, with journalists needing a good general education to be able to relate to and question people from all walks of life. While at the *Cardinal* he wrote that "None the less the great school for the journalist is life, and the great secret of success, perseverance. Nothing that concerns the world to known of should be rejected as common or unclean."

Journalism, Bleyer argued, was not just a study of how to write. It was a study of how to reason and observe. University President Charles Van Hise agreed, and allowed Bleyer to add two journalism courses to the curriculum in 1905. By 1927, the university recognized the study of journalism as a separate school, naming Bleyer its director.

One scholar of Bleyer's later work observed that as his curriculum and ideas about the education of journalists spread from one university to the next,

IT DOESN'T END WITH US

Bleyer never abandoned his ideas that journalists were vital to the functioning of a democracy.[3]

In 1931, Bleyer wrote that "... after thirty years as a university instructor, I am convinced that our college courses in subjects other than journalism do not result in developing in the average student the ability to think logically and apply intelligently what he has learned to his work as a reporter, copy reader, or editor."[4]

At the time of his death in 1934, "Daddy" Bleyer was recognized as the father of American journalism education by numerous scholars in the field. He authored half a dozen textbooks, formed the American Conference of Teachers in Journalism and was a leader in the early days of Theta Sigma Pi, the journalism fraternity. His scholarship on the subject of journalism education is still cited by researchers today.

In the end, he always came back to the words he had written while still a student editor, laboring to make a deadline and filled with the idealism that fueled the *Cardinal*. He valued, above all, the paper's freedom and the education that freedom granted to *Cardinal* staff.

"The college daily should always be for the students and by the students," Bleyer wrote in one of his last editorials at the paper, "and the extent to which this principle is carried out will measure the success of the paper."

Less than a decade after the *Cardinal*'s founding, it was testing that principle. In 1912, a group of students dissatisfied with the *Cardinal*'s coverage founded their own paper, the *Wisconsin Daily News*, and promptly declared "war."

"The *Cardinal* is an old paper owned and controlled by private faculty interests," the News asserted in its first edition, which widely panned the Cardinal's coverage of university events and concerns as excessively boosterish and approving.

The *Cardinal* at that time did devote large amounts of space to such stories as "Hockey Becoming Popular Sport" and treated professors' trips abroad as though they were earth-shattering occurrences. The *Cardinal*, in response to the *Daily News*, produced statements from President Van Hise and other faculty members declaring that they did not provide the *Cardinal* any funding:

> For the benefit of new students we wish, in refutation of this charge, to show you that the form of organization of the *Daily Cardinal* is similar to that of most other student publications and that in no case do 'private faculty interests' own and control. We do not believe that the *Daily News* would charge the *Wisconsin Magazine* or [engineering school publication] *Wisconsin Engineer* with being owned and controlled by private faculty interests or that they would accuse the [alumni publication] the *Sphinx* of being owned and controlled by alumni. We are forced to assume that the *Daily News* has brought this

IT DOESN'T END WITH US

false charge of faculty domination against the *Daily Cardinal* merely to prejudice us in the eyes of the freshman class.

After their initial clash, the *Cardinal* largely ignored its new competitor, breaking silence only to mock the paper as "*sNews*" and "*Sham*" in the *Cardinal's* anonymous campus gossip column "Skyrockets." The two papers' staffs did play one another in sports, and "Skyrockets" joked, "The *Cardinal* accepts the challenge of the *sNews* to bowl on condition those old fellows over there don't roll loaded bombs instead of balls." When representatives of the papers met they didn't let pass the opportunity to score points: "At a Student Government Association party, overheard: *News* reporter to *Cardinal* reporter, 'Don't drink the punch, it's a *Cardinal* sin.' [*Cardinal*] reporter's reply, 'That's *News* to me!'"

This early competition didn't last long. By the fall of 1913, the financial requirements of publishing a daily newspaper were beginning to take its toll on the *Daily News*. The *Cardinal* had every financial advantage, having established offices and a printer a decade before. The *Daily News*, in contrast, had to scramble for printing space and beg or borrow equipment. The *Cardinal* was known to advertisers the community over; the *Daily News* found itself locked out of the town's businesses. The university administration refused to grant parity in terms of paying the papers to print official bulletins; that remained the *Cardinal's* domain despite the *News* editors' pleadings.

The University of Wisconsin in 1912 educated just 4,500 students. It was simply too small to support two daily publications. A new weekly or specialty publication, such as were common on campus already, might have stood a better chance; a second daily was simply overwhelmed.

By January 1913, the *Cardinal's* editorial page boasted the names of two newspapers: "*The Daily Cardinal*, founded 1892, combined with *The Wisconsin Daily News*, founded 1912." The two had not "merged," as the *Daily News* put it in its last edition. The *Cardinal* had swallowed the small paper whole, taking what little money was left and all the talented staff for its own operation. By 1915, the *Daily News* name disappeared from the paper entirely.

---

[1] Carolyn Bronstein and Stephen Vaughn, "Willard G. Bleyer and the Relevance of Journalism Education," *Journalism and Mass Communication Monographs* 166, (June 1998): 3.
[2] Tom Dickson, "A Short History of the Journalism Education," *Knowledge Base* (1999): 3.
[3] Ibid.
[4] Willard Grosvener Bleyer, "What Schools of Journalism Are Trying To Do," *Journalism Quarterly* 8, No. 1 (March 1931): 39.

IT DOESN'T END WITH US

3.

Freedom and Fairness

The Daily Cardinal interests more students than athletics at the university.
— Journalism Professor Grant M. Hyde, The Daily Cardinal, 1931

☙

By the late 1920s, the *Daily Cardinal* had grown to prominence on campus and across Wisconsin. Hidden in that success, however, were the seeds of its future troubles. The *Cardinal* now was considered the voice of the university across the state, and sometimes that voice got too loud and too strident for some of its readers to take.

University of Wisconsin alumni who ascended to political office began to use the paper as an example of the problems they saw in local youth. Bashing the "college communists" was a good way for rural and upstate pols to make points with voters, and the *Cardinal* often gave them ample ammunition.

In 1926, a group of Wisconsin state senators threatened to investigate the paper after student editors published a column entitled "Prohibition — An Injustice To Youth." Editor-in-Chief James Nelson went to see university President Glenn Frank the morning the editorial was published and Frank had already had calls from as far as Milwaukee — eigthy miles away — demanding he curb the *Cardinal*.

It was not an unreasonable request. At the time, most student newspapers were sponsored by their universities, operated as a club or extracurricular activity and funded by the school. Advisors were not just advisors, they were gatekeepers, watching over stories and eradicating any hint of controversy. Journalism

IT DOESN'T END WITH US

programs, those in existence, operated lab papers. These were carefully supervised by professors and designed to teach basic reporting skills, not provide news coverage.

At the University of Texas, the *Daily Texan* was controlled by the "Texas Student Publications" board, a university agency.[1] The University of Ohio's *Green and White* was taken over in 1927 by that university's Campus Affairs Committee, which replaced the paper's own board.[2]

Contrary to that trend, however, the University of Wisconsin had made no formal overtures to either purchase the *Cardinal* or take it over. What methods the university did use to influence the paper — leverage on the professors appointed to its board and the students elected there by their peers — were those of the *Cardinal's* own design.

Nervous about the growing Prohibition controversy, Nelson asked Frank if he intended to censor the *Cardinal* and Frank replied in a letter:

> If there was any such censorship I should take immediate action to have it abolished. If the students of this university can't express themselves honestly and openly through their own publication, then something is decidedly wrong. I certainly shall oppose any attempt to saddle the *Daily Cardinal* with censorship. The only thing for you to remember is that you have a great responsibility on your shoulders and that you must base all your conclusions on honesty and truth.

Usually, university officials were too savvy to let themselves be used to further the goals of some ambitious mill owner or dairy farmer. When the question of sex arose five years later, however, cooler heads could not prevail.

On April 15, 1932, the *Daily Cardinal* published a letter signed only by "Junior Woman," advocating what lawmakers and preachers would decry as "free love." The letter, which university historians David Cronon and John Jenkins speculated might have been written by a male staffer as a lark, classified student sexual relations as "a natural and normal and wholesome method of rounding out their lives, particularly their love lives." [3]

> Why do you who protest think unmarried persons more likely to lose self-respect than married ones? Because written laws and social laws are absolute things to conform to until our legislatures change them? Because married people copulate for the express purpose of producing children? You may answer yes, but do they have procreation in mind? Some married people intend never to have children. Is not much of the sexual relation of married people a rounding out of their lives so that they live as completely as possible?

IT DOESN'T END WITH US

Innocuous as it might seem today, at the time it was a shocking sentiment. Its expression came on the heels of a string of unpopular stands by the paper, among them favoring abolition of the U.S. Army's Reserve Officer Training Corps on campus and scaling back university athletics.

A rural Wisconsin newspaper editor, John B. Chapple of the *Ashland Daily Press*, seized on Junior Woman's "free love" letter as evidence the *Cardinal* was being run by communists, socialists, and "libertarian radicals." Chapple, while unpopular in Madison, had friends among the university regents and in the Wisconsin Alumni Association. Wisconsin was, after all, the state which would elect Joe McCarthy to the Senate two decades later, and it was rumored Chapple wanted to challenge Wisconsin's Progressive governor, Robert LaFollette, in the next election. Chapple had spent the better part of the last year raising money for statewide races through his anti-communist network, the League for Defense of American Principles.[4]

The League sought to intimidate university professors Chapple deemed insufficiently anti-communist, and had found an impassioned adversary in the *Cardinal*. In 1931, Chapple appeared on campus and addressed a mostly hostile student crowd, calling their university "a hotbed of radicalism, atheism, loose moral standards, and communist doctrines." In response *Cardinal* editorial writer Melvin Fagen wrote:

> There is an old saying that the best way to answer the prattling of a fool is to remain silent. But Mr. John Chapple, supreme ass that he is, should not be met with any such weapon. Mr. Chapple is not only a crustacean ignoramus with perverted reasoning powers (there are millions of those in this world) but he is also a deliberate liar and prostitutor of facts for his own selfish purposes.

Fagen's editorial bore the headline, "Mr. Chapple, the Crowd, and Justifiable Homicide."

The "free love" letter handed Chapple a loaded gun. When he became the Republican nominee for U.S. Senate in 1932, Chapple had an enormous platform from which to denounce the paper, and by extension the progressive leadership of the university. Like minds on the board of regents, especially those from outside Madison, backed Chapple and excoriated the *Cardinal*, saying Wisconsin residents made no distinction between the paper and the university.

Regent Fred Clausen of Horicon, Wisconsin fretted that the *Cardinal* "found fault with everything" and failed to "adequately support" campus religious organizations. Clausen told the paper he worried for the young people of the state because the *Cardinal* had been found in high school libraries.

He accused the *Cardinal* of being run by "East Coast" students, anti-Semitic code language he qualified by saying insincerely that he had no desire to drive Jews out of the university entirely.

IT DOESN'T END WITH US

Nonsense, *Cardinal* editor Frederick J. Noer replied in a letter to Clausen:

> Your assertion that there is no thought of trying to 'Hitlerize' the university we accept with wholehearted applause. We believe, however, that you are misinformed as to the composition of the editorial board of this newspaper. It is headed by students from Wisconsin and Illinois. They direct the work of students on the editorial board, and their views naturally dominate the group.
>
> Incidentally, the students from "the East" who are on the editorial board have a deeper respect for the traditions of the university and the state than many of the Wisconsin students that we know, and their respect is certainly not below that of any member of the faculty.

Noer overestimated his paper's standing in the eyes of university leaders, who were heavily influenced by Chapple's growing chorus of discontent. On April 27, 1932, the regents voted to strip the *Cardinal* of its "official" status as the university's newspaper, a symbolic distinction granted by the university in 1904 at the *Cardinal*'s request.

They ordered a committee, made up mostly of the paper's own editors and advisors but including President Frank, to see if the *Cardinal* might be brought under university control in some way. Failing some corrective measure, the regents said, the university would establish its own official newspaper and cut the *Cardinal* out of its business.

Frank, no newcomer to politics himself, schemed for a way to provide the *Cardinal* with more freedom, not less. He got the paper's editors to promise they would not run unsigned letters anymore.

He saw the committee as a way to preserve the paper's editorial independence by giving the *Cardinal*'s critics the impression he was taking the situation in hand. In fact, the committee mandated very few changes.

Frank, like many university officials after him, valued the *Cardinal*'s free spirit and tradition of independence, and balked at outside pressure, especially from anti-Progressive politicians.

Former *Cardinal* editor Willard Bleyer, by now a respected professor, author, and director of Wisconsin's School of Journalism, was named to the committee at Frank's suggestion.

Bleyer then made the most effective argument against any type of university control over the paper: "It would be an expensive procedure in that it would necessitate the appointment of another staff member, and at the same time would make necessary numerous changes as to the time journalism courses are given."

Frank showed he had not changed his mind from the Prohibition flap when he declared the committee's work ended after just one month. He returned the paper's "official" designation and said, "the need for a student newspaper, run by students, without faculty, regent or alumni supervision is obvious. However, that freedom carries with it a necessity for the observance of good taste, a decent respect for privacy, and accuracy."

During the controversy, the *Cardinal's* own editorial page was silent on the matter, even as it ran letters from readers denouncing the paper and all for which it stood. The most prominent staff editorial published during the whole period advocated serving beer in the student union.

Struggles like the ones the *Cardinal* faced early in its existence, traumatizing though they were for editors at the time, made the paper stronger and gave its staff an underdog's intensity, something which would serve it well in later years.

These early run-ins with the university administration and with politicians prepared the editors and reporters to confront those in power, to stand up for what they believed in, and to protect their own right to publish at all costs. At the same time, these early conflicts established the *Cardinal* as a mark for those looking to make a case against students, Jews, "radicals," and academic liberalism in general.

In this, the *Cardinal* was not so different from other campus newspapers, which faced the same growing pains and responded with some of the same vigor. What was unique was the mutual respect displayed between *Cardinal* editors and officials at the university. Both were willing to talk out their disagreements and reach amicable solutions that did not involve takeovers or censorship.

Later, when disagreements between the *Cardinal* and its UW critics took place in more politically charged times, and idealism and academic freedom had come to mean quite different things, the positions staked out by both sides would cost the *Cardinal* dearly.

Cardinal editor Robert Dillett, class of 1934, wrote that the university and its political foes often attacked the *Cardinal* because it was easy to attack. The real problems on campus, he wrote, had nothing to do with its paper:

> One student, living within a stone's throw of the Memorial Union, is living on one meal a day. Hundreds of students are living in uncertainty, dependent upon part-time jobs secured at the student employment office.
>
> It is a critical period for all educational institutions and it is a critical period for the *Daily Cardinal*. If we can secure a mutual appreciation by the university and by the state of their dependence upon each other we shall consider our jobs well done ...
>
> Mistakes have been made in the past. But because we have made mistakes does not mean that everything we have ever

IT DOESN'T END WITH US

stood for is wrong. The answer to our problem is not bending over backwards.

The *Daily Cardinal* began the latter half of the 20th century firmly entrenched in its community, the strongest voice on a growing campus. The *Cardinal* office was the place to go if you wanted your message heard, your words read, and your story believed. Its leaders were never cowed by the powerful and refused to take no for an answer, one of many traditions honored both then and now.

---

[1] Tara Copp & Robert L. Rogers, *The Daily Texan: The First 100 Years* (Austin: Eakin Press, 1999), 21-22.
[2] Norma Jean Jenkins, *A History of A University Student Newspaper*. MS (Ohio University, 1960), 33.
[3] David Cronon and John Jenkins, *The University of Wisconsin, A History: 1925-1945, Vol. 3* (Madison: University of Wisconsin Press, 1994), 280.
[4] Ibid 282

IT DOESN'T END WITH US

4.

Frat Boys and Jewish Kids

[Cardinal board member] Mr. Philip G. Fox, a member of the faculty of the commerce school, made this remark to the gathering: "The liberals on this campus have consistently leaned over backwards to prove that they have no prejudices. That fact proves that they have, and they might as well admit it. It's time the American kids on this campus were given a chance."
— Ruth Bachuber, Daily Cardinal, April 30, 1938

ଔ

The wood-paneled, high-ceilinged room was filled with laughter, the clink of glasses, the clatter of silverware. People kept patting Richard Davis on the back, shaking his hand, congratulating him on his editorship. Good going, Dick. Good on you, Dick. Good job, Dick. Dick's a jolly good fellow.

He moved through them as if in a dream.

Richard Davis's first day as editor in chief of the *Daily Cardinal* was April 29, 1938. He went to a banquet. He gave a speech. He talked with some friends, went home, and got what sleep he could.

He was fired the next morning.

Over the next two months, Davis would lead a staff of dozens out on strike. They would publish a newspaper wherever they could: in an editor's apartment, on a pressroom floor, in the library. His ouster — the culmination of religious and social tension that had been brewing on campus and in the country for years — would lead to near-riots and would tear the university apart. Six decades after, he would find himself unable to speak of that time without pain.

IT DOESN'T END WITH US

Yet his example of leadership in fighting for justice would inspire a new generation of *Cardinal* staff members who, like Davis, took the *Cardinal*'s name into their own hands rather than lose the paper that meant so much to them.

It would serve as a stunning example of what was required of the *Cardinal*'s staff to preserve the paper's freedom, and how far they were willing to go to fight in service of that freedom.

Davis's struggle would prove an important test of the resiliency of the *Cardinal*, then just 46 years old, and demonstrate just how much it had come to matter to its community.

Dick Davis grew up in Manhattan, eldest son of a modestly well-off Jewish couple who sent him to private schools where, he later recalled, "we called our teachers by their first names and were free in talking back to them when occasion arose." The liberal reputation the University of Wisconsin acquired under Glenn Frank appealed to him as it did to many New Yorkers of the time. Despite being a self-described "terrible student – I could not diagram a sentence and still cannot," Davis applied and was accepted to the university in the autumn of 1935.

He majored in journalism but soured on the new Journalism School quickly, after his first professor told him the fiercely conservative *Chicago Tribune* was "one of the world's greatest papers."

Upperclassmen took him aside, seeing his frustration, and told him, "If you want to learn journalism, go to the *Cardinal*."

The *Cardinal* became Davis' second home on campus. Settling into a copy editing job, Davis made friends with the other liberals on the *Cardinal*'s staff, New Deal supporters like himself. They were campus activists who committed journalism on one day and protest on another, following a model they learned from their professors. Davis recalled one day stepping off a bus and seeing his German professor on a soapbox, literally, haranguing passers-by to support the Communist Party. Many *Cardinal* staffers, like Editor-in-Chief Morton Newman, were from New York; many, like Davis, were Jewish.

The University of Wisconsin's Jewish community began with the college's inception and grew in strength and numbers during the early part of the 20th Century. *Cardinals* from 1912 carry the first references to the Menorah Club, the first Jewish organization on campus. The club catered to out of state students particularly, as Wisconsin's native Jewish population was small. By 1938, the overall campus population had grown to about 11,000, and out-of-staters were growing in number, causing some Wisconsinites to feel that "their" university was threatened.

Former Senate candidate John Chapple's 1930s crusades against campus radicalism were far from over, and on the national stage, Joe McCarthy was warming up his anti-communist propaganda machine. Clarence Dykstra, who succeeded the Progressive Glenn Frank as university president, was much more attuned to the wishes of conservative regents from outside the Madison and Milwaukee areas.

IT DOESN'T END WITH US

On college campuses across America, anti-Semitism was common in the early part of the century. Most fraternities and sororities forbade Jews from membership in their chapters. Some major universities — though not Wisconsin — established quotas to curtail the number of Jews enrolled. They also commonly restricted on-campus housing to non-Jews only, moves that were then perfectly legal and supported by public opinion: Surveys from the time showed nearly one in four Americans considered Jews "a menace to our society."[1]

Living in a dormitory along Madison's lake shore, rooming with a gentile boy from northern Wisconsin who became a close friend, Davis felt insulated from all that. He wrote well-received columns on national politics, mostly supportive of President Roosevelt and the New Deal. When he decided to make a run for editor-in-chief of the paper he had come to love, at the end of his sophomore year, he never considered that his faith would get in the way.

The *Cardinal* by this time was a wealthy and well-established organization, with its own offices, press, and non-profit corporation to control its finances. Its editorial staff was overseen by an elected board of control, among them five students elected on a rotating schedule by the student body. Those students — three elected one spring, two the next — voted on major financial decisions and editorial appointments. Three faculty members, appointed by the university president, served as advisors but did not vote.

In a quirk of timing, the outgoing board's last act each spring was to name editors for the following year. The incoming board and the new editors took office after a *Cardinal* banquet at the end of April. The arrangement guaranteed that the outgoing board, who knew the staff and editor candidates best, chose those who would lead the paper. It also set an editor up for trouble if the incoming board did not approve of the outgoing one's choice.

And the *Cardinal*'s incoming board in the spring of 1938 did not approve of Davis.

The campus elections in early April were vicious. Splits had developed between candidates who belonged to fraternities and sororities, traditional bastions of Midwestern conservatism, and those who did not; all-frat slates bested longstanding liberal leaders in student government, literary societies, and the *Cardinal*. The incoming student board members, three "fratmen," as Davis described them later, looked with scorn on the "intellectuals" on the outgoing *Cardinal* board who had reviewed the major choices for *Cardinal* editor: Davis and Roger LeGrand. LeGrand was a journalism student from Milwaukee's newspapering royalty, a poster boy for the sort of Heartland values the fraternities purported to support.

The incoming board was drawn from well-connected and powerful campus interests. John Witte, a sophomore, was the son of Wisconsin professor Edwin Witte, the author of the U.S. Social Security Act. Dorothy Boettiger was the daughter of a Seattle publisher who happened to be Franklin Delano Roosevelt's son in law. Wade Mosby's family had a long past in Wisconsin newspapers.

IT DOESN'T END WITH US

Wednesday, April 27, the night of the meeting at which the outgoing *Cardinal* board was to choose between Davis and LeGrand, Davis got a phone call from Ruth Bachuber, a good friend on the board who had been supporting him. She had been threatened by the head of one of the campus fraternities: Choose Davis and "our" incoming board members will kick him out the next day.

Two of the incoming board members made threats to the outgoing board, according to the *Cardinal's* accounts and Davis's remembrances. Eldon Mueller, a good friend and supporter on the board, told Davis that new board members Mosby and Witte had approached him saying "You're a white man, Eldon, so we're coming to you." Witte told Mueller that "Dick's a good guy, he just had the wrong parents." Mueller was revolted.

Despite such intimidation, Bachuber, Mueller and their fellow board members held firm. Dick Davis would be the editor-in-chief of the *Daily Cardinal* for the 1938-1939 school year. LeGrand would be managing editor.

Mort Newman, the *Cardinal's* outgoing editor, was incensed by the intimidation attempts. While Newman was more politically liberal than Davis and the two often clashed over editorial policy, they were good friends. Newman had made Davis his particular protégé, grooming him to take over the editorship. Newman decided, as his swan song, to mount the strongest possible defense of his successor. On Thursday, April 28, *Cardinal's* front page read: NEW BOARD PLOTS DICK DAVIS OUSTER.

> Shocked by a proposal to oust Richard J. Davis, the newly elected editor of the *Daily Cardinal*, a member of the *Cardinal* board of control disclosed Wednesday night that two new members of the board warned that 'Langdon Street [where the university's fraternities were and are located] does not want another Jewish editor.' Declaring that they are calling a meeting of the board today to oust Davis, the two new members told the *Cardinal* board member that 'we're coming to you because you're a white person.'
>
> Davis was elected editor by the old *Cardinal* board of control Wednesday afternoon after an hour and a half of deliberation. At the same time Roger LeGrand was appointed managing editor, William Lochner, editorial chairman, and Ted Reiff, radio editor.
>
> Robert Taylor, managing editor, denounced in strong terms the projected action of the new board ... "Things like this are a reflection on democracy, decency and the whole state of Wisconsin," he said. "They are better brought out into the open. Davis was elected legitimately and democratically, and he had the great part of the staff behind him."

IT DOESN'T END WITH US

By making both Davis's appointment as editor and the forces moving against him public, Newman hoped, he'd head off the coup attempt with publicity. All eyes would be on the *Cardinal* in the next few days.

The story had a seismic effect on campus. Calls poured into the *Cardinal*'s office, most in support of Davis. A special "emergency meeting" of the outgoing *Cardinal* board was called before the *Cardinal* banquet, and it was combative. School of Journalism Director Grant Hyde, then a *Cardinal* advisor and well-known scholar, characterized objections by Davis, Bachuber and Mueller as the "whining" of "Jewish kids." Bachuber, one of his students but not cowed by his authority, shouted him down and Newman joined her, relating later that Hyde turned "almost purple with rage" at their impudence. The *Cardinal*'s other two advisers, Philip Fox of the university commerce department and Donald Fellows of the business department, remained silent. Nothing was resolved.

At the banquet that evening, Davis looked out at the crowd of people at white-clothed tables. Every staff member, everyone in the room but the incoming *Cardinal* board members, was on his or her feet, cheering him. The ovation went on for more than two minutes.

It was an electric moment: these people had placed their trust in him, their faith. They pledged to stand behind him in spite of well-known opposition. He felt gratified, humbled, and exhausted by the weight of all those expectations.

After the banquet Davis and Newman went back to the *Cardinal* office. Mosby and another fraternity man, Bill Pryor, came in and tried to bargain: Would Davis accept their choice as sports editor? He would not. Would Davis' *Cardinal* editorialize in favor of abolishing taxes on fraternities? Davis could not promise it. Battle lines were being drawn.

The incoming *Cardinal* board met the next day, Friday: Mosby, Witte, and Boettiger, as well as Mueller and sorority member Pauline Coles, both serving a second term and thus well aware of what had gone on beforehand. Davis sat in on the meeting as all editors did and still do. They called themselves to order and read a list of appointments to *Cardinal* positions. Davis' name was not on the list, and LeGrand's was listed for editor. The board members voted: the list was approved.

Davis chain-smoked. The board argued around him, as if he wasn't there. The next morning, the *Cardinal* would tell the story:

> 52 staff members signed statements declaring that "we, the undersigned staff members, are well satisfied with the present choice of executives. We demand that they be retained in their present positions. Any dismissal, without cause, we feel would be sufficient reason for our resigning our *Cardinal* posts and carrying the fight to the student body."

A front-page editorial shouted: "Davis deserves his chance! Will John Witte, Dorothy Boettiger and Wade Mosby have the downright nerve to directly

IT DOESN'T END WITH US

go against the wishes of the *Cardinal* staff? Will they violate the wishes of the student body? Will they subject merit to politics?"

The ouster — and the stated reasons for it —made headlines across the country. It became a symbol of the political struggles to come in the United States. This was to be a journalism war the likes of which professional journalism had not seen in some time. The *Chicago Tribune* — so despised by Davis as a freshman — now trumpeted his cause. The *Milwaukee Journal*, the *New York Times*, the *Christian Science Monitor*, all sent reporters to the *Cardinal* staff meeting that day.

Davis posed for pictures with his supporters, then led them out of the *Cardinal's* offices, on strike. The hell with the opposition, they shouted, they'd publish their own paper as the "true" *Cardinal*.

Thrilling words, but to publish a newspaper you need a printing plant. The "official" *Cardinal* quickly padlocked its presses and locked the strikers out of their offices in the student union. You need typewriters and telephones to report and write stories. The strikers had none. Reporters from other papers pestered Davis: Could he pull this off in less than 12 hours?

He swore at them, saying they'd be out if the paper was in longhand.

Davis and his staff settled on the East Side printing plant, a small operation near campus with outdated presses and mostly broken equipment, as their temporary base. That night the first "Staff Daily" *Cardinal* was published, its nameplate screaming "full campus support." Davis and his staff of perhaps two dozen stayed late enough to pull it off the presses with their own hands.

On Saturday, May 1, 1938, three days after being fired, Davis walked up the campus's main thoroughfare to its highest point, Bascom Hill, on which the university's oldest buildings stand. When he reached the top and looked down, he saw more than a thousand students, almost 10 percent of the entire student body, calling out his name. Someone handed him a bullhorn. Asked in the present day to recall the speech he gave at the rally, he could only remember the way his voice echoed strangely through the amplifier.

Photographs of that mass meeting show Davis standing alone. He is hunched over the bullhorn in his hand, looking nervous and tentative. While it is hard to tell from the soaring rhetoric used in his stories that he was barely 20 years old, in the photographs, his youth and inexperience at leadership are easy to see. A group of young men stand off to his side, wearing white t-shirts and dark slacks. Hands on their hips, they stare him down.

Young though he was, Davis was attracting powerful friends to his side. The following day, Joseph Rothschild, owner of the largest clothing store in Madison, called Davis into his office.

Rothschild told Davis the strike paper could count on steady advertising. Bleary-eyed from lack of sleep, Davis shook his hand and thanked him. That one account sustained the strike paper through its rough first week.

William T. Evjue, the legendary editor of Madison's *Capital Times*, editorialized for Davis in his newspaper. Evjue's piece clarified why this strike was drawing reporters from out of state to watch the battle, why those not affiliated

IT DOESN'T END WITH US

with the *Cardinal* or even the university should pay attention to what was happening:

> The ugly spectre of race prejudice which has been slinking under cover at the University for several years came into the open during the past week. For years, it has been the custom of the University for the outgoing board of control of the *Daily Cardinal* to elect the executive editor of the *Cardinal* for the ensuing year. This was done last week and Richard Davis was named as the editor for the new year.
>
> When the new board of control met, however, Davis was ousted and another student selected in his place. The public reason given for the dismissal of Davis is that: "We have substantial reason to believe that Davis will not be able to work in harmony with all the manifold groups which must coordinate their activities in production of the paper."
>
> That this statement represents a palpable untruth is evident ... the real reason for the dismissal of Davis emanates from a snooty fraternity cabal that quickly uses its newfound powers to serve their anti-Jewish superciliousness. One of the members of the board is quoted as saying, "Langdon street doesn't want another Jewish editor."
>
> The Davis matter is only a manifestation of an undercover feeling that has been growing at the University for some time and with which the University must ultimately deal. There is a snooty fringe in fraternity row which seems to feel that resplendent fraternity pins designate this crowd has having been made of a special brand of clay by the Almighty. They seem to think that their own superior position is enhanced in the minds of their fellows by their contemptuous denunciations of Jews.
>
> It is part of a national phenomenon ranging from the snippy little sorority pledge to the fat dowager in the drawing room that ones own social position can be advanced by deriding the Jews. It has become the 'smart' thing to do.
>
> Perhaps the Langdon Street aristocrats should be reminded occasionally that the University of Wisconsin operates under a constitution which stands as the organic law of Wisconsin and which provides that there shall be no distinction in the

IT DOESN'T END WITH US

rights of citizenship because of creed, race or color. It is a deplorable situation when such manifestations of racial prejudice take place on a campus owned by ALL of the people of this state.

Evjue called for donations to the strikers' cause, putting up $50 of his own money, a substantial sum at the time. The strike staff was pitching pennies into a coffee can to pay their printer's bills; they needed to raise $1,500 for the next four weeks. After that? Davis and his editors huddled in a back office and formulated a plan: They would form their own slate of *Cardinal* board members and petition for a special election to recall those who ousted Davis.

They had a powerful propaganda organ at hand in the strike paper. They used it to campaign relentlessly on behalf of their "strike slate" for the four weeks they published.

"All I ask is a fair trial," Davis said in editorial after editorial. Telegrams came into the dorm where Davis stayed; people pushed them into his hands. "The Progressive Party of the University of Minnesota offers our sincere hope that you will be successful in this fight," one such message read. Davis spent most days and nights at the printing plant. Whenever he tried to attend a class, he'd get called out of it to address some new allegation, some new crisis.

Not wanting a recall, the "official" *Cardinal* and its leaders, including LeGrand, who declined to strike, decided to press their case with the powerful. They appealed to the university to stop Davis's paper from publishing and to cancel the special election.

Witte's father Edwin, a prominent Madisonian who would later have his name affixed to university dormitories in thanks for his service to the community, wrote to Dykstra. He described the entire race issue as a "smokescreen" and said, "I need not call your attention to the fact that when students are branded 'Jew-baiters' they are very apt to become real anti-Semites." In editorial after editorial, Wade Mosby denied he had ever expressed anti-Semitic sentiments. He was misquoted, misinterpreted, misunderstood.

"There is grave danger that this election will throw the campus into another turmoil," Edwin Witte wrote, ridiculing Davis as "the off-campus editor." "The situation, in fact, may become even worse in the fall than it has been during the last month."

The official *Cardinal* mounted a fierce assault on Davis' credibility; not only was he Jewish, he was too liberal, and would "crusade" rather than report. Their first editorial about the controversy said "The *Daily Cardinal* is a NEWSpaper, not a VIEWSpaper. It is a paper for the students, ALL the students, and is dedicated to the welfare of ALL the students." They charged that the strike *Cardinal* was violating second-class mailing laws and called the police to stop the post office from sending out the papers.

Strikers responded by breaking into the official *Cardinal*'s press room and stealing about half the papers there, then throwing them into the lake. They

IT DOESN'T END WITH US

floated up and drifted to shore. The Milwaukee papers were overjoyed at the prank, characterizing the two papers as "engaged in an old-time newspaper war."

Though conscious of the attention the strike was generating off campus, Dykstra was unmoved by the pleas of Witte and others. As in years past, the university refused to involve itself in a heavy-handed way, decreeing one way or the other how the strife should end. Despite the *Cardinal*'s status as the university's "official" newspaper, the dispute was the students' to handle, and they alone would determine its outcome.

The student government agreed to set an election for Thursday, May 26, 1938. The ballot question asked voters to choose between two slates of *Cardinal* board members, one a group of journalism and agriculture students favoring Davis and another, mostly the already-elected incoming board, favoring a new editor.

Election day dawned cloudy and damp. "Today a great injustice will be righted," the strike *Cardinal* said. "Today, in democratic student vote, will end: The bitterest fight which has ever aroused the student body; a battle for a democratic solution of an all-campus problem, the plea to 'give Davis a fair chance' and the publication of the *Staff Daily*."

The official *Cardinal* declared:

> The ballot box decides the fate of the *Daily Cardinal* today. A record vote is expected to pour from every corner of the Wisconsin campus as freshmen and grad students, Greek and independent stream to the four polls to register their sentiment on the question which has shred the student-faculty scene for the past 28 days.

For more than 10 hours, students voted, more than 5,000 of them, the largest turnout in campus election history. According to the *Capital Times*, fraternity houses drove busloads of students to the polls and fined them if they did not vote. Davis stood in line at one of the four polling places, smiling at the poll worker's double take when she saw his name on the ballot. At the end of the day, Davis and Allen Jorgensen, leader of the opposition slate, walked up to Bascom Hall to open the vote totals and announce them to the campus. Dykstra handed them both envelopes and they ripped them open.

Davis: 2,600.
Jorgensen: 2,681.

Walking home that night, Davis heard the parties being thrown on fraternity row to celebrate his defeat. Horns honked and people cheered. A group of drunk fraternity men drove up and asked if he knew where Dick Davis was, saying they intended to beat him black and blue. Davis shook his head, and they drove on.

The election had become a referendum on who had charge of the University of Wisconsin campus. More than that, it had become a determination of

IT DOESN'T END WITH US

who was qualified to lead discussion and inform debate. Evjue savaged the outcome:

> Well, the battle is over and the *Cardinal* is once more safe for fraternity row ... The *Cardinal*'s world should be that of prom queens, fullbacks and tails. Why should the *Cardinal* look out over a world where democracy is yielding to dictatorship and to a world where millions of people face the haunting specter of unemployment, dispossession, poverty and insecurity? Langdon Street is smug and contented and doesn't worry about these things, so wotthehell, let's hear more pleasant things from the *Cardinal*. Instead of discussing Spain, let's hear more about who's wearing whose fraternity pin. Let's have more news about the Phi Gotta Dates, the Uppity U's, and the Snooty Lambdas. Nail some Greek letters to the masthead of the *Cardinal* editorial page.

The "official" *Cardinal* published a conciliatory editorial entitled "Forgive and Forget: It's All Over." Nineteen of the thirty-some strike staff returned to the *Cardinal* to work, and LeGrand offered Davis an editing job. Davis declined.

Davis returned to Madison for his senior year. Coming down the steps of the Wisconsin Union one afternoon, a former supporter recognized him and stopped him. How, the man asked, was Davis able to bear coming back to the campus that had rejected him? Didn't he feel unwelcome?

Davis smiled. "I love this university," he replied. "I won't be driven away from it.

"After all, I know I have at least 2,600 friends here."

---

[1] Irving Kett, "Anti-Semitism: The Deadly Cycle of the Last 100 Years", *Western Defense* (Fall 2004): 1

IT DOESN'T END WITH US

5.

We Are At War

For almost all of the last semester only 3 men were putting out the sports page. This was no easy task when a staff of around fifteen had formerly been used. Now two of the three men have left school and it looks very much as if there might be no sports page at all next semester.
– The Daily Cardinal, January 26, 1944

☙

During World War II, hundreds of women became journalists in newsrooms suddenly barren of staff. Female cops reporters and foreign correspondents, ad sellers and paste-up experts, photographers and rewriters, all replaced their male counterparts who'd traded notebooks for rifles. In Washington D.C. alone, nearly a quarter of the 400 congressional correspondents during the war years were female.[1] Student newspapers were no exception in those years. Male students departing for the draft left jobs that were filled by co-eds previously confined, even in student journalism, to society pages and receptionist duties.

The women who took on those new roles went on to become the first wave of post-war women journalists, the norms rather than the exceptions in newsrooms across the country. At the *Cardinal*, the half-dozen women who put out the paper during the war years – despite overwhelming difficulty – became friends for life.

Working in those offices, under those circumstances, was a test for the women who did it, the first test of their strength and ability to improvise, of their dedication to a chosen path, and of their love for an institution which sus-

IT DOESN'T END WITH US

tained them when other societal mainstays seemed to be crumbling around them.

Female leadership at the *Cardinal* was not unprecedented. Two of William Wesley Young's first reporters were women. Women served on the board of control that governed the *Cardinal* in its early years, approving financial decisions like printing contracts and appointing the top editors. Whole sections were written and produced by female *Cardinal* staffers, sections that went beyond society gossip and other such "women's" news seen in contemporary newspapers. In the early nineteen hundreds, the *Cardinal's* "woman's page" was a bullhorn for female suffrage, savaging President Woodrow Wilson for obstructing votes for women even as the *Cardinal's* main editorial page praised him for his international leadership.

In 1933, the *Cardinal's* lead reporter was a woman, Miriam Ottenberg, who covered campus government and broke major stories about student elections for the paper. Ottenberg would go on to become one of the first women to win a Pulitzer Prize. Despite these advancements, however, certain *Cardinal* departments — sports, advertising, and the paper's top editing jobs — had always been the domain of men, so it would have been easy to abandon the paper in the days after Pearl Harbor, when everyone at the university seemed caught up in greater concerns. Many student newspapers did shut down during the war years. The Cornell *Daily Sun*, William Wesley Young's model for the *Cardinal*, was shuttered for three years.

However, women who took on the jobs of men at the *Cardinal* never considered closing its doors, any more than their male predecessors would have. The independence for which the *Cardinal* already was known, the freedom it granted its staffers, led them to value it more highly than they would have other extracurricular activities.

At 50 years old, the paper had instilled in its staff the virtue that would allow it to continue publishing for the next five decades: an unquestioning, unflagging determination that it survive.

"For those of us who were filling in for the men who had gone, it was our way of saying, 'Hey, you thought this was important, in a way we're doing this for you,'" said Arlene Bahr, who joined the paper in the fall of 1941, before the United States entered the war. "We couldn't go to the front lines where they were going, but we could help save something that had been important to them."

A farmer's daughter from rural Sauk County, Wisconsin, Bahr did her first reporting for her high school paper. She loved the pace of newspaper life: the bustling, social office, the way she felt at home and capable there. When then-Managing Editor Dick Leonard sat her down at the copy desk and told her to start writing headlines, she knew exactly what to do.

"I remember the smell of the building," she said. "It was always heavy with the smell of the hot linotype ink and metal. It was always noisy with the machinery in the back of the building clattering away and the *Cardinal* offices only partially partitioned."

IT DOESN'T END WITH US

The *Cardinal* had its own office facility, newsroom in the front and press room in the back, with a long hallway down one side. Its front window, etched with the *Cardinal's* name, looked out on the campus' main thoroughfare, University Avenue. It published 8,000 copies a day, and was read by everyone from university professors to the groundskeepers. Bahr recalled seeing a janitor leaning against his mop bucket one night, engrossed in the pages she had put together only hours before.

Bahr was at a tea for the University of Wisconsin's journalism sorority, Coronto, on Dec. 7, 1941. The room was filled with newspaper people, and when the reports from Pearl Harbor started to come over the radio, that room emptied as if on fire.

Bahr had one instinct.

It wasn't changing out of her tea dress.

"My immediate thought was that the *Cardinal* would have to publish," she said. "So I went to the office."

When she walked through the doors of the building at 823 University Avenue, she found Editor-in-Chief Robert G. Lewis in his office, a small room immediately inside the door. He was listening intently to the radio. For a moment, they stood together in silence as the world they knew tilted beneath their feet and slid away.

Other staff members drifted in, slowly, and Lewis handed out assignments with the calm steadiness of the military man that, in six months, he would become. Bahr remembered reading copy, the normally boisterous office nearly silent, taut with concentration.

Lewis set the headline, four words in dark, stark block type.

WE ARE AT WAR.

Walking home that night to her rooming house on Frances Street, four blocks from the office, Bahr realized the solemnity in the newsroom was only an echo of a larger silence that had fallen on the entire city.

"I remember that I walked up State Street together around 9 p.m. or so after getting the paper to bed," she said. "It was absolutely quiet on what was often a busy street. No one was out. I can recall looking up at the Capitol building, still lit, and wondering whether bombs could fall on it. And I realized that this was a war that was going to affect us all."

At the time of the attack on Pearl Harbor, the university had been preparing to put itself on a war footing for some time. The College of Engineering in 1940 set up special courses for students who wanted to work "in defense industries," and the Medical School was selected by the United States government to house and train reserve medical units.

Seminars and symposia were held on the subject of military preparedness, and university President Dykstra granted leave to 160 faculty and staff members to work on national defense projects.[2]

The *Cardinal*'s staff took few cues from the paper's own history in the first few days of the war. Coverage of World War I had been far from impartial. Ed-

IT DOESN'T END WITH US

itorials at first chided students who became caught up in "war fever," saying:

> Men are doing and saying things that in their calmer moments they would leave unsaid. The pacifist is silenced, the neutral whom most of us called 'pro-German' holds his peace, and with a few exceptions we seem agreed that now that we are actually at war, there can be only one policy for all of us, and that is to support our government and president ... We need not lose our heads. We are not children or savages; we are presumed to be educated men and women who act under the guidance of reason and are not swayed by every gust of passion or prejudice.

But a few days into the Great War, the *Cardinal's* leaders forgot their own caution. **Editor-in-Chief** Henry Allen gave a speech at a university rally declaring, "We go to war not for a commercial purpose, but to uphold the ideals of democracy. The tax on tea did not cause the Revolution. Cotton and commerce did not cause war in 1860 ... we go as we have gone in former times to fight for an ideal."

Mindful of this pacifistic past, at the start of World War II university students flung themselves with enthusiasm into war activities. A group of student leaders, including Lewis, was named "Student War Council" by the student government. The council coordinated various meetings, fundraisers and volunteer services.

Civilian pilot training programs attracted young people from throughout the state. By the summer of 1943 the university was "feeding and housing the 3,200 servicemen and women assigned to the campus."[3]

As students left for war, however, enrollment began to decline. From the pre-war high of more than 11,000, enrollment dropped by more than half, down to about 5,000 students. Enrollment of male students dropped at triple that rate; from almost 7,700 men in 1940 to fewer than 2,300 in 1944.[4]

It was a decline Marilyn Johnson saw firsthand. Having joined the paper as a copy editor in 1942, Johnson, a newsman's daughter from suburban Chicago, relished the greater responsibility that came with her appointment as "military editor." She liked going out to the campus' Army Specialized Training Program. She would talk to the young men who trained in the silver Quonset huts set up on University Avenue, finding out where they were from, what they planned to do once they got out of the service. The program had been created the prior year by Roosevelt's secretary of war to allow hundreds of active servicemen stationed on college campuses to take classes and receive other technical training until their units were called up.

Which all of Wisconsin's were, three weeks into Johnson's tenure.

"It was world-shaking on the campus because it meant, in the first place, that half the student population left," she said. "It was such a serious thing. If you told anyone they were being called up and they weren't or something, it could have drastic ramifications. All the stories from then on were big bylines and front page stories."

She suddenly had — in addition to waitressing duties at her dormitory, a full load of journalism courses and the odd night on the copy desk — the most important job at the paper.

"I'd spend seven hours a day on the *Cardinal*, seven hours doing class work, and then working five or six hours more because I was self-supporting," Johnson said, wondering. "Looking back, I don't know how we did it."

Little more than autopilot brought her to the office each night, she said. She'd chew a bun or sandwich from the dorm cafeteria as she walked.

One by one she lost not only familiar faces at the Quonset huts, but *Cardinal* co-workers as well, like reporter Marvin Kobel, who entered the infantry and was shipped off to Burma. Former editors Lewis and Leonard went to Germany. In three months, the staff of fifty was a staff of fourteen, all female except for one freshman. The girls recalled him fondly as "Young Jack," and treated him like a little brother.

"So many were drafted, and it left such a vacuum that people who started out one year would end the year as an editor," Jack Geiger said. A gifted student, he started at the university at age 15, and found himself as much a curiosity as his female counterparts, and similarly inconvenienced by societal constraints.

"I was working the night police beat, where most people tended to start out, and Madison had passed a curfew for anybody under 18," he said. "I was the only police reporter in Madison who had to get a special pass from the police."

Finishing out Lewis' term as editor-in-chief in the fall of 1942 was Dorothy Browne. She grew up in Madison and started out as a copy desk girl, setting headlines and reading type. She typed up the handwritten announcements campus organizations brought in and took the typewritten pages to the linotype operators. That "drudge work," she said, prepared her well for moving up at the paper. When she started reporting, she knew exactly how to make it easy on the pressmen who were forever chiding their student charges for being too slow or too wordy.

Browne remembered the changes at the *Cardinal* happening slowly. "One day, you'd look up and somebody wouldn't be there, and you just knew they had gone," she said. "It didn't happen all at once, but in three months, a year, all the editors were gone."

So she found herself next in line for the top job at the paper. Browne's father ran a weekly newspaper on the east side of Madison, and had always encouraged her to enter the profession, regardless of any disadvantages her sex might confer. She took the post with confidence, thinking she would be nothing more than a "caretaker, keeping the business going."

The reaction to her appointment as editor surprised her.

"There was so much hoopla," she said. "The *Milwaukee Journal* ran my picture, with a headline, 'Woman takes over the *Cardinal*.' To me that was nothing. I mean, there was no reason a women couldn't do it just as well or better than a man."

By the autumn of 1942, Bahr remembered, the *Cardinal* was a very different place from what it had been.

"Sometimes," Bahr said, "there were just five or six of us there, putting out the *Daily Cardinal*, running the whole paper. And it became plain to me that someone had to go over and do the business functions or the paper wasn't going to stay alive. I had to sell ads or there wouldn't be a paper."

So, armed with the *Cardinal's* ad rates and little else, Bahr trooped up to the premiere women's store at the time, Yost's, an elegant department store at the end of State Street near the state capitol building. When she walked in and announced her name and purpose, the store's owner did a double-take.

"He was very surprised, he said 'What are *you* doing here?'" Bahr remembered, laughing. "I explained to him that I was selling ads for the *Daily Cardinal*, and after that he was very nice. He was a very loyal customer. He ran ads even before they were profitable. But he was a bit surprised to see me at first."

Not only did she have to adjust to being the only woman – practically the only person – selling advertising for the *Cardinal*, Bahr also quickly discovered that the war had changed the nature of the ads the *Cardinal* could get.

"We had no ads from the men's clothing stores," she said. "And national advertising dropped, except for tobacco ads. The tobacco companies realized that in the military units on campus, they had a captive audience."

Three months later, she confronted yet another uncomfortable reality: "There was no one there to be business manager, except me."

One semester of ad sales had made her the most senior business staffer at the paper. As she had when facing the necessity of those ad sales, Bahr looked at this new responsibility, took a deep breath, and stepped forward. She became the first female business manager at the *Cardinal*, taking responsibility for managing all the accounts at what was then a $10,000-a-week operation, doing payroll for delivery drivers and tracking a sales staff of women who, like herself, had been rewriting copy and answering phones a few months before.

Despite her best efforts, however, the lack of "men's advertising" in the paper hurt it badly. In the 1930s the paper routinely turned profits of $300 to $400 per week, printing campus catalogues and faculty newsletters on its presses as well as the newspaper. Revenues dropped so far, though, that Bahr was forced to dip into the paper's savings to cover the costs of printing eight pages when six months before they'd been dropping fat papers of twelve pages or more onto doorsteps.

Desperate, Bahr approached university officials about a listing of faculty announcements and other official UW news. The *Cardinal* would print it, and the university would pay for it.

It would fill space and provide the paper with a much-needed financial boost while preserving the paper's independence from "official" funding or even wartime censorship.

IT DOESN'T END WITH US

The bulletin was a success, and Bahr hit on another brilliant idea. She approached officers of the Navy and Army units on campus and negotiated contracts that permitted them, for a fee, to print sections in the *Cardinal* aimed specifically at their recruits.

"That became the mainstay of our finances," she said.

So now the editors had pages, but too few reporters to cover the vastly changed campus they served. Greater than the loss of just men at the paper, Bahr said, there was a loss of experienced people to fill positions. The expertise of any *Cardinal* staffer depended largely on the time and attention his predecessor took to training him. The board of control's oversight was primarily and routinely financial, not related to personnel or content decisions. As such, there was little help to be had when sheer lack of people threatened to overwhelm the paper's well-practiced system of training and replacement.

The experienced people took on more and more work, Johnson recalled. "Classes were secondary. The *Cardinal* came first, and bright students flunked out because of it."

One of the frustrations for the *Cardinal* women, and indeed for the students who remained on campus during the war years, was the way the world revolved around war news while they were expected to continue their lives as though nothing was happening. Classes still had to be attended, papers written, and all the while men were dying. The campus reached such a point of distraction that, in a fit of pique one night, Browne dropped the *Cardinal's* usual patriotic prose and dashed off an angry editorial, exhorting students to run for the *Cardinal's* board and for student organizations. "Can't you forget the flag-waving for a moment?" she pleaded. "Except for the Prom King race there was no color, no mud-slinging, in short – no political campaign."

The campus soon settled back into some semblance of normalcy. Worries that the fraternities and sororities, those that were still open, had dominated the junior prom filled editorials, while special Army and Navy sections listed their circulation as "a military secret," a joke that made Johnson smile. Society news invited marriage announcements, more common as men left for duty overseas.

The lulls were always short-lived. On the day in 1943 that Eileen Martinson, a 19-year-old New York journalism student, was named as editor-in-chief, the *Cardinal's* front page headline screamed, "112 Badgers Dead in War."

Martinson channeled her frustration with the war's toll by encouraging students to think of the campus the soldiers would return to see. She encouraged the university to spend money on refurbishing old buildings and erecting new ones:

> What have we to say? We who sit back comfortably and securely, who read of battles and marches, who see in newsreels men shooting and killing and dying? ... What kind of future will they find? How can we prevent hatred and horror and fear and suspicion from once more disrupting their and

our lives and hopes? Will we lose faith again with those who have found their resting places on the shores of the Pacific, in French and Belgian villages, in Italian mud? Will we be able to forget our petty antagonisms, our foolish quarrels, our discrimination and our hatreds? Can we move ahead to broader vistas of freedom and democracy everywhere, by establishing and maintaining these ideals here?

About a month after that column ran, Martinson remembered, she got a letter from a Sgt. Frank M. Rogers, serving overseas. His aunt had sent him copies of the *Cardinal* as a reminder of home, and he had read Martinson's article out loud to his commanding officer.

> I read it slowly because in every word I could hear the thought of millions of men who have left their homes, their work, their studies to rid the world of those who would give control to a few fanatical, soulless individuals. I have heard those questions asked in foxholes, around open fires. There is scarcely a man whose thoughts are not in accord with those you have voiced in your article. I asked my friend, another sergeant, to give me his reactions. He was just as amazed as I to think that a civilian back home, a girl, a college student, was capable of grasping the attitudes of men living in such a different world. Through your writing we again have some assurance of the possibility of the kind of post-war world all of us desire.

Rewards like that kept the women working, even on nights when yet another trusted and trained reporter was leaving for duty overseas, when they recognized another name in the endless lists of dead and wounded.

"We had a feeling that the paper was important and that continuing it was important," Bahr said. "We had a tremendous commitment to the paper, a feeling of great loyalty. I think it had been built initially on the friendships that were there."

Johnson didn't even think about the why or the how after a while. She just went to work, and went to eat, and went home, and felt satisfied in getting the job she needed to get done, done.

"It didn't seem simple at the time," she said, "but it was."

Martinson, in her last editorial after both her term and the war ended, wrote that "four years on the *Cardinal*, observing, watching, fighting, writing, have been an experience which it is impossible to evaluate in words."

> It has developed poise, self-confidence, ability to deal with others; it has been a give and take proposition for only what

IT DOESN'T END WITH US

we have put into it have we received. We have put time, energy, spirit, ideas, and our heart into our work, and we have sincerely and conscientiously tried to carry on in those traditions which were the courageous password of those in whose footsteps we followed. The *Cardinal* is bigger than any of us, and it will always remain that way.

At a *Cardinal* reunion in 1999, Marilyn Johnson Shuman, Eileen Martinson Lavine and Arlene Bahr Chandler sat at a table in a nearly-empty banquet hall.

Martinson had gone on to a job in the promotions department of the *New York Times* and headed a group of mostly women in founding a medical news service. Bahr became associate dean of women at California Polytechnic State University. Johnson wrote advice columns for the *Chicago Daily News* and headed publicity for the UNICEF chapter in northeastern Illinois. They had married, had children, lived to see grandchildren. It was their *Cardinal* years they talked about.

Martinson recalled copyediting errors that doomed what she considered brilliant editorials. Johnson relived nights turning into days without sleep. Bahr laughed when she remembered her roommates' complaints: she came home with her clothes smelling like lead and ink from the hot and smoky pressroom. They sounded, for a few moments, like the soldiers they replaced on the paper. They sat hashing over campaigns long past, reviewing strategies and tactics, decided what had worked and what had not.

The event had ended hours ago, and waiters and waitresses were blowing out candles and stacking up chairs. The three women went on talking, about the smell of the old office, the rush to get pages to press, and above all, how much they cared for – and depended on – one another. Their husbands stood to the side, looking not a little awed.

Martinson pulled a carefully folded photocopy out of her purse and flattened it on the table, and the women bent their heads close together to look.

At the end of 1944, the press release read, the *Cardinal* was rewarded with a prestigious award from the national Associated Collegiate Press, called the All-American Pacemaker.

The award lauded the *Cardinal's* campus news and war coverage, features and editorials, front page makeup.

Even its sports coverage – short-handed staff and all.

---

[1] Emily Yellin, Our Mothers' War (New York: Free Press, 2004), 292.
[2] Curti and Carstensen, *The University of Wisconsin, A History: 1848-1925, Vol. 1*, 405-406.
[3] Ibid, 422.
[4] Ibid, 555.

IT DOESN'T END WITH US

IT DOESN'T END WITH US

6.
Prosperity, Generosity, Challenges

John then compared the expenses and incomes of 1948 and 1949 up through February. Expenses increased more than the income did. Printing costs are $9,000 more than last year. It was decided to change the equipment (four buzzers) on the phone which will save fifty dollars a month. It was also decided not to renew our contract with the wire service; we are not using it enough for the price we have to pay.
– Minutes of the Daily Cardinal Board, March 16, 1949

ଔ

  The decade following World War II began as the *Cardinal*'s golden age. Older editors like Dick Leonard and experienced reporters like Carl Adam came back from the war richer in experience, to write mature and sober editorials about the university's future in a new world order. The paper was fat with advertising aimed at returning GIs, and with increased funds came the sense that the paper was invincible, solid in its position on campus.
  At the beginning of the 1950s, combative leaders like Jack Zeldes – later a top Connecticut attorney and author – and Karl Meyer – who went on to sit on the editorial board of the *New York Times* – took on all comers in editorial battles over emphasis on athletics and academic freedom.
  The paper was fierce in its stances, public with its opinions. Writers pursued stories not only in Wisconsin but out of state, focusing on the plight of minorities, the cost of higher education, and the rights of professors to teach as they wished. The attention the paper drew made it a household name, not always for reasons with which the *Cardinal* staff was comfortable.

IT DOESN'T END WITH US

"It was a pretty contentious, ugly era," remembered sportswriter Arlie Schardt, who wrote a column for the *Cardinal* beginning in 1951 and later became second in command at the American Civil Liberties Union. "The *Cardinal* had a good solid progressive editorial policy, and with McCarthy racing around and right-wing Republicans, horrible people, running the country, there was a hell of a lot of pressure on the *Cardinal*. We were a logical target."

"It was all arguing over freedom of speech and academic freedom," said Leona Protas Schecter, who was editor of the *Cardinal*'s weekly magazine section in 1951. She frequently published stories challenging the wisdom of Madison's two daily newspapers. "We stood up to both the *[Wisconsin] State Journal* and the *Capital Times* and said McCarthy was a bad example for the state. He was against the Constitution. There was a lot of turmoil and intellectual ferment and the *Cardinal* was in the center of it."

She recalled one of the paper's proudest moments was publishing a guest editorial by Young Republican and former student Lawrence Eagleburger, later President George H.W. Bush's secretary of state. Eagleburger castigated McCarthy:

> For the following reasons I feel that Joe McCarthy is not in any way fitted to be either a Republican or a senator: Senator McCarthy is a morally bankrupt man who offers a threat to the nation and the Republican party. He will stop at nothing to promote his own advantage, regardless of the effect these methods may have upon the country as a whole. He has emphasized the Communist threat out of all proportion to its importance and in doing so has ridden to power on the reaction to the false fright he has generated.
>
> McCarthy has slandered many fine Americans simply because they disagree with him or stand in his way. In my way of thinking this is the Senator's worst crime; he has threatened the very roots of free speech and in doing so shaken a foundation stone of American democracy. Who but the bravest of men would dare disagree with an opponent when he knows that he will be viciously attacked by a cowardly liar who hides behind the reputation of his high office and the immunity which the American people have bestowed upon that office in full expectation that it will be used in good faith?

The paper argued for the rights of speakers to come to campus and offer their messages, even when such speakers were considered communists. The *Cardinal*'s viewpoint often prevailed. University authorities were as reluctant as the paper's leaders to curtail speech on campus, fearing that attacks on one person's views might lead to attacks on everyone's.

IT DOESN'T END WITH US

"McCarthy's influence has been powerful in support of educational terrorism," the *Cardinal* editorialized in 1952. "Eighty-nine prominent students — representing Republicans, Democrats and independents — recently lined themselves up against McCarthy in a full-page *Cardinal* advertisement."

The *Cardinal's* editorial staff rode high on such public successes. Jerrold Schecter, campus editor in 1952 and later husband of Leona, recalled that when McCarthy came to campus to speak, the *Cardinal* campaigned to raise money for a liberal lecturer to counter him.

"That was the biggest thing for me, what defined my experience," Schecter said. "The *Cardinal* really did have a strong voice and while we didn't have any political ideology per se, we were very much advocates for free speech."

Unbeknownst to the editorial staffers taking such brave stances, however, the infrastructure that supported their advocacy was crumbling. What would transpire in the next two years would place at risk what *Cardinal* staffers prized most: the ability to speak their minds, to challenge the status quo regardless of the consequences.

The hard times to come would also illustrate that which made the *Cardinal* strongest: the willingness of its staff to fight for its freedom.

The *Cardinal's* finances were precarious during the paper's early years. When William Wesley Young left the *Daily Cardinal* a mere semester after its founding, he did the paper one final service: he paid $165 the *Cardinal* owed to the *Madison Democrat* for unpaid printing bills and office rent. His donation alone allowed the *Cardinal* to break even.

It wasn't until the university granted permission to print official notices — and pay for those notices — that the paper's advertising picked up and its circulation took off. By 1912, when the *Wisconsin Daily News* attempted to break into the student journalism market, the *Cardinal* had every available dollar cornered.

In 1927, the paper had a reserve fund of $8,000, and used that money to purchase a press and rent space from the YMCA — in the center of campus, next door to the student union — to house its new machinery. The Cardinal Publishing Company was founded as a student-owned print shop, employing union laborers and eager learners from the student body to print the *Cardinal* and later, other campus publications.

Such a move was rare among student newspapers, most of which contract their services either to their universities or to commercial printers. In a survey of 200 student dailies by the Gannett Foundation, only nine had their own presses.[1]

By 1940 the *Cardinal's* publishing company, renamed the Campus Publishing Company, was so flush from university and alumni printing contracts that it purchased its own building, a three-story structure on Madison's broad University Avenue.

The company was governed by a separate board of directors made up of university faculty appointed by the regents and advised by representatives of all the student publications printed there, including the *Cardinal*.

IT DOESN'T END WITH US

The *Cardinal* thought of the printing company as its own. It was a heady time for the paper; photographs from those days show students clustered around the building's wide front windows, reading the pages of the paper which were placed there on display every morning.

"It was a dirty, grimy place and it was wonderful because it was ours," said Jean Matheson, editor of the paper in 1952. "It was our own operation and we could be completely independent of the university and its problems."

However, the *Cardinal* had to pay for the printing services Campus, a separate corporation, now provided. It was just as responsible to Campus as it would have been to any commercial printer, and the *Cardinal's* then-profits of roughly $100 a month were not enough to make up for yearly cost increases that ran into the thousands.

By 1950, the *Cardinal* was no longer turning any profit. Its financial records show losses of more than $1,600 that year. Subscriptions were plummeting; one editor reported to the *Cardinal's* board that during a subscription drive, only 10 out of a predicted 60 customers actually signed up. The board offered a bonus to the paper's circulation manager if he could get more than 3,300 paid readers. He failed.

Advertisements were getting thin. *Cardinal* business manager Tom Nammacher, who ran the paper's financial end in 1953, blamed previous editors like Zeldes and Matheson and their frequent editorial disparaging of Wisconsin athletics.

Zeldes had ignited a campus firestorm in 1951 when he wrote:

> In keeping head football coach Ivy Williamson at Wisconsin, the university has paid a great price — not the $2,000 salary hike, but the further subordination of the educational aspects of the university to that monstrous development of public devotion — big time college football.
>
> Two successful football seasons and Williamson's pay — as of the rapid action of two weeks ago — has skyrocketed to $12,500. In awarding the pay hike, the university has departed from the traditional pattern of holding athletic coaching salaries below those of the highest paid teachers.
>
> The new raise indicates that the university thinks he is worth:
>
> • $1,250 more than the university's highest paid teacher and Pulitzer Prize-winning historian
>
> • $500 more than the university's vice president in charge of academic affairs

IT DOESN'T END WITH US

• $3,500 more than one of the country's outstanding atomic scientists who is a professor of chemistry ...

Perhaps these symptoms of educational delinquency are unimportant. Perhaps Wisconsin officials, pointing to bigger and bigger football gate receipts, are right in believing that's the way the public likes it.

Perhaps it's too late to re-examine the conditions that led to the paying of bigger salaries to football coaches than to great history professors, great educators, and university vice presidents.

Maybe so. But we're inclined to believe — as several large national magazines have in the past two years — that the game is getting too big for its britches. The *Cardinal* doesn't believe in turning back the clock but this type of exaggeration of the importance of football over higher education is hardly the type to which a great state university should lend its name.

Nammacher recalled going out to sell advertising after that editorial ran and being unable to get contracts signed because he'd spend most of his days convincing merchants the *Cardinal* was neither anti-university or anti-American.

"Local merchants supported the paper and football was big business for the merchants," Nammacher said. "The editors who preceded me took after the football team and by the time I got there the damage was done. They did nothing to repair the relationships they damaged."

Letter-writers and complainants to the board of regents attacked the *Cardinal's* editors as "out of staters" and "elites," which the young men and women at the paper recognized as euphemisms for the kind of invective Richard Davis had endured 15 years earlier.

"We natives like it and we're the ones who have to foot the bill," one postcard began. Another called Zeldes a "pin-head minority [who does] not represent our views." A *Milwaukee Journal* columnist named R.G. Lynch wrote Zeldes a letter:

> Communists are a plague, Jack. They do not weigh the harm and good of what they want to write, or whether or not it is useful ... Communists are also guilty, frequently, of thinking more about how they will look – of their own personal prestige – than of the affect [sic] of what they write.

Zeldes was unapologetic. Told that a national alumni club was considering withdrawing a $20,000 printing contract from the Campus Publishing Company because of his stand against the coach's salary, a move that would have crippled the printer permanently, he penned an impassioned letter to the *Cardinal*'s board of control.

More than 50 years later, Zeldes could still recite the missive from memory:

> If the *Cardinal* must choose between the principles of an honest newspaper and the very existence of its current physical establishment, I sincerely hope we would choose the former.
>
> I would rather see the *Daily Cardinal* mimeographed than allow a $20,000 contract to be the decisive factor in the suppression of so much as a three-line filler.

Not all of the *Cardinal*'s difficulties could be attributed to its firebrand editorials. The entire university was suffering under a post-war enrollment decline and economic downturn. In the fall of 1950, the *Cardinal*'s Welcome Back issue opened the year with the headline "Estimate 10 Percent Decrease In Enrollment With 16,000 Here."

"New freshman are expected to number about 2,150 with the slight drop from last year accounted for by the smaller number of veterans entering," the *Cardinal* read. "Only 58 of the 1,312 men entering the freshman ranks are ex-GIs, compared with 164 last year."

The following year news was even grimmer, as Korean War draft boards began taking what few young men were enrolling. "University enrollment this semester is expected to drop to about 12,500, officials estimated this week." Only 15 new veterans enrolled in classes. For the first time, the number of men and women on campus was equal.

Subscriptions were the lifeblood of the paper's finances in those days. Advertising revenue was unpredictable, but paid committed subscribers gave the paper a base of income on which it could depend. The *Cardinal* charged three dollars per semester, five dollars per year, and ran about 2,200 copies every day which were either delivered or sold for a nickel. In these lean years it brought in less than $7,000.

When subscriptions dropped, advertising dropped faster. Merchants wanted to be seen by the most pairs of eyes for their money; given the choice of a student daily with little paid circulation and a city daily with thousands of guaranteed readers, the student daily lost every time.

Meanwhile, staff perks and privileges instituted in the first flush of postwar euphoria were not being curtailed. The board of control continued to reimburse editors' trips to other cities for conferences, shell out monthly monetary awards for the best stories, and fund newspaper parties and banquets.

Editors did make some concessions: canceling some news services and buying a radio instead, for example.

Most student newspapers faced their greatest difficulties during the Great Depression, which forced publication cutbacks and even shutdowns at papers

IT DOESN'T END WITH US

like the *Daily Texan*, which discontinued its summer edition, and the *Harvard Crimson*, which lost capital during the lean years.[2] The *Cardinal* had weathered those years surviving on the capital it had built up at the beginning of the century, but now, with postwar spending beginning to wane, it suffered when other papers prospered.

It also had nowhere to turn, unlike other papers of its time. Less than four percent of the nation's 2,000-some campus publications were incorporated in and of themselves, though most claimed some form of "independence," usually meaning editorial rather than fiscal.[3] Papers which received subsidies from university departments could have their shortfalls covered by their "parents." The *Cardinal* had no such assurances.

By 1952 the *Cardinal* was losing upwards of $700 per month and business staffers were quitting in disgust. Nammacher later said that things were so bad that "if you sold three ads they made you the business manager."

That October, the *Cardinal* told its own story in a front-page editorial:

> Financial conditions are forcing us out of business. We are now operating on a week-to-week, month-to-month basis, and unless something is done, the *Cardinal* will perish — permanently …
>
> Income lessened considerably, as did the power to draw advertising, and consequently, this source of revenue was cut. At the same time, the cost of printing the paper jumped. Labor costs doubled. Printers' wages went from $1.23 per hour in 1945 to $2.53 per hour in 1952. Newsprint increased by more than 80 percent.
>
> Today we are caught in the middle. It now costs more than $200 per day to print the *Cardinal*. For the past three or four years we have been living off of the surpluses built up during the profitable post war years. But now that surplus is gone, and we are unable to meet the increased costs from a reduced income.

For a time the campus community rallied around "their" paper. Student government members volunteered to sell subscriptions. Supportive merchants like Jacob Mintz of the popular Campus Clothes Shop held meetings of the local business association to urge members to advertise.

Fraternities and sororities, often at odds with the paper's editors in the past, put aside campus politicking and signed on to support the paper as well.

"The loss of the *Cardinal* to the campus as a whole and particularly to the student body would be disastrous," a student government resolution said. "Therefore we pledge our individual and organizational support to the *Daily*

IT DOESN'T END WITH US

Cardinal in its efforts to maintain financial solvency. We also heartily urge all other students and organizations on this campus to help the *Cardinal* in every way possible, particularly by contributing personnel and subscribing willingly when approached by subscription solicitors."

Staffers tried everything they could think of to stave off disaster. Columnist John Israel spent dark winter afternoons traipsing up and down the campus, trying to sell subscriptions to faculty members.

"Everybody who worked on the *Cardinal* went around knocking on doors," Israel remembered. "We had a commitment that was total. We were desperate for subscriptions to stay alive and we were real in danger of going under. It had to be total."

The crisis broke in the summer of 1953. In the summer session, when the student population at the University of Wisconsin was a fraction of what it was during regular terms, the newspaper published eight-page editions for those students.

The running of the weekly "summer *Cardinal*" was usually left to an inexperienced editor looking to move up in the paper's ranks. In 1953, that was Stan Zuckerman.

The junior-year editor from Brooklyn had looked at the three-month period between spring and fall semesters as a time to catch up on some course work, earn a little money and try to have some fun.

Instead, he spent his mornings in class, his afternoons working a part-time job, and his nights (and early mornings again) in the *Cardinal* office.

"As it turned out, very few of the regular staff and virtually no one newly recruited had any interest whatsoever in sparing time from swimming, strolling, sailing, playing and the occasional course to work at the *Cardinal*," he said. "I think I could count on three or four people to help."

Zuckerman was only peripherally aware of the paper's financial turmoil when he took the position. Business managers like Nammacher were thought of as necessary evils, he said, hostile to the free flow of ideas he and other editorial staffers cherished.

"We despised the notion that the newspaper was a business," Zuckerman said. "We were undiluted purists. The guys who sold advertising were preparing themselves for lives that were anathema to us. We would be newsmen, fulfilling the vital task of supplying a democratic society with the information it needed to make rational decisions. Their role was to raise the money to pay us and stay out of our way. Their presence in the newsroom was not welcome."

One afternoon in late July Zuckerman was making his by now customary round of frantic phone calls, trying to round up enough letters to the editor to fill the regular space for such missives inside the paper. He looked up, surprised, when the manager of the Campus Publishing Company, Mahlon Hinkson, and one of the faculty members on the *Cardinal*'s board, Lester Hawkes, walked in.

They laid a set of figures in front of him. In the last year advertising revenue had fallen by more than $6,000. Subscription sales, which had brought in more

IT DOESN'T END WITH US

than $11,000 in 1952, totaled only $6,650 the following year. Single-copy paper sales had dropped by two-thirds.

In 1951, the paper lost more than $3,000. The next year, the loss was nearly $4,000. Its savings were being drained and soon would run out.

Hawkes and Hinkson explained the situation. The *Cardinal* was by this time so costly to print and so unprofitable that it was endangering the Campus Publishing Company's existence. If the *Cardinal* did not either cut back production or close down entirely, it would take its print shop down with it, depriving the university community of its only student-owned press as well as its paper.

"There was just no apparent alternative," Zuckerman said, "other than a plea to the university for funding – an act we would have seen as a sacrificing our independence."

He and the *Cardinal's* board sat down and worked the numbers. Assuming current advertising revenue, printing at three days a week, the *Cardinal* could cut its losses by two-thirds. It was worth the risk.

Zuckerman said he never considered simply shutting the paper down. "That was unthinkable," he said. "It was a terrible decision but we had no choice, and there was no one else around to share it with me."

He announced the *Cardinal's* fate in an editorial on July 25.

> The publication cutback is being done on a trial basis. If the move results in substantial financial profit, it may be possible to return the *Cardinal* to a five-day-a-week publication schedule.
>
> The main reasons for the financial hardships of the paper are: Decline in advertising revenue, steadily rising printing and operating expenses.
>
> To build up subscriptions, the *Cardinal* is planning a major subscription drive in the fall when house to house canvassing will be instituted.
>
> If advertising revenue does not substantially decline, it is planned to issue frequent 12 page editions, possibly one each week.
>
> Operating expenses are being cut as the *Cardinal* staff will take over several plant operations formerly held by paid employees, such as proof reading and [photographic] engraving making.
>
> *Cardinal* editors foresee no additional respite for themselves, in spite of the publication cutback. Reporters and editors

IT DOESN'T END WITH US

will still be working five days a week to maintain the *Cardinal*'s motto of "Complete Campus Coverage."

His official note might have radiated bravado but Zuckerman was devastated and blamed himself for not finding another way out. "The staff we directed had to live with the decision that I was forced, not to make, but to acquiesce in," he said. "I always wondered if it was a setback that could have been avoided."

For *Cardinal* staffers who worked throughout the following year, however, what they remember is not the hardship of their near-financial ruin, but the fun of putting out a paper. Their financial straits did not affect them editorially, they thought; they still had a paper three days a week and they'd go on doing what they always did.

The *Cardinal* took on the racially exclusive policies of private housing in Madison and continued its anti-McCarthy stance, recruiting James Roosevelt, FDR's grandson, to write guest editorials denouncing the local Republican Party and its tactics. And when the city newspapers mocked the *Cardinal*'s financial troubles, editor Roger Thurrell, who took over from Zuckerman in the fall of 1953, struck back at them.

> We welcome their interest as "sincere youngsters" who are ever ready to heed the sage advice of our professional colleagues. However, we beg to differ with the headline of an editorial which declared the story of the *Cardinal* was a "sad" one. The temporary cutback to three publication days a week does not mark the "passing of a fine tradition," as the *State Journal* claims ...
>
> There need be no epitaphs until the corpse is laid to rest.

While Thurrell helmed the paper's daily operations, Zuckerman and associate editor Richard Schickel found ways to compensate for the *Cardinal*'s diminished production. They convinced Wisconsin Public Radio, along with a local television station, to give them a show, and *Cardinal* editors read the news over the air each night.

The paper was the first in the area to do so.

Reporter Marion Voigt recalled the big stories she covered without fear.

"My first assignment was to cover a meeting of the NAACP, and here I am from Watertown, Wisconsin, which I think had one black family," she said, laughing. "Before I went, I had no concept of what the NAACP even stood for, what its goals were, nothing. But I showed up at the meeting anyway, the only white person in the room."

Dick Carter, who ran the *Cardinal*'s "legislative bureau" from the statehouse a mile away, was able to isolate himself from much of the paper's internal strife.

IT DOESN'T END WITH US

"Those were very upbeat times," he said. "We were all into activism, we were very anti-McCarthy, very liberal in many ways, and it was just a great, exciting time to work."

Recovery from the cutback was slow. In 1954 the paper, turning modest profits, added another day to its publication schedule, coming out Tuesday, Wednesday, Thursday and Saturday, but still falling short of the backing needed to return to a five-day week.

In 1955 a last-ditch subscription drive pushed them over $7,900 in subscription revenue, and the paper began publishing on its former schedule, Tuesday through Saturday, that fall.

In his final column for the *Daily Cardinal* Stan Zuckerman issued a warning to students who took their newspaper, and all the resources available to them on campus, for granted.

> This passivity is outwardly expressed by a striking number of students on this campus who view the enquiring mind as some strange cloudy creature with obvious intent to overthrow the government, the home, the family and all the societal institutions which they demand be above analysis ...

> You can't be too tough on them, all things considered. If they weren't warned before they left for Madison not to become bookworms, if they weren't advised to keep away from the "egg heads," in short, if the population expected anything different from them we might be rid of the "college kid."

> Let's face it. The college world today is neither the best nor the worst of all possible worlds, it's the most possible.

Schickel, for his part, saved most of his ire for the *Cardinal*'s board, who he blasted for questioning the integrity of editorial staffers while business operations remained largely unmonitored.

> In my short span of years, I have had the misfortune of meeting so many people who claim to be experts in newspapers. The tossing of every knife at the *Cardinal* has been preceded by the words "Everybody says ..." Yet strangely, we have always been able to find nearly as many people who oppose the current quack opinion as there are those advocating it.

Zuckerman and Schickel and their dedicated staff left behind a paper better and stronger than the one they found.

Their struggle was a warning to later staff members, who had they heeded it, might have avoided a much worse fate.

IT DOESN'T END WITH US

In 1956, the *Cardinal* and its printing company were strong enough again to make the university that had thus far supported and defended them an extraordinary offer. They would dissolve the Campus Publishing Company, and donate its building, the land on which it stood, and the press that the *Cardinal's* money had bought, to the university to allow the School of Journalism to found a Typographical Laboratory.

In the official university bulletin announcing the offer, the University of Wisconsin's board of regents noted that though they had misgivings about bringing the *Cardinal* under a university roof, the potential educational advantages of the gift outweighed their doubts. "Daily and weekly newspaper organizations in Wisconsin have been pressing for the move, so that students in journalism will have the advantage of an operating print-shop laboratory for courses in 'back shop' work."

The total value of the gift was estimated at more than $125,000; in today's terms, close to $2 million. The Journalism School remodeled two rooms in its lakeside building — where the Helen C. White library now stands — to house the printing equipment, and in the fall of 1956, the *Cardinal* and the press moved in.

The paper's leadership believed that by giving its presses to the university it would strengthen the relationship between the *Cardinal* and journalism education at the University of Wisconsin. It would benefit future generations of students who could be trained in typography and press work, and would give a great state university a foundation to provide a level of practical experience no other school at the time could provide.

Most student newspapers are eventually absorbed by their universities, their staffs taking money and expertise from the "adults" around them. The *Cardinal* did the opposite: it gave both knowledge and treasure back to its university. This gift, its givers believed, would make the *Cardinal* forever a part of the community it had so faithfully served.

This gift, instead, nearly destroyed the *Daily Cardinal*. That moment of generosity would come back to haunt the paper in ways the staff at the time could not possibly imagine.

---

[1] Paul A. Atkins, *The College Daily in the United States* (Morgantown, W. Va.: Communi-Tech Associates, 1982), 10.
[2] Steve Luxenberg, "The *Crimson* Starts Its Next 100 Years," *Harvard Crimson* (Sept. 1, 1973): 1.
[3] Atkins, *College Daily in the United States*, 9.

IT DOESN'T END WITH US

7.

Upheaval

MONTGOMERY, Ala. – *The headlights shine in your eyes. Outside the phone booth you can't see a thing through the glare.*

The men in that car can kill you if they want to, but they're just taking their time. Whenever it strikes their drunken fancy they can roll right over the booth, leaving you and the girl a mess of blood and bones and broken glass.

You want to call the cops. It's night and you're alone, and the phone is right there. But this is Montgomery, Alabama. You don't do that kind of thing here. In this town, when a kid from the North needs help, the last people to call are the cops.
—The Daily Cardinal, March 23, 1965

☙

  Gail Bensinger was on the phone to her brother when the car drove up. She was standing on the edge of a dimly lit parking lot in a white neighborhood in Montgomery, trying to get a story back to the *Cardinal*.
  It was early spring, 1965. No cell phones, no e-mail, no modems, no faxes. She was reading to him from her notebook while he wrote it all down at the *Cardinal* office, and she didn't stop dictating until the tires squealed so loudly she couldn't hear him anymore.
  "Tell them where we are," she said, as the car pulled up and three men got out, shouting at them about Northerners who'd come down to their town to stir up trouble among "their" Negroes. "Tell them what's happening to us."

IT DOESN'T END WITH US

She meant tell the *Cardinal*, tell the paper. Tell the story.

"My older brother was a grad student and he spent most of the time I was down in Alabama hanging around the *Cardinal* trying to get news of me," she said. "I could hear him in the background, getting hysterical, saying 'Gail, get out of there.'"

"That's who you're fighting," Bensinger would later write, home safely and ensconced in the editor's office at the *Daily Cardinal*.

> They're an easy enemy because they're so obviously wrong. It would be harder if they tried to make any sense, but they can't. So all you're up against is the vile language and the billy clubs and the crosses in the night. And while you wait to lose the battles, you sing your victory songs.

The *Daily Cardinal* began the 1960s turning five-figure profits and stashing financial surpluses in its bank accounts. It enjoyed a supportive university administration that refused to be swayed towards censorship by the paper's critics. Its staff included such future journalism luminaries as Jeff Greenfield, the first and only editor-in-chief to serve in the position for two consecutive terms, and the future chief political correspondent for CBS. The paper's reporting garnered national honors; staffers of that era went on to work at the *New York Times*, the *Washington Post*, the *San Francisco Chronicle* and the *Chicago Tribune*.

"I am proud of the *Daily Cardinal*, and deplore the unfair attacks that have been leveled at that publication," University President Fred Harvey Harrington wrote in a March 9, 1965 letter to Wisconsin Gov. Warren Knowles, who had asked Harrington for information in response to state legislators' criticism of the paper:

> The *Cardinal* is one of the best student newspapers in the country, and has been the training ground for many of our outstanding Wisconsin journalists. It reports campus news in a factual manner and opens its columns to expressions of all shades of opinion. I often disagree with the *Cardinal's* editorial positions (sometimes they criticize me); but I do believe that students as well as other citizens have the right to express their own opinions.

By the time the decade ended the *Cardinal* had fallen into disfavor with the university. Its staff had begun to splinter. The paper was on the verge of a complete break with the community it covered and the people it purported to serve. It was tearing itself apart, along with the world around it.

"Last week I submitted my resignation as chairman of the faculty advisory committee," former *Cardinal* board member John Ross wrote in a 1970 letter to a friend who had criticized the *Cardinal's* staunch anti-establishment stance and

IT DOESN'T END WITH US

views on the Vietnam War. "I felt that I could not, even by silence, endorse the editorial positions of the *Cardinal* ... Frankly, I see no major shift in editorial policy at this time unless the student body of this campus speaks out loudly and clearly that they want a shift."

Looking back at the actions of the *Cardinal* staff in the 1960s and 1970s, the *Cardinal's* stands on civil rights, women's liberation, and the war in Vietnam seemed inevitable. Every fight for freedom of speech, every passionate defense of a staff member as "one of our own," every word written on behalf of the powerless against the great, all of it led them to this. This was the path, and there was no other. Or so staffers say they felt, at the time.

Gail Bensinger came to the *Cardinal's* top spot as Greenfield's successor. She was one of the few women editors in those years, when, despite the changing status of women in the workplace since the female leaders of the 1940s, she still had to get permission from the university to stay out past "curfew."

She wasn't in office a month before radio host Bob Siegrist started calling her staff a bunch of commies.

"Oh, that was the year all hell broke loose," Bensinger said. "Every six weeks there was a new crisis, and we had to scramble as hard as we could to get onto the roller coaster before it ran right over us."

Siegrist was a right-wing showman in the model of today's Rush Limbaugh or Michael Savage, who hated communism and higher education with equal fervor. Near the end of Greenfield's term as editor-in-chief, Siegrist had begun needling the *Cardinal* in his broadcasts. Siegrist called the paper a haven for "out-of-state influences," something Bensinger noted was the ever-popular code for "New York Jews."

On Jan. 28, 1965, Siegrist's weekly listener newsletter went from vague allegations of "preponderances of left-oriented journalism" to a specific challenge. Noting that the paper had published a pre-Christmas issue without what he thought was sufficient coverage of the Christian holiday, Siegrist wrote:

> *Cardinal* managing editor John Gruber (New York) insisted that the paper's innocuous look was merely the result of student final exam concentration. Gruber denied that his and his paper's political and ideological outlook was influenced by his residency at 515 W. Johnson St. with Mr. and Mrs. Eugene Dennis Jr., with Michael Eisenscher, and with other known political leftists.

Dennis and Eisenscher had been organizers of campus demonstrations against the House Un-American Activities Committee, against then-presidential candidate Barry Goldwater, and in support of the Berkeley Free Speech movement. Eisenscher's father had chaired the Wisconsin Communist Party, while Dennis's led the national party. Sharing their house, Siegrist implied, meant that Gruber shared their politics.

IT DOESN'T END WITH US

Gruber had grown up the son of a liberal lawyer in New York, and had come to Wisconsin, like many East Coast students did in those days, because the university had inexpensive tuition for out-of-staters compared to other universities of its caliber. He rented a room at the Johnson Street house, close to campus, along with several other students. Neither Bensinger nor any of the other editors had seen anything worrisome in it before Siegrist spoke up.

Siegrist's accusation caught the eye of Republican State Sen. Jerris Leonard, a rising star in the Wisconsin GOP. Leonard, who was then assistant majority leader, said he saw Siegrist's accusations as pointing out a weakness in the *Cardinal's* editorial leadership.

"Reporters and especially editors should avoid appearances of bias," Leonard said in a recent interview. "Many times people can not do much about such relationships, i.e. family members who have extreme bias, but Gruber did not have to 'associate,' live with the likes of leftists. He had options. It showed his disdain for avoiding bias in his important editorial leadership position."

Leonard fired off a letter to the board of regents in which he asked them to investigate Gruber's living arrangements or he would "call for the establishment of a special legislative committee to study the matter and take appropriate action." He also attempted to explain the complex web of associations that led him to deem Gruber suspect:

> Eugene Dennis was the son of the late Eugene Dennis, Sr., former leader of the Communist Party in Wisconsin and the United States. His mother, Peggy Dennis, is a writer for the Peoples' World, the Communist Party's west coast publication, and her writing also appears in the party's *Worker* published in New York. Dennis and his wife attended the founding meeting in California last June of the DeBois Clubs of America, which Herbert Hoover, director of the FBI, has described as "a Communist-oriented youth organization," founded at a meeting "dominated and controlled by Communists." Mrs. Dennis has been listed in the *Cardinal* as head of the Madison chapter of The DeBois Club.

Gruber was unfazed by Leonard's accusations.

"The *Cardinal* is open to all shades of political views," he told the Madison press. "We have had in the past members of all species of political beliefs, far right to far left ... The students, the faculty, the presidents, the board of regents have consistently supported the freedom of the *Cardinal*. I know they will do so now."

He asked the regents to reject Leonard's call for a formal investigation and sarcastically said he would make sure the senator got a subscription to the paper "so he can read more than isolated comments. He might even learn that J. Edgar, not Herbert, is head of the FBI."

IT DOESN'T END WITH US

Bensinger was not a doctrinaire leftist, nor was she a communist. Her own editorials focused on the issues of women's rights, particularly those of women on the Madison campus, and that was where her political sympathies were.

"Writing editorials every day didn't come easy for me," she said. "I realized the guys running a lot of the anti-establishment organizations were just as sexist as the guys everywhere else, so I didn't get involved in a lot of that at the beginning."

Her staff was her family, though, and when they were threatened, she stepped in front of them and took whatever fire she had to take to protect them. She was incensed by Leonard's attack.

"This is a character smear of the worst order," she said in a statement she issued the same day Leonard's press release hit the wires. "If Mr. Leonard has anything to criticize Mr. Gruber for, other than his address, he ought to present his specific charges clearly and honestly."

Reaction from other corners likewise was not kind to Leonard. The chairman of the university's Young Republicans castigated Leonard and Siegrist, defending not only Gruber's right to live wherever he liked, but the *Cardinal*'s journalism as well. "The *Cardinal* has featured regular columns and letters from students of both the right and the left," the club said in a statement. "If more articles from the left appear, it is most likely a sign that the left does more writing."

Wisconsin's daily papers defended the *Cardinal*, saying Leonard's statements were a throwback to the McCarthy era. They astutely diagnosed the *Cardinal* as a dodge for Leonard's real intention, which was to starve the university in upcoming budget negotiations. Kenosha's *Labor* newspaper even recalled the last time the *Cardinal* was subject to legislative salvos: "Not since former Ashland newspaper editor John B. Chapple lambasted the University of Wisconsin in the mid-1930s as a center of radicalism and 'free love' has the university faced such right-wing charges as are now being leveled at it."

On Feb. 5, 1965, the regents met and considered Leonard's letter and the *Cardinal*'s defense. They issued the following statement:

> The Regents of the University of Wisconsin respectfully but firmly adhere to the Board's long established policy of encouraging and supporting freedom of expression in the publication of the *Daily Cardinal*, as well as in all other academic and extracurricular functions of this University.
>
> Guided by the spirit of freedom of inquiry and expression which pervades each facet of the life of this institution, the *Daily Cardinal* has earned a national reputation as a student newspaper controlled and operated by the students through their duly elected representatives.

IT DOESN'T END WITH US

It was, at the time, a radical statement for the regents to make. Other universities were cracking down on their student papers when those papers printed leftist editorials. The University of North Dakota was studying whether or not to disassociate itself from its official student newspaper because of content and coverage similar to what the *Cardinal* was producing. At the University of North Carolina-Chapel Hill, conservative students sued the *Tar Heel*, claiming their student fees were unfairly allocated to what had become a left-wing paper.[1] At the University of Texas, official newspaper advisors began removing material from the paper that they considered "political."[2]

At Wisconsin, the regents valued the ideal of the paper's freedom more than they wanted its occasionally strident voice silenced.

Leonard expressed his disappointment with the regents' decision but accepted it and dropped his threats. Another state senator and ally, Gordon Roseleip of rural Darlington, took up the banner Leonard laid down, and Roseleip's advocacy quickly surpassed Leonard's in both sound and fury.

All through February and most of March, while Siegrist continued his assault over the radio, Roseleip attacked the *Cardinal* in speeches and letters. In one five-page missive to Harrington, Roseleip accused the president of condescending to him and ignoring the threat college communists posed:

> I hope and pray that the day may come when you, as President of the University of Wisconsin, which constantly costs our taxpayers a greater burden, will show those taxpayers that you appreciate their sacrifices, and that you share their concern for what is happening here, by joining in the life and death "game" of defeating World Communism, with the same sort of competitive spirit which our Monroe High School boys showed in winning the State Basketball Championship.

Roseleip's entry into the fray didn't frighten Bensinger or her staff. Leonard, who would become assistant attorney general of the United States and end his career as a trusted advisor to President George W. Bush, had solid Republican credentials and powerful allies, and thus proved a real threat.

Roseleip, on the other hand, Bensinger said, was "a goofball."

"There had been a very famous taste test in the legislature that year, between butter and margarine," she recalled later, noting Wisconsin's dairy-state pride. "He was the only legislator who flunked. At the time, nobody took him seriously."

Harrington concurred, writing jokingly to one regent that Roseleip's latest angry letter was "a real prize."

"At the time, we didn't think there was anything to worry about," Bensinger said. "It was only later that we realized they could have made a lot of serious trouble for us."

IT DOESN'T END WITH US

Despite their continued verbal barrages, Roseleip and Siegrist got no further action from the regents. The campaign against the *Cardinal* did Leonard no favors, either; he lost a U.S. Senate race in 1968.

The failure of Leonard's and Roseleip's attacks only emboldened the *Cardinal*. The freedom the regents affirmed and which Bensinger so strenuously defended led to some of the best journalism the *Daily Cardinal* ever published.

Less than a month after the regents' decision, a group of Madison students chartered a plane and planned to fly to Montgomery, Alabama, to witness and assist civil rights workers in registering blacks to vote.

The Madison campus that spring had been full of "sympathy demonstrations" for blacks fighting for civil rights in the South. As far back as William Wesley Young's days the *Cardinal* advocated greater equality for minority students, taking on students' segregated housing and fraternities' exclusionary rules.

Shortly after a black minister was beaten to death while protesting in Selma in 1965, Madison ministers backed by Governor Knowles organized their own march, raising money for local civil rights organizations and expressing sympathy for the Southern demonstrators.

On March 17, a call came into the *Cardinal* office for reporter Dave Wolf, who had been covering much of the local civil rights movement. He told Bensinger the plane, rented by the leftist Student Non-Violent Coordinating Committee, had spots available for *Cardinal* reporters. Would they go?

It was barely a decision. Yes, they would go. Yes, they would sleep on the floor of whatever kindhearted and sympathetic Southern families would put them up. Yes, they would spend three days watching women and children beaten with police batons and thrown bodily into paddy wagons.

Yes, they would stand in a phone booth and shout their leads over the long-distance lines as three men circled them, shouting threats.

"Dave did the bravest thing that night," Bensinger said. "He whipped out his notebook and started interviewing them. I said into the phone, 'We're fine.' They wouldn't answer any of his questions so we just walked back to SNCC headquarters."

The stories Bensinger filed from pay phones and borrowed rooms are some of the most powerful, she said, that she ever wrote.

> The placards carried by the white supremacist group were more militant than SNCC's. "Who Needs Niggers." "Niggers Go Back To Your Leader Johnson." "Stand up with Wallace," they read.
>
> One placard portrayed a huge black face, and read "Will this be our new Uncle Sam?" At one point the woman who carried it turned to spectators and said, "Kingfish – that's him."

IT DOESN'T END WITH US

A minister closed the 25-minute rally with the warning: "It is time somebody stood up, somebody stood for Jesus, and stood up to ungodly race mixing and violence."

The crowd then retreated for a block and dispersed ...

Soon afterwards a police van appeared and the police bodily lifted the demonstrators and placed them in the wagon. Bystanders applauded and laughed. Shouts of "harder" were heard.

The editorial she penned once she returned, that terrifying moment in the headlights of an oncoming car now a memory, is one of the most passionate the *Cardinal* ever printed.

> American citizens cannot turn to the law or to the voting booth, and it is upon these two institutions that America lays claim to be the most free democracy, the best-ordered nation, the most rational government in the world. We proclaim our virtues throughout the world — we beg the world to do it our way. Who the hell should do it our way when we don't?
>
> What good is an independent judiciary when the judge who is untouchable speaks in his court of "niggers" and "chimpanzees?" What good does it do to elect a semi-literate voting registrar who asks citizens to interpret parts of the Constitution that the Supreme Court still hasn't managed to figure out?
>
> What good does it do to have a sheriff protect the peace of a community when in all likelihood he is responsible — either directly by participation or indirectly by consent — for the murder of those who want to upset this miserable status quo? Not much ...
>
> All our sacred, beloved institutions fell apart once before because the drastic changes which were needed could not emerge from within the system.
>
> Somehow we had better figure out a way to bring them about by way of the law and the voting booth pretty damn soon, while we can still convince ourselves they can work.

"It was a year of just one thing after another," said Bensinger, who went on to work for the *Washington Post* and head the international desk at the *San Fran-*

cisco Chronicle. "It was the year the whole world came crashing down on this nice isolated college campus, and everything snowballed after that."

---

[1] Louis E. Ingelhart, *The College & University Campus Student Press: An Examination of Its Status & Aspirations & Some of the Myths Surrounding It* (Terre Haute, Indiana: National Council of College Publication Advisers, 1973), 6-8.
[2] Copp and Rogers, *The Daily Texan*, 88.

IT DOESN'T END WITH US

IT DOESN'T END WITH US

8.
Breakdown

In May, a block party held by students of the Mifflin-Bassett St. area was busted up by city police. Numerous other block parties before this incident had been ignored if not helped by police. The residents of the Mifflin-Bassett St. area are known to be the more radical active students of the community. In the police riot that ensued almost one hundred students including two city aldermen (also students) were arrested, not to mention thousands of dollars worth of property damage caused by the widespread and indiscriminate use of mace, tear gas, and police cars.
– The Daily Cardinal Unorientation Issue, Summer 1969

ଔ

    In the autumn of 1968, the Students for a Democratic Society held its annual convention in Boulder, Colorado. The leftist political organization had begun recruiting on the Madison campus and the *Cardinal* needed coverage of its events, but lacked the resources to send reporters to the convention.
    The *Cardinal* relied instead on its subscription to the University News Service, a wire service that gathered reports from college campuses all across the country, to grant it access to SDS happenings.
    On Oct. 22, 1968, the news service sent over two stories about different SDS factions feuding in the run-up to the group's presidential election the next month.
    Both reports prominently featured the name of one of the rival SDS parties: The Up Against the Wall Motherfuckers, "informal anarchists from New York." They featured exchanges between the Motherfuckers and their rivals, de-

IT DOESN'T END WITH US

scriptions such as "they're about as exciting and spirited as a lukewarm fart in August."

The Motherfuckers' leader was quoted as saying, "The fucking society won't let you smoke your dope, ball your woman, wear your hair the way you want to. All of that shit is living, dig, and we want to live, that's our thing. Action, not this bullshit rapping."

Night Editor Rob Gordon pulled this copy off the wire. Both stories ran inside the paper, on pages six and nine. Editor-in-Chief Greg Graze didn't even notice them at first. Two days later the *Cardinal* ran a story about a speech by Milwaukee draft resisters. The story, written by reporter Deena Compton, quoted men who had burned files in a military draft facility as saying that resistance was "teaching souls to touch each other rather than fucking with minds."

That story ran on the paper's front page.

That was all it took to begin the end of the *Cardinal's* affiliation with the University of Wisconsin.

"The *Cardinal*, while it tried to remain objective and keep a third-party perspective, did give a lot of coverage to the protest movement, and then as now reporting bad news leads to charges of liberal bias," Graze said in a recent interview. "Anger at the *Cardinal* had been building for years and this was what finally tipped the balance."

Graze had grown up in the *Cardinal* of Bensinger and Greenfield, the paper that sent reporters to Montgomery and defended itself from outside attacks in the strongest terms. He had seen the *Cardinal* rally the community behind its cause of press freedom. The paper's status as a campus institution had always protected it from the capriciousness of politicians and gadflies. The idea that the university would attack the paper over the printing of a four-letter word, while university-age men died in a war, struck Graze as childish and absurd.

The board of regents which had so staunchly defended the *Cardinal* in 1965 was no more. Regent chairman Arthur DeBardeleben, who fended off Roseleip and Leonard, had retired. Kenneth Greenquist, another strong Cardinal supporter, had also left the board. They and two others were replaced by representatives from rural and suburban areas, where anti-war and anti-establishment sentiment were not nearly as strong as they were in the city of Madison itself.

The campus climate was also vastly different. Between Bensinger's Cardinal and Graze's lay the Dow Chemical riots of 1967, chronicled by David Maraniss in his Pulitzer Prize-winning book *They Marched Into Sunlight*. Students protesting the chemical company's recruitment fair on campus were tear-gassed and beaten by city and campus police in a brutal attempt to disperse the crowd. University leaders, under pressure from alumni and city officials, expelled the organizers of those protests, spurring further unrest.

The military draft was, by the time Graze assumed the editorship of the *Cardinal*, taking thousands of men each month and sending them to Vietnam. The

IT DOESN'T END WITH US

American public was divided in a way it had never been before. The harder that draft-age men and women resisted, the stronger the backlash they faced.

"We were a lightning rod," Graze said. "People were upset with liberals, upset with campus radicals, upset with the anti-war movement. We were there."

College newspapers across the country were facing controversy because of actions like those of the *Cardinal's* editors. The University of North Dakota was studying whether or not to disassociate itself from its newspaper because of articles it deemed "irresponsible." The University of North Carolina-Chapel Hill was taking fire over a "vulgar reference" its paper published about the university's president.[1] At Pennsylvania State University, four student journalists were arrested for "circulating obscene literature" after their underground newspaper, the *Water Tunnel*, published scatological drawings.[2]

Public pressure was mounting on Wisconsin's regents like never before. It was harder for the regents to justify publicly defending students like Graze, who printed patently profane material, than it was to stand behind a young man like Gruber, accused of communism because of his associations.

On Nov. 1, 1968, regent Bernard C. Ziegler, a wealthy industrialist from rural West Bend, Wisconsin, led the charge. He proposed, and the regents adopted, a resolution reprimanding the *Cardinal* "for the use of language that is considered by the standards of this country to be unacceptable for public use.

"Furthermore," the regents wrote, "it is the intention of this board to take appropriate action whenever language standards are violated in any subsequent issues of that or any other University newspaper."

Ziegler also told the *Wisconsin State Journal* that Graze and the other the student editors should be expelled, something the staff took personally. The editorial the *Cardinal* ran the next day was brief and to the point, and titled "Up Against the Wall, Re—ts."

> The shibboleth of "obscene" or "unacceptable" language which the regents have chosen to use against the *Cardinal* in this case is patently absurd. This generation of college youth has come to realize that the concept of obscene language is merely one aspect of the institutionalized hypocrisy in our daily lives: an interest which camouflages a genuine concern with the quality of our daily lives.
>
> The charges against the *Cardinal* are as insidious as the minds which made them in the first place. But aside from the feeble charges, the *Cardinal*, like any other journal, is under no obligation whatsoever to answer for its policies under any condition prescribed by any outside authorities or individuals. Consequently, although the *Cardinal* staff has determined a policy on the standard of English to be used in the newspaper, it is an internal matter and will remain so ...

IT DOESN'T END WITH US

It is obvious that if it were not the *Cardinal* or obscenity it would be the dorms, the Union, the leftist groups, [student government] WSA, the fraternities and sororities or something else. Only last Saturday it was reported in the Madison press that regent Ziegler has suggested that the board have its own "agents" to "investigate areas of concern."

He said he made his suggestion because of alleged reports of obscene language and the expression of "immoral thoughts and actions ... in several classrooms." He said that the agents would be auditors, hired directly by the Board to report on activities in classes and conditions in the dorms and the Memorial Union ...

Thus let there not be a shred of doubt in anyone's mind of the immediate and eventual intent of the regents. And for this reason, the *Cardinal* has chosen to resist in every way, legally and extra-legally, the totalitarianism of this group. For if the *Cardinal* dies at the hobnail boot of the regents, the blood will be on 34,000 hands and no student group or individual will be safe from the guillotine.

The editorial was signed by the entire staff and the five elected students who, along with three professors, made up the *Cardinal's* board. The *Cardinal* student board members then sent a letter to the regents declining their request for a meeting.

The Board firmly believes that the editorial policy of the *Cardinal* is a matter solely within the jurisdiction of its directors and editors; that language standards are an integral part of editorial policy. The Board also concluded that the newspaper's editorial and news policies reflect the responsible judgments of the editorial staff ...

The directors and editors of the *Cardinal* are always willing to explain the newspaper and its policies to any individual or group in an appropriate setting. But the *Cardinal* will not participate in an arena which has the atmosphere of a tribunal.

Editorials and letters from one board to the other escalated the situation into an all-out war that ended up on the news pages of the *Washington Post*. Graze had been stringing for the *Post* for several months, writing articles on campus unrest, protest and politics as a correspondent, so his Washington, D.C. attorney father was surprised to read his name in a story instead of above it.

IT DOESN'T END WITH US

"My father came all the way out from Washington to meet with [university vice chancellor Robert] Atwell to express his displeasure at what they were trying to do," Graze recalled. "I don't know what he said but they dropped the expulsion effort."

The situation was not as combative as news reports of the time made it appear. While the *Cardinal* published editorials advising the regents to "stuff their obscenity charges into their shirts with whatever else is in there," Graze went to work behind the scenes to try to mitigate the damage. He and Atwell met privately at the faculty club and Graze told Atwell he had reprimanded Gordon for using the unedited wire copy containing profanity.

"I explained that I had worked for the *Washington Post* and that I was a serious journalist, I wasn't just in this casually," Graze said. "I took a strong stance against what the regents were trying to do but I had made it clear to the editor responsible that I wasn't happy with what got into the paper."

Graze defended the quotations in the draft file story as language "conveying the power and emotion of the subject," and Gordon resigned from the paper. Graze thought that was the end of the situation.

During the controversy the *Cardinal* garnered support from student leaders, many of whom had themselves been involved in disputes with the regents at one time or another. The faculty of the Journalism School, while critical of the *Cardinal*, issued a statement supporting the paper's freedom to "publish without fear of reprisal."

On Jan. 10, the regents met and voted punish the *Cardinal* the only way they could. They voted 4-3 to strip the *Cardinal* of the only material benefits the university yet granted it: free office space in the UW's journalism building on Madison's Henry Mall, a small cul de sac off University Avenue.

The *Cardinal* had moved to Henry Mall more than a decade earlier. Its editorial offices occupied the front of the old brick one-story building, while the typography laboratory, containing the *Cardinal's* donated presses and typesetting equipment as well as photography space, occupied the back. The space had been granted as part of the 1956 donation of presses and assets by the Campus Publishing Company, but past generosity paled before present outrage.

Beginning in fall 1969, the regents' resolution read, the *Cardinal* would have to pay $125 per month to rent the space its offices — two small offices for the editor-in-chief and business manager and one large newsroom — took up.

The regents also discontinued nearly $6,000 in annual subscriptions purchased for faculty and summer students.

At the time, the *Cardinal* was bringing in more than $160,000 per year through subscription and newsstand sales (for five cents per copy) and advertising. The paper had $80,000 in reserve cash in various savings accounts, and, Graze noted, the recent controversy only made the paper's circulation go up.

"Advertisers loved us because everybody was always talking about the *Cardinal*," Graze said. "We were getting all the attention, and our circulation peaked at about 17,000, which was the most it had ever been."

IT DOESN'T END WITH US

Seeing no real financial downside despite the inconvenience of rent, buoyed by the support of student groups and the journalism faculty, the *Cardinal* made no further move to fight the regents' punishment.

Its final editorial on the subject was less about press freedom and more about the prevailing political climate. The university, the paper pointed out, was being used.

"Lacking a more substantive issue, the state politicos are using the *Cardinal* as its whipping boy," it read. "And not only is the paper to feel the brunt of the attack, but the state legislature is using the issue to slash the University's budget request, including faculty salary increases and funds for special projects and programs."

Graze still tells the story with a kind of breezy bravado. Robert Taylor, who was on the *Cardinal*'s board, remembered it differently. Taylor, a professor of journalism, was also communications director for the university president, and soon after the controversy began he wrote in a note to Harrington, "Attended a most somber *Cardinal* Board meeting this noon. It was a group of almost-scared young people, waiting for the blow to fall ... my feeling is that the [*Cardinal*] board is under considerable strain."

The controversy didn't so much blow over as become subsumed; in February 1969, the campus's black student groups went on strike from classes, demanding a black studies department and more equitable treatment by the university. Leftist student groups quickly followed, striking in solidarity, and on Feb. 13, Governor Knowles called in the National Guard.

The *Cardinal*'s headlines about itself were buried now, beneath pictures of soldiers pointing guns in students' faces.

The *Cardinal*'s war with the regents wasn't over. The following summer, the *Cardinal* cemented its status as a radical newspaper in the style of the underground papers becoming more popular on campuses across the country. In the process, it proved that there was still one last thing the university could take away.

Each year the *Cardinal* published an issue mailed to incoming freshmen. In years past it had been an inoffensive guide to the university, explaining the history of the institution, and mostly contained "puff pieces" on campus dignitaries and area eateries which advertised in it. No one took it seriously, least of all the *Cardinal* summer staff who were at the end of their terms when it was published.

Allen Swerdlowe had more ambitious ideas. To Swerdlowe, managing editor in the summer of 1969, the issue was a chance to tell incoming students about the real university, the one he experienced as a *Cardinal* reporter.

"I wanted it to be a political issue, to explore the politics of the university rather than tell kids where the bookstores were," he recalled. "It was more about dismantling the façade that the university created through its propaganda, about us being the propaganda chiefs rather than the university."

Swerdlowe conceived the Unorientation Issue as a kind of record album. The issue unfolded in sections, the first explaining the events of the '68-'69 school year, including the regents' attack on the *Cardinal* and the National Guard response to the black student strike. A satirical graph correlated students' political awareness with their sexual activity, charts outlined the structure of the University of Wisconsin from president down to student, and a whole page instructed incoming freshman what to do if they were tear-gassed.

The lead story began, "Last year saw the systematic increase of student repression on the University of Wisconsin campus." On the cover was a photo manipulation: the regents as scowling puppet masters, pulling students' strings.

Swerdlowe delivered the pages to the *Cardinal*'s printers on Aug. 25. They looked down at it, up at him, and then back down at it again. They sighed, and started setting the type.

"They were a bunch of guys trying to support their families and we were a bunch of snotty kids," Swerdlowe recalled. "It can't have been easy for them, but they did their jobs despite our interference."

The university leadership, still smarting from the *Cardinal*'s attacks all year, was not so resigned. Every year since 1935, the university mailed home the paper as part of its orientation materials. In years past, the university had paid for the production of that issue. In 1969, because of the stripping of all university subsidies, the *Cardinal* paid for the issue, but still needed to obtain incoming students' names and addresses from the UW.

Normally, the *Cardinal* provided the printed papers to the University News and Publications Office and the office affixed second-class mailing labels and sent the issue out.

But when Swerdlowe and summer editor Dennis Reis presented themselves and 5,500 copies of the Unorientation *Cardinal* at the publications office, Publications Director Harvey Breuscher refused to turn over the mailing list or mail the papers himself. Breuscher later told the *Wisconsin State Journal* he objected to the "anti-establishment, anti-university" positions in the paper. He told Swerdlowe the paper was not acceptable because its masthead proclaimed it was "sent to all incoming freshman by the University of Wisconsin."

Cardinal board member Taylor, in his capacity as vice president of the university, advised President Harrington that they should withhold any mailing permits until that line was removed from the paper. While Taylor ordinarily was sympathetic to the *Cardinal*, "this year's edition is something else," Taylor wrote in a letter to Harrington.

> It is a 60-page attack on the University and contains four-letter words ... in view of the *Cardinal*'s statement that the University is sending in this edition, it seems wise for us to make it very clear that we are not — by denying the *Cardinal* the use of our list of freshman names and home addresses.

Swerdlowe, who had spent the better part of his summer on the issue, was incensed. He and Reis claimed censorship. They then went to what they would

IT DOESN'T END WITH US

only identify later as "another student organization" that had the mailing list and copied it to make their own labels.

The following day, Aug. 26, Taylor and fellow *Cardinal* advisor and journalism professor Lester Hawkes called a meeting with Reis, *Cardinal* Business Manager Anthony Mullen and incoming Editor-in-Chief Steven Reiner.

They sat and talked about how to delete the offensive copy and reprint the paper in time for mailing. Taylor advised Mullen to tell the Madison post office that the *Cardinal's* second-class mailing permit was no longer valid.

While they met, the *Cardinal* summer staff worked, gluing labels onto the already-printed edition. Taylor and the others emerged from their meeting to announce to the Madison press that the papers would be revised to the university's satisfaction.

On the night of Aug. 29, Reis, Reiner and others took the original, unrevised papers out of the *Cardinal* office and loaded them into the trunk of Reis's car. The next morning they took them to the Madison post office, where, according to Taylor, Reiner and Reis told the Madison postmaster they were authorized to mail them on behalf of the *Cardinal*.

The postmaster accepted the papers.

Out they went.

Harrington and the regents were angry to say the least. At their September meeting they asked Taylor who had first designated the *Cardinal* the "official" paper of the university, and whether the line the *Cardinal* included in its masthead about its status could be in some way formally revoked.

When Reiner heard of the regents' request from Taylor, he didn't argue the point. He simply deleted the line without editorial comment or notice.

"When we did 'Unorientation' it was about sticking it to the university," Reiner said. "There was always this tension about what the *Cardinal* was. Was it a dutiful university paper, an arm of public information for the university? Or was it an independent student voice that would do what it wanted to do, within the bounds of decency and reason? I think we'd always straddled those lines, and now we were coming to a tipping point."

This incident, like the obscenity fight, hardened the *Cardinal's* stance against the university during a politically polarizing time. In a "welcome" editorial in the first issue of the 1969-1970 school year, Reiner wrote,

> Unable to speak for anyone else, we will speak for ourselves. Still surviving after one death threat after another the *Cardinal* still remains, very much alive and kicking. Long ago we realized that our life was tenuous and that something somewhere along the line would have to be bartered if we're to continue to live.
>
> Thus internally we undergo, reprehensible as it might seem to some, a degree of self-policing. We estimate our value, we

IT DOESN'T END WITH US

think about what we can accomplish as long as we live, and we choose to give away a point or two to the opposition.

That we did last year in the four letter word controversy. That is what we will do again this year.

Reiner may have found the *Cardinal* to be comparatively conciliatory. Most outside observers did not. After the *Cardinal*'s published obscenities in 1968, a university alumna wrote an impassioned letter to Harrington. In it she pleaded for him to do something to bring back the university of her youth, a university that in all likelihood only existed in her sepia-tinted memories, but a university she held dear nonetheless.

> It may be that that is one aspect to which the board of regents has not given enough thought. The University is the property of, and the concern of, the people of this state. And when the board of regents allows the official paper of the University of Wisconsin to print such items as have appeared during the last few weeks, and especially during the past week, then it is losing the respect of the students and of the citizens of this state, and I think that without respect for authority, no institution can long exist.
>
> Respect from children to parents is a necessity, but it must be respect that is earned. In family life, earned respect plays an important part in the preservation of that unit of society, and once it is lost, then the whole structure is weakened.

She went on to rail about drugs in the university rooming house where she once lived, the loose morals of students compared to those in her day, and the temerity of students referring to professors by their first names, cosmetic concerns that Harrington could have done little about. Threaded throughout this letter and others like it was a very real fear about what was happening to the campus, the community and the country, and a very real pain at what she felt was being lost. It was typical of many letters Harrington and others in authority received about the *Cardinal*, and it is easy to see how they might have swayed the regents' opinion.

The *Cardinal* did not cause campus riots nor resistance to the war, though its staff covered the one and felt itself a part of the other. What the paper was in 1969, more than anything, was what it was in the mid-1930s for John Chapple and in the early 1950s for the Young Republicans: a convenient target for a community's rage. Its transgressions up to that point could all be put down to the foolhardiness and arrogance of youth, the pressures of a daily deadline, and a sincere desire to reflect a world which was falling apart around it.

IT DOESN'T END WITH US

With flattery and incentive, at this point the board of regents might have co-opted the *Cardinal*. With tolerance on both sides, what happened to the paper in the following decade might have been averted. But as the regents stripped the *Cardinal* of the trappings of respectability, they made it easier for the *Cardinal* to see itself as outside the university, and when pushed, to push back.

"We felt very passionately about things," Reiner said. "And I think like any bad relationship, it was unfortunate. It was unfortunate that the relationship between the administration and the students, the administration and the *Cardinal*, had soured and that everybody was acting in a not very constructive way. The administration was overreacting."

Stripped of the rent-free space it had been provided following the 1956 press donation, stripped of its official status as the university's newspaper, the *Cardinal* ended the 1960s almost entirely alienated from the university it had been founded to cover.

At the time, Graze said, and Swerdlowe echoed him, "We didn't think they could do anything else to us."

They were right, in a way.

What happened next, the *Cardinal* did to itself.

---

[1] Inglehart, *College and University Campus Student Press,* 46.
[2] Seth King, "Defiant Students Keep the Underground Presses Rolling." The New York Times (May 19, 1969): 1.

IT DOESN'T END WITH US

Above: The first issue of the *Daily Cardinal*. Students paid pennies to have the paper delivered to their dorm rooms.

Left: William Wesley Young, founder of the *Daily Cardinal*.

IT DOESN'T END WITH US

Above: *Cardinal* night editors Norm Jacobson and James Gordon Bennett put the paper to bed in 1937. **Below:** The paper's business office in 1942.

IT DOESN'T END WITH US

IT DOESN'T END WITH US

The *Daily Cardinal's* business staff, 1943: Velma Kort, Betty Born, Arlene Bahr, Lillian Mueller and Joyce Malm.

The Daily Cardinal

CARDINAL BUILDING
811 University Ave.
Golden Jubilee Year — Complete Campus Coverage
ADVERTISING F. 5000
EDITORIAL F. 5001
VOL. LI, NO. 65 — UNIVERSITY OF WISCONSIN, MADISON, TUESDAY, DECEMBER 9, 1941 — FIVE CENTS

WE ARE AT WAR!

Native Filipinos Battle Jap Raiders

They men are typical of the Filipinos enduced into U. S. Army service recently by order of the President. [...] Moros and Tagalogs, representing the three most prominent types in the Islands are shown here. They [...] active service during the bombing of Manila.

Students Dazed At Jap Attacks

'What Will Happen to Me?' Is Question of Wary Campus

Dazed at Japan's declaration of war, every student yesterday asked, "What will happen to me?"

The men on the campus will be hit the hardest since those deferred because they are students or because they have physical disablements will be reclassified and re-examined. A probable result of the war will be a "speeding up of and tightening the operation of selective service."

The campus as a whole will be affected differently than in the last war when the university became an army training camp, it was indicated yesterday by Comptroller A. W. Peterson. "There is no sense in getting panicky," he warned. No measures have been taken yet.

Answers on the campus will carry on with their Effective Service work to help the men in the armed forces already under supervision, it was learned. The most important thing, Dean of Women Louise Greeley declared, is that the women remember that they are students and to be calm in the crisis.

Hysteria Hit Campus In Last War

By STAN GROWACKI

The university campus during the first World war was alive with feverish excitement and, unlike yesterday's sudden declaration of war against Japan which left Americans stunned, students in 1917 had been stirred to such a frenzy that they all but de— [...]

Faculty members generally were shocked at the status of the nation, or even that of the campus. They were agreed, however, that it was right that the United States should enter the war actively shoot— [...]

Above: *Daily Cardinal* Editor-in-Chief Cliff Behnke (center) confers with staff members over the day's pages.

Left: *Cardinal* photographer and reporter Neal Ulevich.

IT DOESN'T END WITH US

The Daily Cardinal.

UNIVERSITY OF WISCONSIN.

VOL. XI. NO. 181. MADISON, WIS., TUESDAY, MAY 27, 1902. Price Five Cents.

GRAND MASS MEETING
TO-NIGHT. EVERYBODY COME.

A POPULAR PLAY

WILL BE PRESENTED BY SENIOR CLASS.

"Because She Loved Him So," Made Famous by Gillette—Exceptionally Strong Cast—Miss Lamont and Mr. Pyre Direct.

The cast for the Senior class play is now hard at work and rehearsals are being held daily—afternoon and evening—under the direction of Miss Lamont, instructor in elocution, with Mr. Walton H. Pyre, the season just closed with Otis Skinner, as coach. "Because She Loved Him So," is a comedy in three acts adapted from the French of Brisson and Le Clag by Wm. Gillette. It is decidedly a high class play and was last presented to a Madison audience about three years ago when it was achieving such a grand success with Gillette in the title role of John Weatherby. The committee have chosen another Gillette play believing that it cannot help but please a university audience and because of the favor with which "The Private Secretary," a Gillette play, was received when presented by the Harmsfoot Club on February 21.

"Because She Loved Him So," affords an excellent opportunity for a variety of parts. The character parts are excellent and the straight parts have a coloring that gives each of them a distinct individuality of its own.

The cast of the play is exceptional this year in that nearly every member has had previous experience in university dramatics.

John V. Brennan, who takes the leading role of "John Weatherby," is recognized as the best actor in the university, having achieved great success in "A Colonial Girl," the dramatic contest and in the title role of "Rev. Robert Spaulding" in "The Private Secretary."

Elizabeth N. Shepard is also well known in 'varsity dramatics, having taken leading parts in the Dramatic Contest of last year, "Nance Oldfield" and "The Private Secretary."

Dwight E. Beebe previously appeared in university dramatics in "A Colonial Girl," in the Dramatic Contest, and as "Sydney Gibson, the Tailor" in "The Private Secretary."

Freda D. Stolte, also had a leading part in "The Private Secretary" and in the "Red Domino" performance of this year.

J. D. Patrick appeared in the Haresfoot performances of the last two years and in the Glee Club play "The Professor's Daughter" two years ago.

Mary H. Swain took a leading part in the "Hector" cast in the dramatic contest of last year.

J. G. McFarland and F. O. Letser had appeared in the Dramatic Contest.

The cast is exceptionally fortunate in having the combined assistance of Mr. Pyre and Miss Lamont in staging this play and a most finished production may be expected.

The cast is as follows:

Oliver West, a London artist, J. Barrow Patrick.

Gertrude West, his wife, Freda D. Stolte.

John Weatherby, Gertrude's father, John V. Brennan.

Mrs. Weatherby, his wife, Elizabeth N. Shepard.

Louisa Donicla, a Spanish woman, Mary H. Swain.

Mr. Marsh, a Portsmouth lawyer, James G. McFarland.

Thomas Weatherby, Gertrude's brother, Dwight E. Beebe.

Margaret, servant at Mr. Weatherby's, Laura K. Sage.

Rev. Lyman Langley, Dean of Waterford, Fred O Letser.

Julia Langley, his daughter, Mary Stoppenbach.

Susan, maid at Oliver West's, Marie O. Hinkley.

Albert Pritchard, servant at Oliver West's, John A. O'Meara.

Mr. Jackson, and Mr. Breslin, Nicholas Kirch and John F. Powers.

PROF. BRUCE TO GO

Second Offer From North Dakota is Accepted—Will be Head of Law Department.

Professor Andrew A. Bruce of the law school faculty has received a second and more flattering offer from the University of North Dakota and has accepted. The new position is that of head of the law department of North Dakota institutions.

The University of North Dakota is the only institution of higher education in North Dakota. It is rapidly growing and is experiencing a phenomenal growth. It is for these reasons that Professor Bruce deems it advisable that he accept the opportunities for advancement being so much greater at a younger institution.

It is understood that the salary named in the new offer is considerably larger than that received here.

Tennis Team Victorious at Minneapolis.

Notwithstanding the heavy rain fall during the last few days the University Tennis team defeated Minnesota team by a score of 4 to 0, winning the four matches played. The fifth match, however, remained in a tie and the sixth set bowing played owing to rain.

In the doubles Boye and Helmholz defeated Payne and Wyman, 7—5, 6—1, 6—1. Seaman and Morley defeated Smith, 6—7, 6—4, 7—6. In the singles, Morley defeated Northrup, 6—2, 6—3. Mosley defeated Northrup, 6—2, 6—3. Seaman defeated Gillette, 6—7. Helmholz tied Wyman, 4—6, 7—5, 1—4, rain.

In the final round of tournament at Madison Helmholz defeated Seaman 6—2, 6—4. Therefore Boye and Helmholz will represent Wisconsin at Chicago in the intercollegiate, which begins on Tuesday, May 27. The tennis team this year has made a better showing than ever before, winning both the dual meet with Chicago and Minnesota. Great things are expected of Boye and Helmholz at the intercollegiate for they have both been playing in excellent form.

—Sidney Olsen, '02, left last evening for Hibbing, Minn., where he will take up engineering work under E. J. Longyear, a prominent engineer at that place.

ANOTHER FRATERNITY

CHAPTER OF SIGMA NU TO BE INSTALLED HERE.

Robert O. Holt, Instructor in French, is the Prime Mover—Chapter to be Composed of Men Prominent in College Activities—The Members.

Robt. B. Holt, when seen this morning, said that he had received word last evening from the Grand Recorder of Sigma Nu fraternity that the charter had been granted to the petitioners at Wisconsin. The granting of this charter brings a course though strong national fraternity, Sigma Nu was established at Virginia Military institute in 1869, and its rapid progress since that time has been phenomenal, as there are now forty-five active chapters. Its chapters are located in all sections of the country, though perhaps strongest in the south, and while it is young in years, the chapter roll includes many men of national importance.

The installation of the Wisconsin chapter is to take place at Keeley's hall Wednesday evening, May the 28th. Following the installation exercises a banquet will be held at which time toasts by visiting Sigma Nu and neophytes will be given. Several delegates are to be present from the Chicago Alumni association, Northwestern university, University of Indiana and other chapters of this division.

A complete list of the chapter members here follows:

Otis B. Dahle, M.; Herbert S. E. Washburn, Racine; I. O. Hobbard, Westfield; C. A. Ulmer, New York City; Albert O. Hinn, Fennimore; Julius H. Warner, Windsor; R. M. Trump, Milwaukee; John A. Froelich, Madison; Chauncy W. Wotton, Madison; Ralph O. Plumb, Manitowoc; Robert D. Buchanan, Rio; Nicholas M. Schantz, Hartford; W. O. Hotchkiss Eau Claire; D. C. Washburn, Racine; C. B. Williams, Fennimore.

The members have been quite active during the past few months in their work. They have already secured their quarters for next year. The house to be occupied by the fraternity the coming year is 613 Francis, the house formerly occupied by the Phi Gamma Delta fraternity.

Robert D. Holt, the prime mover in the organization, has been at Wisconsin for three years and during the last year has filled the position of Instructor in French. He was elected to the Phi Beta Kappa society as a tribute to his scholarship. Before coming to the institution he was a student at Vanderbilt University at Nashville, Tenn., and it was there that he became a member of the Sigma chapter of the organization which is to be started here.

EDWIN BOOTH SOCIETY.

The following will give selections at the regular meeting of the Edwin Booth Dramatic Society, Wednesday evening, May 28: Joseph Kuffend, Arnold L. Gesell, Charles Lenart, John V. Brennan, J. O. Patrick, G. E.

Beebe, Harry C. Johnson, J. A. O'Meara, J. F. Powers, Nicholas Kirch, Wm. Ryan, J. O. Miller.

This will be the last meeting of the year and election of officers will take place. A full attendance is therefore desired. The meeting will be held in the Music Lecture room, Library hall.

Secretary.

INSPECTS UNIVERSITY REGIMENT.

Annual Inspection by Captain J. J. Bradley 16th U. S. Infantry.—Military Notes.

For two hours this morning the U. W. Corps of Cadets looked their best while Captain John J. Bradley, 16th U. S. Infantry inspected the work done by the military department. The regiment fell in at 9 o'clock, the staff and corps was first examined, then battalion and regimental formation was gone through with, then came dress parade and inspection of the companies. This was followed by battalion and company drills. Captain Bradley introduced an innovation by asking questions of the men and some humorous answers are reported to have been given by the excited privates.

The regiment will drill again on Thursday, after which there will be but one drill more this year, that of the parade on decoration day. On this occasion the regiment will escort the old soldiers, when dress parade will be held on the campus at which Company D will be presented with medals and the officers with their commissions. After this ceremony the men will be awarded blank cartridges, and the season will be ended with plenty of noise.

The target squad has been out on the range every Saturday and will have its competition shoot probably on Monday afternoon. A gold medal will be presented to the winner and the results sent in for the intercollegiate contest.

INTERSCHOLASTIC ARRANGEMENTS

Seats on Sale Thursday at 12 o'clock at O'Neill's—General Admission 50 Cents, Reserved Seat $1.

Active preparations are being made at Camp Randall for the Interscholastic meet, to be held there Saturday, May 31. The bicycle track is being rolled and graded, and the running tracks are being attended to so that there will be nothing in that respect to interfere with a good contest. Crowds will be kept off the grounds by means of a temporary wire fence which is being erected, and several regular police will be engaged in addition to the student police which will keep the field clear of the onlookers.

As there are to be over thirty high schools represented, many of which are quite well known in athletics, it is impossible to make any definite prediction, but the Milwaukee – West Side and Madison High schools are mentioned among the most prominent point-winners.

Reserved seat tickets will be on sale at 12 o'clock Thursday at Borton & O'Neill's drug store. General admission will be 50 cents and reserved seats $1.

IT DOESN'T END WITH US

This *Cardinal* photograph shows the first major campus moratorium on ending the war in Vietnam, Oct. 15, 1969.

Right: State Sen. Gordon Roseleip, who assailed *Cardinal* Managing Editor John Gruber over living with "known communists."

Below: Police in riot gear confront partiers on Mifflin Street. Protests and clashes between police and students in housing there became common in the late 1960s. *Cardinal* editors purchased helmets and gas masks for reporters who ventured into "Miffland" to cover the violence.

The *Daily Cardinal*'s front page, showing a negative of a photo of the aftermath of the Sterling Hall bombing in August 1970.

Above: Workers clean up debris from the bombing.

Left: Former *Cardinal* staff member David Fine is taken to jail after his arrest in connection with the bombing of Sterling Hall.

IT DOESN'T END WITH US

Each time the *Cardinal* has moved offices, its green semi-circular copy desk has moved with it. **Above:** The desk in the Union, early 1940s. **Below:** In the *Cardinal's* then-new home in Vilas Communication Hall in the early 1970s.

The *Daily Cardinal* board, including Editor-in-Chief Bill Swislow (center) and board member Robert Taylor (right), deliberates whether to donate $5,000 to David Fine's defense fund.

Above: Press Brigade members Rob Siebers, Mary Jo Ross, Jone Satran and Steve Kerch. **Below:** Standard Press Party members Debby Schindler, Deborah Jaliman and Milo Geyelin with the Dane County Sheriff.

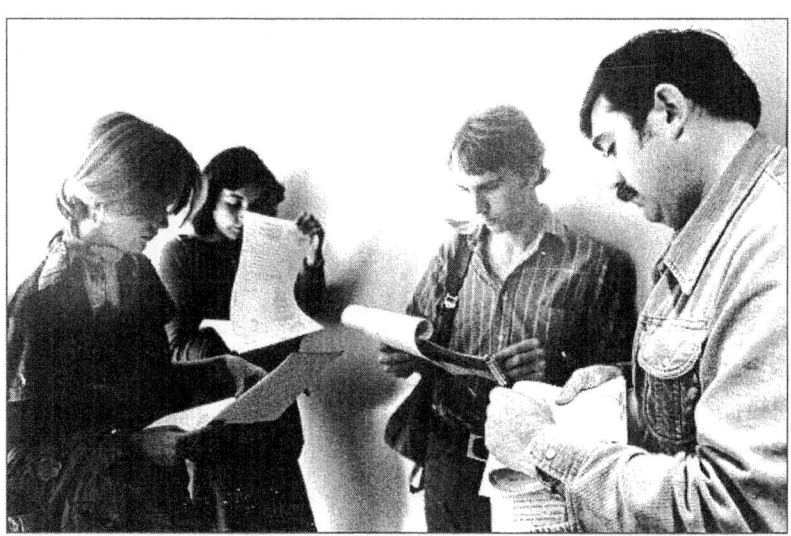

IT DOESN'T END WITH US

The Daily Cardinal

VOL. LXXIII, No. 83 — University of Wisconsin, Madison, Wisconsin — Friday, December

WESTWARD, HO!

USC's Deadly Duo

PETE BEATHARD — HAL BEDSOLE

Rose Bowl Game Will Pick National Gridiron Champs

Once-beaten Wisconsin clashes with undefeated Southern California in the Rose Bowl January 1, 1963, in what shapes up to be one of the biggest post season games ever played. USC and Wisconsin are ranked 1-2 by both wire services making the game a genuine national championship.

The battle pits a fancy, imaginative Trojan offense against Wisconsin, the top scoring major college team in the nation. USC used numerous variations on the "T" and "I" formations while the Badgers usually run from either a pro-type or wing "T" formation.

Defensively both teams stack up as "tough" with neither giving up more than two touchdowns in any of their games.

If the Badgers capture the opening kickoff they will start Pat Richter and Ron Carlson at the ends, Roger Pillath and Andy Wojdula at the tackles, Steve Underwood and Mike Gross at the guards, and Ken Bowman at center.

Joe Cassidy at the fullback spot Jim Nettles or Louis Holland at left halfback and Ron Smith at the right halfback spot with Ron VanderKelen at quarterback. VanderKelen is the Big Ten's leading scorer and Wisconsin's master. He is no and Mike Horan at fullback.

Holland, the lead guidance man in the Badger's attack was the Big Ten's leading scorer and touchdown maker. Knick, the no 2 sophomore to crack into the Bowl unit, is yet to lose yardage as a Badger.

If Wisconsin stacks on defense, there changes will probably be made: Larry Howard at ends in place of Richter, Jim Jay instead in place of Carlson, Jim Nettles at quarterback, Jim Purnell at fullback and Jim Nettles at halfback.

MILT BRUHN

LOUIE HOLLAND

UCLA Here Saturday; Cagers Shooting Is .504

This Saturday at 1:30 p.m. the basketball team will try to extend its two game winning streak against the University of California at Los Angeles (UCLA) in the Fieldhouse.

Coach John Erickson will probably use the same five that beat Marquette by 17 last Tuesday. These probable starters are Ken Siebel at center, Mike O'Melia and Don Hendrickson.

Kojekus will go into drive into his bench with Lonnie Ostrom, Jim Bohen, Bob Wills and Ken Siebel. According to Erickson, Siebel above his injury is recovering faster than expected, will see action this Saturday.

UCLA, quarterbacked in the NCAA last year by two hobbies back from four first team, from surging guard Walt Hazzard was rated the No. 1 team by the NCAA.

After 50 games this season, the Badgers are shooting a fantastic .504 from the field (121-240). This tremendous shooting percentage makes a happy contrast with the 42 percent the Badgers have in both Milling. The 6-2 senior is 8 for 8 from the floor in the two games he has appeared in.

Other Badgers hitting more than 50 percent: Jack Brens (9 of 17); Tom Gwyn (10 of 17); top scorer for the season is Siebel who in 5 games scoring guards Mike O'Melia (18-37) and Tom Hendrickson after netting on...

Wisconsin, although with 19 points is averaging little against Miami because of his injury. Going into the Miami game, he was getting better than nine rebounds per game.

Siebel is scoring with 113 points for a 18.5 average. Second behind him is averaging with 78 points. Siebel is averaging 32.1 in 19 point per game on 16 points and Hendrickson has a 9.5 average in 22 points.

ROBERT COLEMAN
Jewelers
DIAMONDS — SETTINGS
631 State Street
CE 5-4144

Onion Rings 40c
HOWARD JOHNSON'S RESTAURANT
OPEN 6:30 A.M. to 11 P.M. EVERYDAY

THE KAPPA SIGMA'S
with
Ron VanderKelen
and
Brother
Don Hendrickson
and the
Rest of the
BADGERS
a successful
Rose Bowl Trip

Prepare for
A BUSINESS CAREER
in the following NIGHT SCHOOL courses
☆ Beginning typing
☆ Advanced typing
☆ Electric typing
☆ Gregg Shorthand II
☆ Speedwriting Shorthand (beginning same)
☆ Bookkeeping
☆ Accounting
☆ Wisconsin Real Estate

STUDENTS MAY ENROLL NOW
Accredited by the Accrediting Commission for Business Schools, Washington, D.C.

FREE PLACEMENT SERVICE

Madison Business College
215 W. Washington Ave.
2ND SEMESTER DAY SCHOOL CLASSES BEGIN

IT DOESN'T END WITH US

Above: The *Daily Cardinal* printed in the Typography Laboratory after the Campus Publishing Co. donated the presses and assets to the university. **Below:** Printers Phil Holen and Orv Larson gathered with *Cardinal* staff.

IT DOESN'T END WITH US

By James Rowen
Reprinted, 1969,
from The Daily Cardinal
425 Henry Mall
Madison, Wisconsin
All rights reserved
— 35c —

IT DOESN'T END WITH US

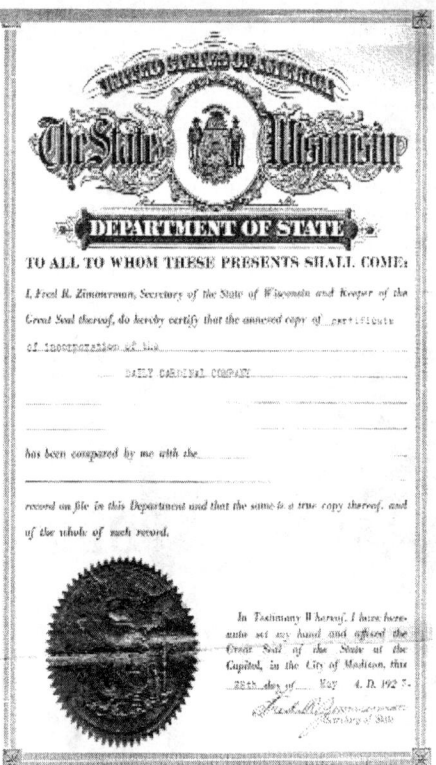

Top: The *Daily Cardinal* board discusses the *Herald* takeover, watched by Madison press.

Left: The *Cardinal's* original articles of incorporation.

Above: Dick Ausman

IT DOESN'T END WITH US

Above: *Cardinal* staffers Meghan Henson, Bill Whittaker, Kathy Litt, Peter Kafka, Jon Schatz, Abigail Goldman and Gregory Larson in Washington DC covering the Campaign for Peace in the Middle East, 1991. **Below:** Stephanie Anderson and Syrentha Savio prepare for the paper's 100th birthday, 1992.

IT DOESN'T END WITH US

PRESIDENT IS SLAIN

The Daily Cardinal

Centennial Issue   April 4, 1992   The University of Wisconsin Madison

100 years of *Cardinal* spirit

William Wesley Young, pictured here, founded the *Cardinal* with $300.

Our face and fight have changed over a century's passage, but our message and passion have not. *The Daily Cardinal* has seen the Spanish-American war, the downfall of Hitler and 15 University administrations come and go.

Walk into our office and find those who thrive on deadline pressure and the ground breaking stories, hard-core sports junkies, activists who lead rallies, critics of the University's low minority recruitment standards and those who simply want to do something they'll never be able to do again.

We have come from blue-collar, suburban and elite families. We read the *Village Voice*, *Sports Illustrated* and *Spy* magazine; we watch "Star Trek" and cheer at football games. We skip class to pump out our eight-page paper, we find something to grouse about in each issue, and every so often we congratulate ourselves on a job well done.

The Daily Cardinal is the last place we will work where the most senior staff member wields the same power as the newest at our staff meetings, and has the same power to mold the shape of our pages. One person, one vote.

They've called us radicals, they've called us hippies, they've called us pawns of the establishment. We're feisty, we're intelligent, we're brainy and we're damned good journalists. We call the bureaucracy on inconsistencies and injustices. We scoop the city papers in our news coverage.

The bylines on our pages change from day to day, and every year our editors' desks are infused with new blood. But the passion, idealism and hard work of 100 years remains consistent. Within the pages of our paper and the confines of our office, a debate rages between philosophers, journalists, activists, careerists and cynics. But it is this spirit that flavors our pages; this is *The Daily Cardinal* of 1992.

Pin-up girls decorating the *Cardinal*'s office in 1948 have been replaced by Madonna and Karl Marx by the 1992 staff. The staff's faces have changed over 100 years, but the idealism and activism have not.

KING MURDERED

IT DOESN'T END WITH US

THE BADGER HERALD

'Daily Cardinal' ceases publication
Outstanding debts force shutdown; paper might resume printing in April

Students gain access to teacher evaluations

Above: The *Badger Herald* on Feb. 8, 1995. **Below:** The *Cardinal* office, cleaned out and shut down in the summer of 1995.

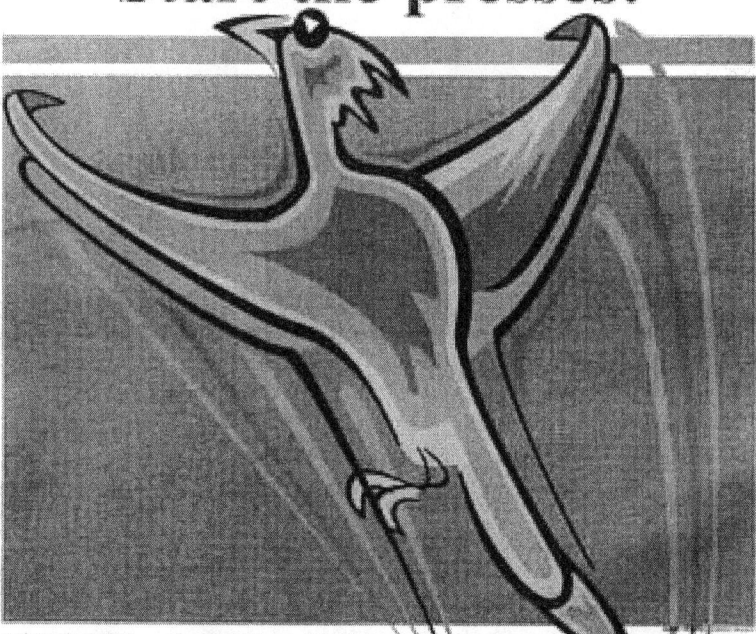

IT DOESN'T END WITH US

Above: Business Manager Vince Filak and Editor-in-Chief Mark Wegner burn a copy of the *Cardinal*'s debt settlement as Managing Editor Matt Schwalbach watches. **Below:** *Cardinal* alumni review their old papers and talk about their experiences at a 1999 *Cardinal* reunion.

IT DOESN'T END WITH US

The Daily Cardinal

Serving the University of Wisconsin–Madison community since 1892

VOLUME 111, ISSUE 7 · WEDNESDAY, SEPTEMBER 12, 2001 · DAILYCARDINAL.COM

TERROR IN U.S.

Deaths estimated in the thousands

By Danielle Szulczewski
THE DAILY CARDINAL

The country watched with horror Tuesday as a series of hijacked and crashed airliners resulted in what many will feel as the most profound act of terrorism in American history.

As of 2:30 a.m. CDT Wednesday press time, news services reported more than 1,200 fatalities in New York City and more than 700 in Washington, D.C., independent of the victims of the plane crashes.

At 8:45 a.m. EDT Tuesday, American Airlines Flight 11, a Boeing 767 jet en route from Boston to Los Angeles, hit the north tower of the World Trade Center in New York, according to CNN. U.S. Attorney General John Ashcroft later said the hijackers took Flight 11 by force with knives.

At 9:03 a.m., 18 minutes after the first attack, United Airlines Flight 175, flying from Boston to Los Angeles, crashed into the center's south tower.

At 9:40 a.m., the Federal Aviation Administration canceled all flights, a first in American history. Shortly afterward, all incoming international flights were rerouted to Canada, followed by the closing of the Mexican and Canadian borders.

Five minutes later, American Airlines Flight 77, departing from Dulles Airport near Washington, D.C., en route to Los Angeles, struck the Pentagon in northern Virginia.

The crashes at the World Trade Center resulted in the collapse of the south tower at 10 a.m., a 60-foot portion of the Pentagon at 10:10 a.m. and the north tower of the trade center at 10:29 a.m.

According to a transcript from United Airlines Flight 93, flying from Newark to San Francisco, tears shown near Johnstown, Pa., approximately 80 miles southeast of Pittsburgh at 10:10 a.m. News services reported the U.S. officials believe the flight could have been heading for another Washington location. Reports of

CRASHES, page 4

United Flight 175 from Boston to Los Angeles crashes into the south World Trade Center tower in New York City at 9:03 a.m. EDT Tuesday. For eyewitness accounts of the attacks in New York City and Washington, D.C., see page 3.

NEWS ANALYSIS

Experts elaborate on attacks' implications

By Ron Sykes
THE DAILY CARDINAL

Many U.S. citizens awoke across the country Tuesday to startling images on the television.

The World Trade Center destroyed, the Pentagon in flames, four commercial airplanes hijacked and used as weapons against America.

America is not new to acts of terrorism, either domestic or foreign. The Oklahoma City bombing was only seven years ago, and the perpetrators of the 1993 bombing of the World Trade Center were supposed to be sentenced today.

The difference between Tuesday's attacks and the acts of the past is the sheer magnitude of the actions that exposed the vulnerability of Americans cities, according to Stan Schafer, a professor of history at UW–Madison.

"Once upon a time you had to have a club to kill someone. ... Now were so technologically advanced there's so many ways to attack," he said.

According to Schafer, the United States has become overly dependent on its own advancements, opening itself up to many different forms of attack.

"You can get to a city through the air, water, a sewer system—those all provide channels of attack for terrorists," he said. "The very things that we believe enhance our lives can be turned against us to harm our lives."

In contrast to Schafer's emphasis on technology, Professor Yehuda Lukacs of George Mason University in Fairfax, Va., argues that the rise of terrorist attacks is inherent to the American political and social system.

"I think that any country that is free and democratic is vulnerable to such a magnitude of attacks," he said.

Audrey Keith Coates, a research fellow in

ANALYSIS, page 4

UW students react to East Coast disasters, administrators speak at evening vigil

By Christina Thulf
THE DAILY CARDINAL

The terrorist attacks in New York City and Washington, D.C., have affected people around the world, with students at UW–Madison proving to be no exception.

Shortly after hearing the news, the local Red Cross filled with potential blood donors, with a wait that reached three hours during the day.

Members of the UW–Madison women's tennis team divided their energies would be best directed by helping those who are now suffering.

"We went to practice, and we didn't think it was a good day to practice, so we came here," said Katie Dougherty, a senior on the team, awaiting her turn to donate blood. "It's terrible as the situation is, we're out here in Wisconsin ... this is the only way we could help."

Mark Shields, the regional spokesperson for the Badger-Hawkeye Region, Madison Locations for the Red Cross said the center had brought in a record amount of blood today.

"The outpouring of support from the public is very touching," he said. "UW has a great tradition of supporting the blood supply and that support will be very important in the coming weeks."

Some students who said they wanted to help but could not because they had to attend class, thought the university should have handled the situation differently.

"Not only for safety reasons should they have shut down classes but out of respect and consideration for those people who were killed," said Todd Schreiber, a UW–Madison senior from Manhattan. "And for people like myself who are from New York and for the people who have friends and relatives in New York, to give them an opportunity to find out about the people they care about."

Schreiber spent the day trying to get in touch with family, eventually learning that his father, who was working very duty two blocks away from the World Trade Center, saw the second plane hit the tower.

"It's so surreal and very eerie," he said. "I feel kind of weird not being there ... watching my city on television in Madison."

A number of other students expressed shock at what occurred early Tuesday.

"I woke up this morning and I thought it

STUDENTS, page 4

Two UW–Madison students clutch their candles as they read a song sheet during a vigil on Library Mall Tuesday evening.

"...the great state University of Wisconsin should ever encourage that continual and fearless sifting and winnowing by which alone the truth can be found."

IT DOESN'T END WITH US

IT DOESN'T END WITH US

9.

Bombing

There are some, perhaps many in the movement who see one and only one way of renewing and strengthening the fight for change. Several of those people, whoever they are, were responsible for the firebombings of the Red Gym, the Primate Lab and the State Selective Service headquarters in the last four days.

They call themselves the Vanguard of the Revolution. They are indeed. They have chosen to initiate direct action. They have chosen to show to those both in and outside of the movement that the immobile and repressive position taken by this nation can only be countered head on in the streets with bombs and guns ...

And if acts such as those committed in the last few days are needed to strike fear into the bodies of once fearless men and rid this campus once and for all of repressive and deadly ideas and institutions then so be it.
– The Daily Cardinal, Jan. 6, 1970

ଓଃ

The meeting went on for hours, Len Fleischer said. Hours.

"It was like the tortured conversation you have at the funeral of a good friend," said Fleischer, editorial page editor of the *Daily Cardinal* in the fall of 1970. "A disaster had happened, and we had to figure out what to say to the campus about it."

By "we" he meant the thirty-five *Cardinal* staff members all crammed into *Cardinal* Editor-in-Chief Rena Steinzor's college apartment.

IT DOESN'T END WITH US

Less than three blocks from the *Cardinal* offices, a university building sat scarred by explosives, surrounded by shattered glass. Shortly before dawn, Aug. 24, 1970, anti-war radicals calling themselves the New Year's Gang had set off a bomb next to Sterling Hall, the building that housed the university's controversial Army Math Research Center.

The explosion killed Robert Fassnacht, a 33-year-old postdoctorate physics researcher, and injured four others. A nationwide search began for the bombers, four young men: 24-year-old Karleton Armstrong, his 19-year-old brother Dwight, 18-year-old David Fine and 22-year-old Leo Burt.

Burt and Fine had been *Cardinal* staff members.

The bombing's effects rippled out from the Madison campus like a wave through the anti-war movement. University historians Cronon and Jenkins wrote:

> ... the New Year's Gang had killed not only Bob Fassnacht but the strategy of revolutionary violence as well, in Madison and to a considerable extent in the nation as a whole. The gaping hole in Sterling Hall was a continuing reminder of the enormous explosion that shocked the campus community as had few events in the university's long history. Student radicals could and did point out that the bombing had merely brought the war home, that it was an example of what the United States was daily inflicting on the Vietnamese people ... to the anti-war but peace-loving idealists who comprised the great bulk of the UW student body, Armstrong's bomb also brought home the horrors of violence, whether in Vietnam or Madison.[1]

Journalist Tom Bates, who wrote about the bombing and about the *Cardinal* in his 1992 book *Rads*, said in his book's introduction that the bombing was "a turning point."

> The physical damage to the university was frightful, but even more sobering was the news that a brilliant young physicist who had nothing to do with the Pentagon-funded think tank had been killed in the explosion. For the Madison Left, with which I identified, it really was as though the sky had fallen.[2]

The meeting went on for hours.

"It was a long, agonizing conversation about what we should say about this," Steinzor said. "Some people were absolutely horrified and disgusted by the violence. No one exactly embraced it, but some people did feel that something very serious was happening to people we knew, and honestly believed we were all equally responsible."

IT DOESN'T END WITH US

The AMRC had been under *Cardinal* scrutiny for nearly a year. Reporter Jim Rowen published a series of articles that had detailed how the center, founded in 1955, had been doing work that advanced the war in Vietnam, tying the campus directly to the war. He followed that series, Profit Motive 101, with more detailed stories about the ways in which academic research benefitted what the *Cardinal* characterized as the forces of imperialism. A story about a UW professor who tested LSD and other drugs on rats in order to determine its use as a chemical weapon concluded:

> Weapons are made to be used. Herbicides and poison gases have been recently used in Vietnam by the Americans and in Yemen by the Egyptians, but still the University continues its complicity with the Pentagon arms researchers. Since some faculties and administrators choose to cooperate with the military, perhaps students should make known their feelings regarding such research on campus.

The campus shortly before the bombing was "a haze of tear gas," Fleischer said. Protests were daily occurrences. Arrests were so common that prior to university speeches and films, student leaders passed a hat around for donations to a bail fund. Steven Reiner said one of his major purchases for the year had been state-of-the-art gas masks for all *Cardinal* reporters.

"I convinced the board of control to pay for them before we went to cover the first big march on Washington," he said. "We got four big boxes of these brand-new, very expensive gas masks, which of course we thought were very cool. But we needed them, and we used them quite often."

From December 1969 through January 1970, arsonists struck university buildings, attacking the Primate Laboratory, the Army Reserve Officer Training Corps building and the county draft offices. The vandals called the *Cardinal*, claiming to have the capability to "plant bombs around the school."

"We have enough straights in our organization so that we can get away with it," the *Cardinal* quoted the caller as saying. "We can shut this University down in a day if we want to, because we've got pretty powerful stuff."

"We felt back then that there was a war going on in the United States," Fleischer said. "It wasn't just in Vietnam. Students had been shot at Kent State. All kinds of things were happening. We didn't feel like we were into gratuitous violence, it was just that the stakes had been raised that high. The campus and the country were in a state of literally armed confrontation."

Some students, particularly those who lived and studied some distance from the center of Madison's far-flung campus, went to class and tried to ignore the ferment.

For others, the atmosphere of protest and engagement was the purpose of their presence, and the *Cardinal* was the center of the action. Fine and Burt were among those caught up in the movement. Fine wrote editorials and

IT DOESN'T END WITH US

columns and Burt covered the increasingly violent protests that took over and shut down the center of campus:

> Carrying torches, demonstrators massed on the Library Mall after leaving the Union rally, before marching up Lathrop Dr. toward the Army Math Research Center.
>
> Breaking windows in the Center and Sterling Hall, the protesters moved onto Charter St. and out onto University Ave, where they barraged a passing police car with rocks, shattering several windows ...
>
> Several people, said to be police agents, broke from the ranks of the march to block attempts to smash windows in [retailer] Rennebohms. At that point, a burly plain-clothed policeman attacked a protester, bear-hugging him in the middle of University Ave.
>
> He was promptly set upon by a score of demonstrators who sought to free their companion.

During that same time, the *Cardinal* was becoming more and more radicalized. "Underground"-style newspapers were publishing at college campuses across the country; the *Cardinal's* style, especially on its editorial and features pages, emulated their provocative rhetoric and freewheeling narratives. In this it was not alone. "Some university-sponsored student papers are also becoming more radical," the *New York Times* reported. "The *News*, a Boston University paper, published an edition last November containing photographs of a couple in positions of sexual intercourse, as a protest against dormitory visiting hours."[3]

The *Cardinal* under Reiner had altered its decades-old layout and typefaces to more closely echo the casual, modern feel of *Newsday*, he said. Reiner wrote editorials, at the end of his term, that "today would get me thrown in Guantanamo Bay," declaring that if violence was the only way the anti-war movement could make any progress "then so be it."

"There was lots of discussion and lots of screaming and debating and lots of back and forth about what the paper's editorial stance was going to be," he said. "And I may have thought in my head that what I was doing was walking some sort of line, but in the end, it pissed a lot of people off."

The *Cardinal* became an instigator, cheerleading for the violence taking place on campus as the anti-war movement grew fractured and fractious. "To the pious and angered critics of the young bombers and saboteurs," the *Cardinal's* editorial page read, "Look at them. They are your children."

Steinzor joined the *Cardinal* in 1967, in the fall of her freshman year. The granddaughter of immigrant labor organizers in the New York garment indus-

IT DOESN'T END WITH US

try, she had come to Wisconsin looking for an education as a reporter. She found it on the *Cardinal*'s city desk.

From a city hall reporting job she moved on to become editorial page editor under Reiner. In the spring of 1970, she was elected to succeed Reiner as the paper's top editor.

"Rena had been the city editor, and she was very, very, very passionate about ... everything," Reiner said. "Especially about politics and feminism."

She was the first editor-in-chief to be chosen by the *Cardinal*'s election model of selecting leaders, where every staff member, from top brass down to copy checkers, has one vote on who should run the paper the following year. It was a system — one still used today — that she and Reiner had pushed for, feeling they could not advocate for true democracy in other societal institutions while tolerating a hierarchy within their own.

"It used to be that editors were selected at a meeting in some big fancy place, that had to do with the chancellor," she said. "Instead of that, we had the *Cardinal* staff casting ballots. There was really a big rebellion against anything that smacked of unwanted authority or authority exercised by people who didn't have their futures on the line."

Steinzor had gone home for the summer to visit family, and she was in California with her grandparents when the bombing happened. "I don't remember who called me," she said. "But someone called me and told me what had happened. I was in total shock."

Managing Editor Ron Legro had been asleep in his off-campus house when the noise of the explosion knocked him up and out of bed. With Steinzor out of town, he had the responsibility of assigning and editing most of the copy that would be needed for the *Cardinal*'s fall registration issue.

"I hustled down there, and of course it had all been roped off. There was lots of confusion and the *Cardinal* was basically a spectator," Legro said. "The cops weren't going to let the *Daily Cardinal* into that crime scene. We couldn't get near it.

"So we just started working, because when we put out our fall issue, it was going to need a ton of articles about Sterling Hall."

They needed not only articles, but an editorial. The involvement of former *Cardinal* staff members was all over the news by the time Steinzor returned to campus; a hunt was underway for Fine, Burt and the Armstrong brothers.

The city — the country — was watching what the *Cardinal* would say.

Editorials then were written by consensus, by general agreement, which meant different factions of the staff — mostly left and far-left, though conservatism lurked on the sports desk and in the business office — had to come around to a common point of view.

Two weeks after Sterling Hall was bombed, the staff had difficulty even finding a common point.

"By this time, a lot of us were taking the violence on campus pretty personally," Steinzor said. "During protest marches, police would single out *Car-*

IT DOESN'T END WITH US

dinal reporters. We had a photographer who'd been clubbed in the face and pretty badly injured. In the mind of someone dealing with that, it's hard to make the distinction between what we would and wouldn't have done. We couldn't renounce them. Things got blurry."

Staffers argued back and forth. Some, Fleischer said, wanted to say the bombers had gone too far. Others, Steinzor remembered, wanted to praise the bombers' intent.

Legro said it was surreal. The headlines were about their friends, their colleagues. They didn't want to believe the police, the news reports.

"In the newsroom, Leo Burt was a prince among thieves," Legro said. "Kind-hearted, light-hearted, thoughtful and intelligent and — this was unusual in our crowd — without a bad word for anyone around him."

It went on for hours.

"There were voices saying, 'Don't do this,'" Steinzor said. "Those voices were eclipsed."

Steinzor wrote the editorial:

> In the aftermath of an act of sabotage which shook this society to its foundations, we are left with victory and defeat, failure and success.
>
> The bombing of the Army Mathematics Research Center destroyed an object of widespread political hatred and struck a blow to the American military machine. It also killed a man.
>
> The AMRC was a physical and symbolic installation whose sole purpose was to serve the strong arm of American economic interests across the globe. This military arm of our government has been the most violent instrument in the history of the world and has stolen from, murdered and destroyed the lives of people in the countries from Cuba to Vietnam, as well as those at the bottom of the social ladder within its own turf.
>
> AMRC personnel and the administration of this university would have the people of this community and the country believe that the Center was engaged in "pure" mathematical research which had an incidental function in the perfection of weapons of death by the army.
>
> Such an assertion sets up both a false dichotomy and a lie. The AMRC, along with thousands of installations like it throughout the country, are the jugular vein of American militarism. The idea of pure research in such a context has

IT DOESN'T END WITH US

about as much moral credibility as the idea of efficient and painless genocide did when it was advanced thirty years ago. Over and over members of this community asked those in power to discuss the AMRC's purpose with them. They were refused.

Over and over again members of this community stated that they opposed what the AMRC stood for and what it was doing. They were ignored. Finally, some members of this movement decided to stop talking, to stop asking that the place be shut down. And so they blew it up.

A powerful and offensive physical attack was launched and completed. Damage was material and symbolic.

But the bomb that went off that Monday morning did more than simply close down the AMRC. It killed a man, destroyed years of research that would have benefitted mankind. Robert Fassnacht's death is a tragedy. Those of us who love life enough to revolutionize it must and do realize that. We mourn Fassnacht as we mourn the others killed in the struggle.

However, we distrust those who would have us mourn Fassnacht in a vacuum. The very organs used to sell the death culture that is America have been making capital out of Fassnacht's death for days. There is something perverse about the majority of opinion makers in this country who have endorsed mass murder in Vietnam and then manipulate the death of an individual in an effort to silence those who would stop them.

We mourn Robert Fassnacht because we love life. His death has been used in the power structure's effort to reinforce the bizarre status quo that is this country. This is not what his death means to us.

If Robert Fassnacht had died in Vietnam, if he had been yellow or black, he would be a line in a news story, a number. And it is that reality that some of us have already died to change and will struggle to change.

But the question that remains, in the final analysis, is the content of the future of this movement.

IT DOESN'T END WITH US

The AMRC has been destroyed. In order for its physical and symbolic destruction to have any meaning beyond this specific point in time, the movement from which the bombing sprang must be expanded. People must be reached and talked to. We must turn out from ourselves. This is not the first time that the *Cardinal* and others have called for the organizing of a mass base. But now more than ever, we need unity and we need to organize — to talk with people outside this immediate, sheltered community.

And we need to figure out, collectively, the most important question of all:

Where do we go from here?

Hardly anyone who read it got past the word "victory."
"Everybody freaked out," Legro said. "People had been waiting to see what we would say, so the mainstream press picked up on it right away. The regents went berserk, and the *Cardinal* was labeled an enemy."

The backlash was national. The editorial was reprinted in papers from California to Maine.

"I write in response to your editorial, excerpts of which appeared in the *New York Sunday Times* on September 27th," wrote Stanley Kravit of Missouri in a letter to the *Cardinal*:

> I realize that excerpts do not always do justice to the content or intent of an original writing. To the extent that these accurately reflect your editorial, I am nauseated. If you do not know that violence of this nature is philosophically self-defeating, you are unbearably naive.
>
> If you do not feel in your mind and heart that it is morally self-degrading to condone it, you have forfeited any claim to the respect of your peers. If you do not comprehend that the forces of repression — forces which will use this incident for condemnation far in excess of its criminal aspect — are getting stronger every day, you are critically uninformed.

While rural and out-of-state opinion of the *Cardinal* had been low for more than a decade, student and local opinion had supported, or was at least in line with, the *Cardinal* right up to the beginning of the more violent anti-war protests.

As students began attacking merchants on State Street and professors in the classroom, however, local opinion began to turn against the paper.

IT DOESN'T END WITH US

Madison's *Capital Times*, so staunch a defender of the *Cardinal* during the Davis strike and amid charges of radicalism in the early 1960s, published a front-page editorial calling the paper a supporter of "terrorism."

Steinzor appeared on the Today Show, which used her and the *Cardinal* as an example of leftist student activity on college campuses. Letters poured in to the *Cardinal*, accusing her and her staff of "unholy hubris:"

> I have you on TV right now. Nuts with your left-wing liberal newspaper. Nuts with your liberal revolutionary ideas.
>
> The best and most sensible people in America are thoroughgoing conservatives.
>
> I grant you the privilege of your views, but America doesn't need them.

The editorial was not the end of the *Cardinal*'s coverage. As the FBI publicly made its case against Burt, Fine and the Armstrongs, Steinzor criticized their evidence and affidavit in the *Cardinal*'s pages. She wrote that "people within the movement have said that they feel the affidavit is being used to pressure potential informants."

The FBI was interviewing *Cardinal* staff members, including Legro, who had last seen Fine and Burt at a party at his house a week before the bombing. Rumors flew through the office: A staff member was an informant, was snitching on fellow *Cardinal* reporters, was really an FBI mole.

"There was a feeling of being besieged, not just by the public which was so angry with us but by the police and the FBI as well," Legro said.

The university's journalism faculty went on the attack against the *Cardinal* in the pages of the *Cardinal* itself. Professor William Hatchen, then the Journalism School's assistant director, said the paper "has in the past encouraged and abetted violence and destruction, which I consider irresponsible." Other professors called the paper "reprehensible" and said it was "an organ of opinion, which should not be the sole function of a student newspaper."

"The *Cardinal* had turned from progressivism into various kinds of radicalism," said William Blankenburg, who joined Wisconsin's Journalism School faculty shortly before the bombing and would later become the school's director. "Not all of it was coherent."

Nor was all the *Cardinal*'s content high-minded and motivated by a desire to spur discussion about the issues of the day, Blankenburg said.

"They ran large photos of genitalia that you could look at to see whether you had a venereal disease or not," he said. "They wanted to raise hell, and they were very good at it."

Major advertisers deserted the *Cardinal* in droves. The University Book Store, a solid advertiser in the paper for decades, and First Wisconsin National

IT DOESN'T END WITH US

Bank, both pulled their advertising. Many smaller accounts also declined, and from Sept. 1970 to Dec. 1971, the *Daily Cardinal* lost more than $19,000. Its total net worth declined from $90,000 to $65,000.

Faced with this decline, the *Cardinal* encouraged its detractors. Editorial staffers rejected full-page ads, which could have netted the paper hundreds of dollars, because those ads' sponsors operated in a manner contrary to the paper's editorial stances. Most damaging of all, the paper's editors often ran ads next to editorials decrying those ads, with a cartoon drawing of a finger pointing directly at the "offensive" business.

The practice was seen by staffers as a brave way of "taking their money and screwing them with it," as former campus editor Joan Walsh later wrote:

> Alongside an ad from South Africa-based De Beers diamonds, for instance, we ran a long, tortured exposé of conditions for blacks in De Beers' mining camps written by yours truly. We were ham-handed and self-righteous and close-minded in our way, but we were willing to let ideas clash.[4]

What Walsh and other editors saw as their righteous skewering of oppressive forces would create an anti-business reputation that would follow the *Cardinal* for decades. As late as the early 1990s some national chains refused to advertise with the *Cardinal* because of just the practices she praised.

The paper's editors were not thinking of the future.

"It's hard for people to imagine," Steinzor said, "but we really did feel like the French Resistance. I remember sitting in front of the television, watching the blanket bombing of Cambodia and just being overwhelmed. We took a deep responsibility for what was happening, and we felt it was our obligation to deal with this. I'm not trying to justify it. Obviously in retrospect we didn't understand how some things would come across, because we were so passionate and so young."

The repercussions were not just financial. In a 1970 readership survey half of all *Cardinal* readers found the paper biased and partisan, even though they shared the views that led *Cardinal* staffers to oppose the war. Half of all students found violent protest "somewhat" or "completely" justified, and all but two students (of 260 polled by the *Cardinal*) wanted the U.S. to leave Vietnam entirely, but still, the same margin held unfavorable views of the *Cardinal*.

The year before, a group of right-wing students had founded a weekly conservative paper to counter the *Cardinal*. The *Badger Herald* was just one of many conservative papers springing up on campuses across the country, but whereas other "official" student papers froze out their new competitors, the *Cardinal* was driving its audience the *Herald*'s way.

Prior to the publication of the fall 1970 registration issue, Steinzor said, the *Cardinal* had had a chance to expand its circulation beyond the campus and become a city daily rivaling Madison's two metropolitan papers.

IT DOESN'T END WITH US

After the bombing, she said, that dream was dead.

"The *State Journal* editorialized in favor of the boycott, and said the *Cardinal* was the tool of the little baby devils," she said. "They said real red-blooded Americans should have nothing to do with us ever again. When I left, the *Cardinal* was defensive. It had been tested and imperiled."

Despite its losses, the *Cardinal* was never in the kind of danger that might have curbed its staff's actions. It still had its generous surplus upon which to draw. Its board of directors granted the staff a wide latitude, criticizing but never attempting in any formal way to stop them.

"Everybody at the paper knew we had this big fat endowment," Legro said, referring to the paper's savings account. "And all we thought it meant was that we could do whatever we wanted. If you had that now, you'd hold onto it, try to get it to make money for you in perpetuity. We just thought about how we were going to spend it."

During the late 1960s and early 1970s, the *Cardinal* did groundbreaking journalism. Rowen's Profit Motive 101 series is unrivaled as investigative reporting on the UW campus, and his methods are taught to incoming staffers today. Reiner's editorials and the *Cardinal's* protest coverage remain some of the most vivid writing the paper ever printed. Reporter Peter Greenberg was invited by NASA to come to Florida and cover the launch of the Apollo 14 moon mission; the *Cardinal* was one of only 10 college papers in the country to be granted access:

> At "T- 1:10 and counting" the VIPs had already begun filling the wooden bleachers two miles from [launch pad] 39A. To continue the picnic attitude that seemed to surround the mission, NASA hostesses presented each incoming VIP with five souvenir postcards of the flight, and a stamp vendor was located nearby next to the refreshment stand and port-o-sans.
>
> It wasn't just Woodstock. It was also the Super Bowl. I half expected to see Anita Bryant wheeled out on a fifty-foot orange to sing the Battle Hymn of the Republic.

The journalists at the *Cardinal* during this time — editors Reiner and Greenberg, writers Rita Braver and Walt Bogdanich — would go on to become some of television and newspaper journalism's most celebrated names.

"The paper did good things, interesting things," said Reiner, who is now a producer for CBS News. "It was a solid paper, a beautiful-looking paper, and it still represented as much as possible the breadth of life on campus. Nobody ever said, 'We're seizing the sports pages to run the Communist Manifesto.'"

All of that accomplishment was subsumed by the era's vicious politics. By the death of Robert Fassnacht and the arrests of Fine and the Armstrongs. By the *Cardinal's* description of the bombing as a "victory and a defeat."

IT DOESN'T END WITH US

"I was devastated afterwards," Steinzor said. "I don't think I ever said to myself, 'I wish I hadn't written that,' but I did very much regret what it had done to the institution. A lot of institutions suffered during that time, and the *Cardinal* was one of the ones that did."

Even so, Steinzor said, she would write that editorial again. To do otherwise, she said, would have betrayed the *Cardinal*'s traditions of freedom and advocacy, betrayed the loyalty of the staff, and betrayed her own conscience.

"It took me a long time to be proud of what I had done," she said. "It took me a long time to be glad that in a moment of moral challenge, I had taken a stand."

After she graduated, Steinzor got a job working at the *New York Post*, processing letters to the editor. She went to law school. When she applied for a government job, she was turned down.

"I had an FBI file, with quite a large label on the front of it that said 'This woman hates the United States government and wants to see it destroyed by violence,'" Steinzor said. "The file consisted almost entirely of clippings from the *Cardinal*."

Fleischer dropped out of college midway through his junior year, when his term as editorial page editor ended. Disillusioned with his university experience and with the growing violence of the anti-war movement, he moved to a farm in rural Wisconsin, determined to stay out of the fray from then on.

"We really were young people confronting a really gigantic problem," he said.

"Not to sound defensive, but that has to be understood. These were very large issues, war and violence and inequality, and we were grappling with them every day. The tenor of the times has to be remembered and explained."

Legro graduated and went out the West Coast to work for the Gannett newspaper chain.

"I remember leaving the paper and feeling bad for it as an institution, feeling bad for many years afterward," he said. "I was pained by the struggling they had to do to overcome this problem that had developed for them in the community."

Karl Armstrong was found and arrested in February 1972 and subsequently convicted. His brother Dwight was caught in 1975 and scheduled to go on trial the following year as was David Fine. Leo Burt was never found.

As the Vietnam war drew to a close, the *Cardinal* began to turn its attention away from instigation and back toward what it had once done best: covering the campus.

After Steinzor's tumultuous term, *Cardinal* staff members elected leaders who began to deal with the repercussions of their predecessors' actions. Steinzor's successor, Patrick McGilligan, cut the paper's Saturday production in order to save money.

The new business manager, David Starck, put a stop to the cost overruns which had become common in the past several years.

IT DOESN'T END WITH US

"By the time I started at the *Cardinal* the business problems had begun to straighten themselves out," said David Newman, who took over the editorship from McGilligan. "What I was called on to do, more often than not, was to mediate staff disputes and keep the paper on an even keel. For me and my staff, things were going really well."

The good times would last until 1976, when the Sterling Hall bombing once again became the *Cardinal's* main story.

---

[1] Cronon and Jenkins, *The University of Wisconsin, A History: 1925-1945, Vol. 3*, 519.
[2] Tom Bates, *Rads* (New York: Harper Collins, 1992), xi.
[3] Seth King, "Defiant Students Keep The Underground Presses Rolling," 1.
[4] Joan Walsh,"Who's Afraid of the Big Bad Horowitz?" Salon.com (March 9, 2001): 2-3.

IT DOESN'T END WITH US

IT DOESN'T END WITH US

10.
Revolutionaries

We reaffirm our intention to donate $5,000 to David Fine's legal defense. Our conviction that such a contribution was right and proper remains unchallenged. We reaffirm our intention to reestablish worker control at the Daily Cardinal. We urge the faculty members of the Cardinal Board to reconsider their veto, to vote to approve the staff's donation. We urge our readers, we urge journalists within and without Madison, we urge all who care about a free and independent press to place all available pressure on the faculty members to reconsider their vote.
– The Daily Cardinal, Feb. 5, 1976

◘

From the time of the *Cardinal*'s founding its leaders always answered to the student body as a whole. William Wesley Young's staff of 1892 were popularly elected at a student mass meeting before the first issue came out. Later, when the *Cardinal* was formally organized as a corporation, it was governed by a board of control, later called a board of directors: five students elected by the whole student body, the editor-in-chief and business manager, and three faculty members appointed by the university chancellor, usually members of the journalism faculty.

According to the *Cardinal*'s bylaws, codified in 1938 following the Davis strike, the three faculty members held veto power over any financial decisions made by the staff or student members.

The student members were often former or current *Cardinal* staffers themselves. Absent some raging controversy, interest in a post monitoring the fi-

IT DOESN'T END WITH US

nances of a college newspaper was minimal. Consequently, desk editors often moved to the board of directors when their terms running news or editorial page were completed.

For decades the board had chosen and approved editors, usually relying on the counsel and consensus of staff members to put forth candidates. After the Davis strike, none of the board members were eager to overrule staff choices even when — as in the case with Steinzor, Reiner and others — editors made questionable decisions with regard to coverage.

However, at the start of her term Steinzor spurred a change that would lead to some of the biggest *Cardinal* controversies of the next 30 years: the editorial elections.

The process, which is still in place today, worked like this: Candidates for editorships presented themselves at special staff meetings. Anyone, from a copy editor to a former staffer to a reporter who had just started the previous week could come and ask the candidate questions. Hypothetical, journalistic, political, personal. Then the candidate or candidates left the room while the staff deliberated and voted by anonymous paper ballot. One staffer, one vote.

Announcing the change after she became the first editor-in-chief elected by this method, Steinzor wrote in an editorial that the new procedure freed the paper "from the constraints of tradition and artificial power relationships." In addition to Steinzor, the staff had elected six new editors; the meeting lasted twelve hours.

The paper's board of directors still had to approve the editors, but this was rarely a source of conflict. Even when individual board members objected to a tone or direction the paper took, they preferred to influence the editors who were there, rather than fire them and force open confrontation.

Bill Swislow joined the *Cardinal* shortly after this change took place. Raised in the Chicago suburbs, Swislow attended Madison because his older sister had attended the UW and praised it. He rose in the *Cardinal*'s ranks from the copy desk to the editorship because of his pocket calculator.

"The copy editors all used this plastic sheet that went over the typewritten pages and they used measurements on it to estimate how many column inches a story would be," Swislow said. "I was the one who worked out with this calculator a chart that would help you do the counting more accurately, so I got elected copy editor."

The *Cardinal* in 1975 was still the paper Steinzor and Rowen had envisioned. Its average staffer was twenty-seven years old, unusual in its former editors often staying to put in years after their student days were done, graduate students making up a significant portion of the staff. Editor positions were salaried. Reporters were paid by the story, up to twenty-five dollars per piece.

The pay was not exorbitant by journalism standards, but it did serve as an inducement to experienced editors to remain on the staff.

If the *Cardinal* — if any student newspaper — has an unsolvable weakness, it is the turnover inherent in a student publication. Every four years it reinvents

IT DOESN'T END WITH US

itself according to the will of its staff. During Steinzor and Rowen and Swislow's days, ex-editors often stayed on for years. They wrote columns, copy edited, and continued to influence the paper's direction for good and ill.

Swislow was politically leftist when he arrived on campus and he found the *Cardinal* welcoming and exciting.

"It was a blast," he said. "It was a world unto itself. Everybody was basically left, or at least center-left, and they were interested and engaged in what was going on."

The *Cardinal* he joined was also more financially stable than it had been in years. Newman's leadership, while maintaining the paper's political stances, had not antagonized advertisers directly the way Steinzor's had, and his successor, Sam Freedman, took an even more moderate stance. In 1970, the *Cardinal* lost $11,000; in 1975 the paper ended the year with $14,000 on hand. It had cash reserves of more than $50,000 and further equity in equipment and supplies.

The trials of the New Year's Gang continued to be front-page news in all the Madison papers. Dwight Armstrong was scheduled to go on trial in 1976. As was David Fine.

On Jan. 25, 1976 the *Cardinal* office was buzzing. Staffers were returning from their Christmas breaks, getting the paper ready for its registration issue, the largest of the semester. Elections for editorships for the 1976 calendar year were being held that afternoon. Swislow was contending for editor-in-chief. At nineteen, he would be one of the youngest top editors in the paper's history.

"It was an uncontested election, which was ridiculous, but nobody else wanted the job," Swislow said. "I was ignorant, I had no real reporting experience, and the people who would be working for me, some of them were older than me by seven years."

His time in the office and the fact that he'd worked hard on the copy desk — plus his leftist politics — made him an acceptable choice. His staff was filled with younger *Cardinal* writers, who respected the old guard that was on its way out.

"It was pure democracy, in that whoever walked in the door set the policy," said Steve Kerch, a Rockford, Ill., native who became Swislow's managing editor. "But there weren't very many people who knew the production side of things, which is where I stayed. A lot of the younger kids just didn't have that training."

Besides the elections, there was another item on the agenda. A $5,000 donation to David Fine's defense fund.

The older editors and ex-editors present — David Newman, Jim Rowen, among others — saw Fine as a symbol of all that the anti-war movement had been trying to achieve. They also felt loyalty to him as a fellow *Cardinal* staffer. In feeling that the whole world was arrayed against them as students and as journalists, they felt a need to protect their own. And David Fine was one of their own.

Some of the newer and the younger staffers, however, did not see things in such black and white terms. The backlash against the Sterling Hall bombing on campus had dampened down anti-war activity, the bombers' actions hurting, rather than helping, their cause. While Karl Armstrong had had a certain charisma that drew followers, David Fine did not share it. Even after his arrest, in the Madison press and especially in the *Cardinal*'s pages, Fine continued to posture for left-wing revolutionary uprisings, and to the younger *Cardinal* staff members, he started to look like a caricature of the politics they admired.

"He did not represent any kind of virtue," Andrea Schwartz, who would become Swislow's fine arts editor, said bluntly. "The ideal we had in mind, of a fair trial and justice for all, was a good one, but our representative was horrible."

"'This isn't three years ago,'" Kerch remembered someone arguing. "Everyone knew we didn't have the best example of the anti-war movement, some innocent persecuted victim, we had the worst example. But people felt that we couldn't *not* do this, that it would somehow invalidate everything that we had done in our history."

The older, more strident voices held sway. Swislow said he was affected by the appeal that Fine "was desperate and had really believed in what he was doing, and that the killing [of Fassnacht] was an accident."

The staffers voted by paper ballot and then a small group of editors, Swislow among them, went into a tiny office off the main staff meeting room to count them. They told the staff the vote hadn't been close: 31 in favor, five against. Though staffers later tried to assert that the vote had been closer than that, the damage was done.

The *Cardinal* planned to announce the donation in the Jan. 27 newspaper. But someone tipped off the *Capital Times*, and that paper scooped the *Cardinal* on its own story. Whitney Gould, a former *Cardinal* staffer herself, wrote the *Capital Times* story, quoting Swislow in his first act as editor-in-chief.

"We want to see him get a fair trial," he told Gould, referring to Fine. "And the only way he can do that is if he has the money for a defense. Since he is also a former staff member, we felt a certain amount of solidarity."

The *Cardinal's* editorial, on Jan. 27, went much farther than "a certain amount of solidarity" and Swislow's politic remarks about judicial impartiality. Headlined, "We Support David," it read:

> David is being tried by the government against which his anti-war activities were directed, the same government which is responsible for hundreds of thousands of deaths in Indochina. This is a political trial. The United States chooses to prosecute those who opposed its criminal activities in Indochina rather than answer for its own guilt.
>
> The *Daily Cardinal* has strongly supported anti-war activities. For it to come to David's defense is a continuation of those commitments. We believe that David is innocent of the charges brought against him. As an anti-war activist and es-

pecially as a former staff member of our paper, he deserves our full support. Only with the strong monetary and political support of the community can his efforts to secure a fair trial succeed.

The *Cardinal*'s actions ripped the scab off a wound that went deep on the Madison campus, and in one stroke undid the good will built up by more moderate editors. It made the *Cardinal* once again a focus for all those angered by the anti-war movement.

The *Cardinal* was not the only campus organization to publicly support Fine. The Wisconsin Students Association, the student governmental body that, unlike the *Cardinal*, actually operated based on student fees and university funds, had decided to donate $2,000 to Fine's defense weeks before the matter came before the *Cardinal*. The move drew some student protest, but it was the paper which bore the brunt of the criticism.

All the Madison papers excoriated the *Cardinal*. Outside the city the reaction in Wisconsin was even more virulent. The *Kenosha News* called the staff's action "A Cardinal Sin," and the Racine *Journal-Times* referred to "a plague of immaturity" which had diminished the *Cardinal* for more than a decade.

"Such a donation," the *Journal-Times* warned, "if approved by the rubber-stamp *Daily Cardinal* board, removes the appearance of any objectivity in the student paper's coverage of the story and upcoming trial."

The rubber-stamp reference, which had truth in it, riled the faculty. It made what could have been a reasonable discussion about the amount the *Cardinal* wanted to donate — which at the time constituted more than a third of the paper's profits from the previous year — into a political showdown, a shootout at the *Cardinal* corral.

A showdown, in particular, between Swislow and Professor Robert Taylor.

Taylor knew from *Cardinal* internal strife. He had been Richard Davis' managing editor in 1938 and had watched as the dispute over the paper turned the campus upside down. That lesson stayed with Taylor as he ran interference for the *Cardinal* during some of its more difficult periods in the 1960s, drawing on his university contacts to keep the administration from coming down too hard on the paper.

He was, by 1976, the *Cardinal*'s elder statesman and the closest thing the paper had to an institutional memory.

> The students didn't see him that way. They saw a symbol of university elitism and power, a man standing in the way of what they felt was right. Taylor, to them, was an obstacle to be knocked down, preferably hard.

"He had a historical view and at the time that was a detriment to us," said Mary Jo Ross, who was Swislow's city editor. "You have to remember, we

IT DOESN'T END WITH US

thought we were acting out of principle, but we confronted [Taylor] in the worst possible childish manner."

The board met on Feb. 4 to approve the paper's elected editors, read the monthly financial reports and consider the Fine donation.

Ross said the meeting was the most bitter thing she'd ever witnessed. Students questioned the faculty members about their loyalty to the *Cardinal*, about their allegiance to the university, about political precepts that had little to do with the debate. Finances, the one guiding factor in the faculty's oversight of the paper, were never even mentioned.

"I remember one editor asking Taylor a very long involved question and Taylor would pause while he answered and the editor said, 'Answer, pig.'" Ross recalled. "[The questioner] wasn't twenty years old. It made no sense. We were nineteen or twenty, and it was so easy to get caught up in things."

All but one student member of the board voted in favor of the Fine donation. The faculty veto was unanimous. For students looking for something to rebel against, this denial was just one more outrage in a series of outrages. The students walked down to their offices in a state of anger and dejection. Someone — Swislow can't remember who — called David Fine, who came into the *Cardinal* offices to commiserate with his former comrades. The Madison papers published photographs of the accused bomber standing side by side with the paper's top brass.

The paper the next day carried a front-page cartoon of a vampire-bat-like creature feeding on a corpse labeled "*Cardinal*," while a figure of justice blowing a trumpet for the free press stood above, burning torch in hand. Former city editor Alan Higbie wrote the accompanying story, headlined, "Knifed in the Back: Faculty Board Stabs Paper."

Higbie quoted Fine saying, "By vetoing the overwhelming majority of the *Cardinal* staff, the faculty members of the board join the growing conspiracy of officials who are determined to deny me the fair trial the paper's contribution would have helped insure."

The story of the *Cardinal* staff versus board dust-up was carried in every paper in Wisconsin as the latest outrageous actions of campus radicals and domestic terrorists. East-coast news organizations, many of whom had older *Cardinal* alumni on staff, ran the story as an example of anachronistic Madison, home of the diehard hippies. Dean of Students Paul Ginsberg fretted that, as usual, the *Cardinal* was damaging the university's image.

Swislow gathered the staff together. They would strike, he said. They would unionize and get legal representation and force the board to accede to their demands. Taylor wrote soothing memos to university higher-ups urging patience and expressing his confidence in his ability to broker a compromise.

Taylor called Swislow and Kerch up to his office and explained the situation frankly. If the *Cardinal* staff went on strike, it would do several things. It would isolate the paper further from the community. Once begun, it would be hard to stop. It would cut off income from the Typography Laboratory which

IT DOESN'T END WITH US

printed the *Cardinal*, forcing the Lab to seek other clients, including competitors.

Further, Taylor confided, the faculty's veto power was a responsibility the present members considered a holdover from *Cardinal* eras past and a weight they did not want on their shoulders, as it could lead to future conflicts like this one. Could a compromise be reached?

Swislow offered one: Make the paper's board completely democratic. One member, one vote, on every issue that came before it, no vetoes. Only student members would be able to approve hiring and firing. In exchange, Swislow would drop the strike threat.

"We said we were going to go on strike, and it was nicely argued but it was totally absurd," Swislow said. "There was no way we had the money to do it, no matter how big we were talking."

Taylor agreed, and on Tuesday, Feb. 10 the *Cardinal* board met again to consider amendments to the paper's articles of incorporation and bylaws. The amendments not only converted the board to a purely democratic model, they also specified things like "all sexual pronouns would be removed" from official corporate documents, and stated that the faculty board members could not overrule the staff board members' election of editors, a measure that would become important later.

Taylor and the other faculty members had a demand of their own: an additional faculty member, bringing the total on the board to four. The students agreed, and the meeting which had begun with anger and accusations ended with hugs and handshakes all around. The *Cardinal*'s headline the next day read: DEMOCRACY WINS. Ginsberg, who had attended the meeting, told the *Cardinal*, "I'm going home feeling very good. They really hammered it out."

Everyone thought it was over.

As part of the agreement reached at that February board meeting, the *Cardinal* faculty members stated that the amendments to the *Cardinal*'s bylaws would be placed on the Spring 1976 student government election ballot.

It was not an outlandish suggestion. According to the *Cardinal*'s own founding documents, any changes to the paper's structure had to be approved by students, though that requirement had been largely ignored in years past. Amendments, the faculty and staff both thought, would pass easily, without comment.

The night of the April 28, 1976, Mary Jo Ross and about twenty other people were crammed into a house a fellow *Cardinal* staffer rented on Hancock Street, not far from the Madison capitol building. They had been out leafletting all day, asking students to vote in favor of the proposed board amendments and in favor of new board members, a four-person slate of current and former *Cardinal* staffers calling itself the Press Brigade.

For much of the weeks leading up to the election the Press Brigade candidates thought themselves unopposed, as candidates for the *Cardinal* board often were. However, anti-*Cardinal* sentiment had not abated. In late February then-

IT DOESN'T END WITH US

State Rep. George Klicka, a Republican from suburban Milwaukee, introduced a resolution demanding the university "take action" against the *Cardinal*. Though it was quickly defeated, the measure served to remind people across the state of the ongoing controversy.

Still, the upcoming student elections were cause for optimism for Swislow and his staff. The *Capital Times* published a story less than a week before the scheduled April 27-28 vote declaring "little opposition" for the *Cardinal* board amendments. The Press Brigade slate looked poised for an easy victory.

Five days before the election, a new slate of candidates emerged. Calling themselves the Standard Press Party, student government rep Charles Heisinger, history students Deborah Schindler and Milo Geyelin and genetics major Debra Jaliman presented themselves at a student government meeting. They declared themselves candidates for the *Cardinal* board because they believed in "straight journalism."

"By this we mean, first, honest journalism," Heisinger told the student government at the time. "Journalism which is based on unfabricated fact. Second, informational journalism rather than the opinionated variety; opinions and persuasive essays should be labeled as such. And third, journalism which encompasses a range of ideas permitting readers to make sound rational decisions for themselves."

Heisinger said following those principles might require vetoing staff elections of editors who did not meet the Standard Press Party's, well, standards.

The *Cardinal* staff's reaction was one of amusement. "We never thought they'd actually win, first of all," Schwartz said. "The *Cardinal* was perceived as being run by this bunch of elite leftists, and it was bizarre and surreal and intensely frustrating to see these people come in who were obviously way over their heads."

The election battle was brief but bitter. The SPP distributed fliers showing a *Cardinal* editor passed out over his typewriter with the caption, "Every year ... teachers go back to teaching, students go back to studying, and the *Cardinal* goes back to sleep." Coverage in the *Capital Times* and *Milwaukee Journal* portrayed the SPP as moderates on a politically polarized campus.

Ross fired back at the critics, saying the non-journalism students of the SPP should "come in and start to work from the bottom up" if they want to affect the *Cardinal*, according to a story in the *Capital Times*. Press Brigade fliers trumpeted the four *Cardinal* editors' experience and urged students to consider all the endorsements the slate had received: several aldermen, State Rep. David Clarenbach, the Green Lantern Eating Co-op and the United Farm Workers Support Committee, among others.

On election night in the house on Hancock, Ross had her finger in one ear and the phone pressed to the other, shouting down the line for Kerch to give her the election results. Kerch was at the *Cardinal* office, reporting on all the student government contests and referenda on the ballot. The Press Brigade campaigned hard. Their opponents were inexperienced nobodies.

IT DOESN'T END WITH US

They were more than optimistic. They were confident.
They lost.
"Everybody was standing around the phone, staring at me, and I had to tell them," Ross said. "It felt like the end of the world."
Worse, in retrospect, the board's amendments had passed. Student members alone now controlled the hiring and firing of editors and had a numerical advantage on the board as well, five students to the four faculty.
"We succeeded in putting the students in control but we lost the students we wanted controlling it," Swislow said.
The SPP board members wasted no time exercising their newfound authority. On May 6, the incoming board members, who were now a majority of the student voting members on the board, rejected the *Cardinal*'s choices for editors for the summer session. These were usually routine jobs given to editors who wanted to train for a higher position. Geyelin said staffers Shelagh Kealy and Tom Woolf, who had been elected jointly to the position, should submit applications and résumés to be considered for hiring.
Kealy refused. "It's not right," she said, according to a *Cardinal* account of the meeting. "It's for the staff to decide."
Swislow told Geyelin if the SPP members wouldn't approve Kealy and Woolf, he'd stay on as editor in Madison throughout the summer.
Fine, Geyelin responded. We'll fire you right now.
On May 13, the SPP-controlled *Cardinal* board met and voted 4-1 to terminate Swislow and business manager John Eugster, effective May 22, and open the positions up for applications. Eugster, who had presided over a $12,000 profit so far in 1976, was praised by those who terminated him and told by Geyelin that if he reapplied, he'd have a good chance of getting the job back.
"I was just fired," Eugster responded, incredulous. "Why should I turn in an application to you?"
Swislow did two things right away. He called for a petition to recall the newly elected *Cardinal* board members. He gathered the staff and told them he and Eugster would sue to get their jobs back, and to listen to Kerch, who remained as managing editor.
"The rest of our staff was still editors, they had just fired the two of us," Swislow said. "And we refused to leave."
In fact, Swislow and Eugster went to court and requested a temporary restraining order preventing the new board from hiring any replacements for them. A Madison judge granted the order and called a hearing on June 22 to consider whether the two should be given their *Cardinal* positions back.
The result was a surreal month in which Geyelin, Schindler, Jaliman and Heisinger presided over a staff hostile to them and which balked at any suggestion they had. Kerch tried to make sure the paper was publishing each day. Swislow, Eugster, and the Press Brigade members met with the board or conferred with their lawyers, while Geyelin and Schindler brought in friends of theirs who they suggested should be on staff.

IT DOESN'T END WITH US

Less than two weeks after the firings the *Cardinal* delivered nearly 7,000 signatures on its recall petition to the student government, but there would be no recall election. Government reps told the *Cardinal* it was too near the end of the year for a new election. The staff and board would just have to work things out.

The board had no interest in doing so. On June 1 the SPP-controlled board installed Patti Elson, a journalism student and wife of local attorney Edward Ben Elson, as Swislow's replacement. A business school grad student, Steve Smith, was appointed to replace Eugster. Patti Elson and Smith called a meeting for the following Friday to address the current staff, and began hiring new editors and reporters.

Swislow beat them to the punch. Declaring he would not leave his post, he told the staff they would publish their own paper independently of the new board and editors. Their June 21 edition, traditionally the first of the summer academic session, would be known as the "Staff *Cardinal*."

Unlike the strikers of Davis's time, the *Cardinal* staffers did not go out looking for their own office space. They shared the paper's offices with their adversaries. A June 15 headline in the *Capital Times*: "Fight Ends in *Cardinal* Lockout."

> The altercation began when two "Daily" *Cardinal* members, reporter Richard Chamberlain and advertising manager Joe Colletti, were interrupted by "Staff" *Cardinal* editorial page editor Matthew Fox while they were working in a small room off the main office.
>
> "Fox and his buddies were screaming and yelling about our door being closed," said Colletti, "and he started going through a pile of mail on the desk we'd just gone through." A shoving match between Fox, Colletti and Chamberlain ensued and Colletti finally called the UW police officers.
>
> The officers calmed things down and left, but soon afterward, Colletti said, he called Dean of Students Paul Ginsberg. Ginsberg asked the police to return and clear the office, "to ensure that people were not physically and verbally abused."

The "official" *Cardinal* staffers would be allowed back in, Ginsberg decreed, while the Staff *Cardinal* would have to find a new home. Ironically, it was at the offices of the *Badger Herald* that the staff settled, working around the conservative weekly. *Herald* Publisher Tom Burton told the *Capital Times* he supported the striking *Cardinal* staffers out of a common sense of obligation to press freedom.

IT DOESN'T END WITH US

"The staff was one hundred percent united," Swislow recalled, a note of pride in his voice. "Some of them knew some of the SPP staff socially but no one ever defected to join them because they had run against us and they didn't have a clear agenda. They thought they could just show up and clean house."

On June 21, the Staff *Cardinal* published a thick paper covered with a drawing of an old-fashioned newsboy, a stack of *Cardinals* under his arm. In an editorial it declared itself "The Real *Cardinal*."

"We have said before that the *Cardinal* is not merely a corporation, or a logo, or an office. It is the people who put out the newspaper every day. Our summer registration issue demonstrates this fact."

While the Staff staff remained united, the SPP was falling apart. After Ginsberg declared the *Cardinal* office off-limits, Elson declared a "temporary suspension of operations," which Heisinger and the other SPP board members ignored. Before their "official" *Cardinal* was published, Elson gave an interview to the *Capital Times* disavowing the issue.

While Heisinger and the SPP board tried to put out a paper, Elson negotiated a compromise. The Staff *Cardinal* staffers could return to the office and their paper could be printed by the Typography Laboratory. Its first strike issue had been put out by a printing company in north suburban Black Earth.

So Swislow's staff had a front-row seat for the difficulties Elson and the SPP members were facing. Schwartz said there was a moment she knew the new staff would never overtake the old: "At one meeting somebody on their staff, one of their editors, stood up and said, 'What's a pica?'" referring to a unit of measurement in newspaper design.

"He thought it was a typewriter," she said. "At that moment we could relax, because we knew these people had no idea what they were doing in the office."

"We were spending twelve hours a day working on our *Cardinal*," Swislow remembered. "They were just students, they had no idea how hard it was. We were fanatics. We were willing to do anything."

Not only that, they were, with the odd camaraderie which develops in stressful situations, enjoying themselves. Among Swislow's papers and clippings of stories about the strike is a fictitious press release about Heisinger giving an order to one of the *Cardinal's* longtime printers and getting hit in the head with a tray of lead type for his trouble. A satirical list of new "rules" for *Cardinal* staffers instructed female editors to wear "a blouse and dress or nice pantsuit. Bras must be worn! Let's look neat."

By the second week of the summer session, Elson and the other SPP members gave up. Swislow and Eugster dropped their lawsuit. On July 1, the *Cardinal* announced that Elson would share the remainder of the summer editing job with Woolf, one of the staff's original choices for editor, and the papers would merge back into one.

The next day, all SPP members resigned from the board. Elson, despite her intention to co-edit the summer papers, never set foot in the *Cardinal's* offices again.

IT DOESN'T END WITH US

"I think she saw what it looked like and gave up," Higbie said. "Most students leave for the summer. They [the SPP] didn't want to sit and nurse this thing for months. I think they simply lost interest."

Schwartz said the old staff stepped in and continued publishing without a hitch. "We came in and it was as if we were saying, 'What bad dream was this?' It didn't seem like it had been real."

David Fine never did receive $5,000 from the *Cardinal*. In the hue and cry over the strike, the two *Cardinals*, and the fight for control of the paper from top to bottom, the thing that caused it all was forgotten. Fine was convicted later that year and paroled three years later.

The fight over money for Fine and control of the *Cardinal* left lasting scars. Swislow left Madison for Harvard the next year. He began working for the venerable Harvard *Crimson*, one of the country's first student newspapers, but the lessons of the *Cardinal* were hard ones to unlearn.

"I lasted three weeks," he said. "It was too hierarchical for me, too strict. I said, 'I'll go study.'"

Today he said that while he does not regret the strike itself, he regrets the factionalization of the staff, the emphasis on politics over newspapering that he said he helped foster. "The *Cardinal* was very shortsighted," Swislow said. "It was not the legacy that was left to me or that I wanted to leave to others who came after me."

Robert Taylor, the faculty board member who spent much of his time opposing Swislow and his staff, was likewise embittered by the *Cardinal* staff's hostility. During the controversy, a professor at upstate University of Wisconsin-Stevens Point had written a public letter of support for the students and opposition to Taylor.

Taylor responded, noting that that professor's university was similarly embroiled in controversy and offering his services in return for the professor's interference:

> Dear Lee,
>
> I clipped the note of thanks enclosed from today's *Daily Cardinal*, noting that you, Paul Soglin, Paul Ginsberg, the Madison Co-Op Garage and others stood firm with the *Cardinal* Staff in its recent joust with the powers of evil I represented on the *Cardinal* Board of Directors.
>
> While I was unaware of your help in this matter, I think it is only proper that I notify you that I have formed the Friends of Undergraduate Cohabitation Kommittee-Stevens Point to help your students in a struggle for "freedom" not too unlike the *Cardinal* crisis.

IT DOESN'T END WITH US

> I have not yet had an indication of support from Soglin or Ginsberg, but I'm fairly certain I can line up the Madison Co-Op Garage.

In 1999, the *Daily Cardinal*'s alumni association instituted awards for the paper's most distinguished graduates. Robert Taylor had at that time logged more than three decades as a board member of the *Daily Cardinal*, and an award for extraordinary service to the institution was named in his honor. Looking out over a crowd of people applauding at a ceremony that year, Taylor recalled the two strikes in *Cardinal* history, one he participated in, the other he opposed.

"I was on the losing side both times," he said. Appreciation for his work had been a long time coming. "It's been 34 years and this is the first time anyone ever said thank you."

Three years later Swislow's former staffers, remembering his leadership during this divisive time, nominated him for the service award. Schwartz, now married to Alan Higbie, said she'd never forget Swislow, all of 20, standing up to university officials and demanding the right to lead the *Cardinal* as he saw fit.

"He was very brave," she said. "He did what he believed in and he really was a hero."

The association asked Taylor if he would object to his award being given to a one-time opponent, someone who had faced him down, in pursuit of his goals for the *Cardinal*. Did Taylor hold a grudge?

Taylor thought for a moment, then said with a chuckle. "No. He's grown up quite a bit."

IT DOESN'T END WITH US

IT DOESN'T END WITH US

11.

Competitors

There are rational people in our community who can see through the ravings of power-mongers who fashion allegations out of thin air in order to facilitate the elimination of a 95-year-old daily campus newspaper. We at the Cardinal go to school, maintain part-time jobs, and have social lives. But for many of us, putting out the newspaper is our highest priority.
– The Daily Cardinal Staff Opinion, March 10, 1987

ଔ

Many colleges and universities have more than one student publication. Often one publication is sanctioned and subsidized by the university and another publishes on its own as an alternative. The University of Missouri-Columbia, for example, publishes one newspaper as a class requirement for its journalism students while an independent group of students publishes its own paper without official university oversight.

Some have a daily paper and a weekly paper with different areas of coverage or emphasis: specialty papers abound for college students' diverging interests.

The competition, especially in many college towns where the students are the only target market or where the overall population is small, can be fierce, and sustaining a publication beyond the ambitions of its founders is incredibly difficult. Often independent publications will begin, last a few years with meager advertising budgets, and die out when their editors graduate. Often it is impossible to find successive generations of students investing in an idea, especially when that idea is just one of many options available to them.

IT DOESN'T END WITH US

The University of Wisconsin-Madison is the only college campus in the United States which has two student-run, non-subsidized daily newspapers competing against one another.

The *Daily Cardinal*. And the *Badger Herald*.

From the time of its founding, the *Cardinal* had competitors, though rarely any which took on the newspaper head-to-head. The 1912 appearance and subsequent demise of the *Wisconsin Daily News* had done little to shake that era's *Cardinal* staffers, but in 1957, a far more serious competitor had emerged. The *Wisconsin Herald* was backed by a group of wealthy Madison businessmen who felt the *Cardinal* was not sympathetic enough to their interests. Their student representatives gave *Cardinal* reporters $50 job offers. The *Daily Cardinal*'s managing editor, Alan McCone, quit to join the new staff and business staffers followed him.

Despite those defections, the newspaper didn't survive. The advertising market was locked up by the *Cardinal* — its dominance of the campus entrenched — and few students were interested in a new voice. The *Wisconsin Herald* did not last the year.

Few observers gave the *Badger Herald* that long.

The *Herald*'s history tells it this way: In the summer of 1969, the *Cardinal* was turning increasingly toward an underground newspaper sensibility, a tone not merely liberal nor even radical but in fact near-anarchic: directions for making Molotov cocktails and escaping detection during riots littered the news pages.

Its editorials were a mix of countercultural buzzwords and inept coverage of regional "worker issues" that often had little to do with the campus. For the *Herald*:

> The idea was to create an alternative voice on a campus, a voice that would cast the protests in another light and challenge common ideology.
>
> Gathered in the back of the Brathaus, the *Herald*'s founders, Patrick S. Korten, Nick Loniello, Mike Kelly and Wade Smith debated late into the night about how to establish such a voice. "How about revitalizing *Insight and Outlook* [a student magazine that had died in the early '60s]?"
>
> No, they decided, that would be too boring. After the sixth beer, their vision became surprisingly clear: "How about starting a weekly newspaper? A newspaper that would focus on Madison and issues facing UW students?"
>
> After several months of fundraising, scrounging for desks and typewriters, and renting offices where the Sunroom Café

IT DOESN'T END WITH US

now stands [above Steve & Barry's on State Street] the first issue of the *Badger Herald* was published Sept.10, 1969.[1]

That paper was a small, black-and-white tabloid similar to the *Cardinal* in appearance and distributed free across the campus and downtown area. It was published once a week.

In its first issue, a front-page story attacked the *Cardinal* and praised campus conservative groups. Its lead editorial was headlined, "A Monopoly Ends."

> Welcome to the pages of the *Badger Herald*. You, and others like you in the University of Wisconsin community, are about to witness a significant departure in the history of student journalism on the Madison campus. Since April 4, 1892, there has been but one newspaper here, and that newspaper, in spite of its official status, has considered itself "independent." It has made all sorts of moves in recent years designed to strengthen that contention.
>
> But there has been one big flaw in the running of "The Official Student Newspaper of the University of Wisconsin," and that has been its monopoly status. The basic human drive for competition has been by default directed at the university administration, rather than at a competing newspaper, and the result, in the judgment of many, has been mediocrity at best, and demagoguery at worst.
>
> Seventy-seven years is enough. It is time there was a truly "independent" student newspaper at Wisconsin, one which competes in the open marketplace, and must make its editorial decisions on the basis of that competitive market. A newspaper is not truly worthy of its name until it is clear of the artificially protective and restrictive atmosphere of "official student newspaper" status.

Korten, a political science major from Milwaukee, got involved with the conservative movement from the day he arrived on campus. He started working as a student announcer on Wisconsin's university radio station, which gave him a front-row seat for the anti-war demonstrations then sweeping the campus.

He also joined the Young Americans for Freedom, a right-wing political student group, and rose in its ranks to become chairman of the UW branch. Korten said he and his fellow "serious conservatives" were numerous on campus, but felt marginalized by the more vocal liberal students.

One day he and his fellow YAF officers were discussing the *Cardinal*, and lamenting the lack of a similarly strong voice for their views.

IT DOESN'T END WITH US

"We said, 'Enough is enough. What this campus needs is a decent newspaper,'" he said. "The *Cardinal* at the time was a paper that wore its ideology on every single page. There was no subtlety about it. It was not a newspaper in the strict sense of the term. It was an opinion journal that purported to cover the news."

The *Herald*'s goal, however, was not to overtake and erase the *Cardinal*, he said. It was to compete with it.

"We operated on the assumption that the *Cardinal* would continue as it was, and we would be the alternative. We thought a campus like Madison deserved a real newspaper and at the time, it didn't have one."

Conservative newspapers had begun appearing on college campuses across the nation at the time Korten and his YAF friends had their brainstorm. Stanford, Duke and the University of California-Berkeley all hosted right-leaning publications at the time the *Herald* was founded, reactions to their liberal "official" papers.

What Korten would only describe as "seed money" paid for small offices off-campus, where the paper was headquartered and composed. The *Herald* was not well-received on campus at first, Korten said. He and the other editors endured threats from radical student factions, even as more conservative elements cheered its arrival.

"When things were dicey, I would sleep on an Army cot in the *Badger Herald* office with a fire extinguisher next to me," he said. "We rolled chain-link fence across the windows. It was nasty, and the threats were serious. The left did not like us."

The *Herald* was determined to succeed, doing so by being what more ideological papers often find it difficult to be: A business.

"The second person we ever hired was a business manager," Korten said.

Previous would-be competitors began as daily newspapers, fast spending whatever start-up money they had on a punishing 5- or 7-day schedule. The *Herald*'s weekly production scheduled allowed it to save some of that early money. Whereas previous *Cardinal* competitors pursued the same advertisers valued by the *Cardinal*, with middling results, the *Herald*'s founders and backers exploited an advantage the *Cardinal*'s previous opponents had not touched.

In early days the new paper, vulnerable and mindful of university administrators' disapproval of the *Cardinal*'s present direction, Herald editors appealed to regents and professors critical of the *Cardinal* for moral and financial support.

Wisconsin Alumni Research Foundation president Walter Frautschi, stinging from Jim Rowen's 1969 *Cardinal* exposé of the regents' involvement with the Army Math Research Center, chipped in $50 to the *Herald*.

According to a *Cardinal* article in the fall of 1969, "*Herald* editor Patrick Korten reported that Regent Gordon Walker, Racine, made a financial contribution to the *Herald* at the Oct. 17 regent meeting and that other regents offered their verbal support to the *Herald*." Others on the *Herald*'s contributor lists, filed with the university and uncovered by *Cardinal* reporters in the late 1980s,

IT DOESN'T END WITH US

were local corporations and politicians who had been criticized by the *Cardinal* as well. They translated their anger into financial help for the *Cardinal*'s rival.

Korten said he was very determined that the *Herald* steer clear of any official university affiliation. "We didn't want their money or their active public support, we just wanted to compete with the *Cardinal* on an equal basis," he said. He said he didn't recall the individual contributions.

For the first five years of its existence, the *Herald* accepted financial counseling and auditing services from the university free of charge, according to internal university memos uncovered by the *Cardinal*. On the *Herald*'s board were three university-appointed professors, mirroring precisely the *Cardinal*'s bylaws. Those professors lobbied aggressively for the *Herald* to receive preferential treatment from the university.

"Personally, I would rather see one strong, independent newspaper, covering campus events and expressing student opinion, than two weak periodicals," UW Professor James Fosdick, then one of the *Herald*'s advisers, wrote to Dean of Students Paul Ginsberg. Fosdick urged Ginsberg to continue providing "financial counsel for the *Badger Herald* so that they will have every opportunity to 'make it' financially as an independent student newspaper organization."

While accepting university help itself, the *Herald* was engaged in a campaign of disinformation against the *Cardinal*, saying the *Cardinal* was subsidized with state tax dollars, a claim sure to inflame out-of-town conservatives. The *Herald* made much hay out of the *Cardinal*'s location in a university building, ignoring the fact that the *Herald* had been offered similar quarters and declined them. The *Cardinal* defended its location by pointing out the building stood on land donated by its publishing company in 1956.

The *Herald*'s rabble-rousing was successful. A church in Sarasota, the 15th Ward Republican Club of Milwaukee, the Fort Atkinson Women's Club, all gave money to the *Herald*. All told, donations in the first five years of the *Herald*'s existence totaled more than $12,000.

Records filed with the *Herald*'s university advisors indicated that of the paper's 200-some donations in the first year of its existence, more than half came from out of state, and of those from Wisconsin, most were not from Madison.

The *Herald* was an attractive cause because it proposed to fight liberalism in the heart of the midwest. Madison, in no small part because of the violence of its protest culture there, was ground zero to those who wanted the counterculture movement stopped.

The *Herald* played to that audience, soliciting in arch-conservative publications like the journal *Human Events* for contributions to fight the liberals on their own ground. The new paper scored a considerable coup in 1971, when renowned conservative writer William F. Buckley agreed to speak at a fundraising dinner for the *Herald*. The engagement was only the second time Buckley ever agreed to forgo his usual speaking fee; the first was for his brother's election campaign.

IT DOESN'T END WITH US

The paper hailed Buckley as "Chairman Bill" and sold more than 700 tickets at $15 apiece. Buckley's remarks, transcribed in the *Herald*:

> I want to join you in honoring and encouraging a few young students who chose rather than to yield to the lure of despair, rather than to simply nurse their vouchmerits through their college years, to fight back. And notwithstanding that the effort would require thousands of hours of work, much of it menial, in an atmosphere hardly hospitable to the defense of conservative principles.
>
> One might as well undertake to found a Republican paper in the basement of Buckingham Palace as a conservative paper in Madison, Wisconsin. I find it altogether astonishing that they have come so far in so short a period ...
>
> Reason can not reach the revolutionary vapors on which the young revolutionists are stoned. What is required, I think, is among other things, a premonitory sign, a sign of firmness, a sign of resolution ... That sign is variously shown in decisions of the Supreme Court, acts of Congress, manifestos by our poets. And in relatively simple resolutions by young citizens such as the editors of the *Badger Herald*, whom I proudly salute.

However, Buckley's rhetorical largess did little to contain the *Herald*'s mounting debts. In its first year the paper had lost more than $10,000 because the cost of printing it out of town were crippling it.

In 1970 the *Herald* launched a campaign to secure the university's printing services, at that time contained entirely in the UW's Typographical Laboratory, the shop established by the *Cardinal's* Campus Publishing Company 1956 gift to the university.

The manner in which the campaign was conducted sheds much light on the relationship between the *Herald* and the university. *Herald* editors' letters to university officials are chummy, as from one friend to another. Korten particularly played the sympathy card, something for which his paper would later deride the *Cardinal*.

"It has been a long, tough year for the *Badger Herald*," Korten wrote in a warm and informal letter to Regent Bernard C. Ziegler, a frequent critic of the *Cardinal*. "There are times when we considered getting cots and sleeping at the office, since we seem to live here anyway ... our request is simply to obtain permission to print our paper on the university press."

Ziegler, no fan of the *Cardinal*, agreed. According to the minutes of a board of regents meeting on June 12, 1970:

IT DOESN'T END WITH US

He stated that he had assured the *Daily Cardinal* representatives that any arrangements that the Regents worked out would not be in conflict with their schedule at the printing office, and would not in any way put an undue financial burden on the *Daily Cardinal*.

He explained that by this he meant that, if the *Badger Herald* were allowed to use University facilities, they would be charged proportionately for the use of the space and the printing, so that there would be no subsidy on the part of either paper.

Whereas previous competitors had been met with strong opposition, the *Cardinal* treated the *Herald* as a joke, refusing to consider it a threat. The *Cardinal* protested briefly, but settled for having the *Herald* on presses its revenues had purchased, satisfied that the *Herald* would be charged fair rates for the same work for which the *Cardinal* paid.

Later, Korten's successor Nick Loniello lobbied UW Journalism Professor Lester Hawkes to persuade national advertising organizations, which placed ads on behalf of large corporations, to include the *Herald* in its listings of potential Madison media outlets. Hawkes, once a *Cardinal* adviser, wrote letters to the national ad companies urging them split revenues for which the *Cardinal* had worked for decades with the *Herald*, which was then only two years old, as a matter of "fairness."

Through the years the *Herald*'s staffers internalized the myth Korten and his successors helped construct: The *Cardinal*, which had never taken donation funds from the university, was state-subsidized, while the *Herald* was not. The facts were complex, the myth was simple, and the myth endured.

However stubbornly it refused to acknowledge the shoulders on which its staffers stood, the *Herald* took the springboard its donors gave it and used that springboard to soar. Throughout the late 1970s and early 1980s, as the *Cardinal* concentrated more and more on fanning the dying embers of a radical movement splintering after the end of the Vietnam War, the *Herald* was doing what few newspapers do well: marketing itself to the campus and the advertising community as a new and exciting voice.

When the *Wisconsin Daily News* had tried to gain access to the *Cardinal*'s loyal advertisers in 1912, *Cardinal* representatives rushed to secure their relationships and make sure no interloper could steal their clients away. When the *Daily News* spread misinformation about the *Cardinal*'s ownership, saying it was controlled by faculty interests, the *Cardinal* did not let such falsehoods pass unremarked. When the *Daily News* asked the university's leaders for "parity," for equal distribution of university advertising and other business, the university stood by its first newspaper, and refused to give away to another paper something the *Cardinal* had worked hard to earn.

IT DOESN'T END WITH US

At every turn, the *Cardinal* failed to heed the warning signs the *Herald* sent up, never repulsing gut-level attacks from the *Herald* with anything stronger than a sarcastic editorial. Never, according to the minutes of the *Cardinal*'s board of directors, did the paper consider legal action against the *Herald* for its claims, preferring to ignore the upstart and hope it went away. Perhaps it is forgivable, given that the *Cardinal* had survived nearly 100 years of struggles from within and without, always escaping with its life, if not its prosperity, intact.

However, Dick Ausman gave the *Cardinal* plenty of time to see him coming.

Ausman, a business major from Merrill, Wisconsin, joined the *Badger Herald* when he was 18. His older brother had been the *Herald*'s business manager and got Ausman involved, first as a circulation volunteer.

"He needed somebody to deliver the paper and I was the only one he could convince to get up that early," Ausman said.

From that lowly post he became circulation manager and then, when his brother graduated, business manager. He became publisher of the *Herald* in 1985, after taking a year off from school. Ausman said he knew exactly what he wanted to do with the *Herald*: take what was a weekly paper every bit as politically polarizing as the *Cardinal*, and turn it into a world-class journalistic training ground, apolitical in its news pages and ruthless in business.

"I saw what other college newspapers were doing," he said. "They were doing true training for journalists. These were places where people who wanted to learn how to write and edit could come and do that. So I came in to improve the *Herald*, moderate the paper, and make it successful."

Within days of assuming the position, Ausman began pecking at his paper's rivals. His first antagonistic act was to call the city's property tax assessor's office and initiate a tax audit of the *Cardinal*'s property, a shot across the bow that should have warned the paper that the *Herald* was serious. The *Cardinal* admitted to irregular record-keeping, paid some owed back taxes willingly, and remarked on Ausman no more that year.

At the same time, Ausman concentrated on making the *Herald* an equal competitor with the *Cardinal*. Ausman took the *Herald* daily on Nov. 10, 1986. Its editorial board quoted Korten's original "statement of purpose" and said:

> Of late the *Herald* has, we believe, come into its own as a serious, relatively straight-forward and fair-minded newspaper. A number of factors — among them the business success of the paper and the structural limitations of a weekly — prompted our decision to try daily publications for the remainder of the semester.
>
> The responsibility of which Patrick Korten spoke in 1969 will remain an indispensable credo at the *Herald* ... Encouragement from our partisans and detractors alike has bolstered

IT DOESN'T END WITH US

the confidence of the staff and made us all acutely aware of the salience of the institution. Publishing a daily paper is surely the greatest challenge any of us has ever undertaken; it is a challenge made doubly difficult by the discriminating nature of a university audience. We think we're up to it.

What the editorial did not mention was that in addition to turning daily, the newspaper also was now listed on the advertising rate cards for Madison Newspapers, Inc., which had printed the *Herald* for the past several months. When businesses bought ads in the city's largest papers, the *Wisconsin State Journal* and the *Capital Times*, they were offered space in the *Herald*'s pages at the same time.

This new convenience broke the *Cardinal*'s near-monopoly on local advertising, the ease of buying ads in all three papers at once proving attractive even to businesses that had had decades-long relationships with the *Cardinal*.

The line on the MNI rate card went unremarked and unchallenged by the *Cardinal* for nearly a decade, even after the *Cardinal*, too, began printing its papers with MNI.

"They allowed us to happen," Ausman said of the *Cardinal*. "They were off in their own little world and we were doing what I thought was in our best interests."

Ausman's main strength in attacking the *Cardinal* was a study of its history. The *Badger Herald* counted among its writers Edward Ben Elson, husband of Standard Press Party hire Patti Elson, who had tried and failed to lead the uprising against the *Cardinal* in 1976. Elson's tactic of gaining seats on the *Cardinal*'s board through the usually uncontroversial all-campus elections attracted Ausman's interest.

"I got copies of the *Cardinal*'s incorporation papers and looked over them," he said. "I found this avenue to take control of the *Cardinal*, and I used it, and it was perfectly legal, it was within the law. You can say it was a sneaky thing to do, but it was the best means to accomplish the end I had in mind."

That end was one student newspaper on campus. Ausman said he would have accepted dueling editorial pages, but the paper itself would be run by *Badger Herald* staff, according to *Badger Herald* business principles. One paper, Ausman said, could have challenged the *Capital Times* or the *Wisconsin State Journal* for dominance in downtown Madison; two campus papers, he believed, could only bleed each other dry.

In November 1986, the largest party vying for power in the university's student elections was a joke party called Bob Kasten School of Driving. Its name was a play on Wisconsin's U.S. Senator having been caught driving under the influence, and its members were pranksters and rabble-rousers. The party promised to use its power to accomplish such lofty goals as putting hundreds of goldfish in campus fountains. Its embrace of triviality won it converts among the usually disaffected student body, who voted the BKSOD's entire slate into office in December.

IT DOESN'T END WITH US

Included in that slate were winners of three seats on the *Daily Cardinal*'s board of directors: students David Atkins, Rita McConville and Brian Lawton.

"We had no idea who these guys were," said Tim Carroll, who had been hired as business manager for the *Cardinal* just three months before. "They were totally stealth candidates. The editorial staff started looking into it and they kind of found out they were Dick Ausman's people, but nobody was really sure."

The new board members took office and laid to rest the *Cardinal* staff's uncertainty. On Feb. 25, 1987, Atkins sent out a letter calling Editor-in-Chief John Keefe, Carroll, and Diana Kaufman and Eric Rasmussen — *Cardinal* staffers already serving as board members — to a meeting at his apartment.

Keefe and Carroll went expecting a "meet and greet' session with incoming students, who they imagined would be curious about the paper's operations and interested in working with the current staff.

They walked into the apartment with open minds.

They walked out with pink slips.

"They called the meeting to order, said they had a motion to fire the business manager and the editor in chief, and then they made a motion to appoint Dick Ausman business manager of the *Cardinal*, and the editor of the *Herald*, Brian Beneker, as the editor of the *Cardinal*," Carroll said. "We were in total shock."

Atkins, Lawton and McConville voted yes; Kaufman and Rasmussen voted no, and that was that.

"It was insane, it was deeply surreal," Carroll said. "I was sitting there and they were talking about me like I wasn't even there. I was just in disbelief, and then really, really pissed off that they would try to do this."

At the time of the elections, Keefe had been editor-in-chief of the *Cardinal* for less than eight weeks. A junior majoring in journalism, he was still figuring out how to manage his often-unruly staff and put the paper together. Suddenly, he was thrust into the quintessential corporate intrigue. He had to learn about mass media law, open records acts, and the ways in which company bylaws could be manipulated by those who knew them well.

"I never felt like they'd successfully take over the *Cardinal*, but I was worried we'd lose on some legal technicality," Keefe said. "They were clearly trying to pull as many dirty legal tricks as possible and I was worried we were at a disadvantage because we just didn't know how to be as tricky as they were."

Keefe's staff, not privy to the legal maneuverings of the paper as much as their boss was, saw only usurpers — and responded accordingly. The evening after the board meeting, Keefe was out attending classes, and several members of the *Herald* staff, including Beneker, attempted to assume their new positions.

"I got back from class and people were coming up to me telling me, 'They were here, they tried to give us orders,'" Keefe said, laughing. "'They said we're the new editors and we said no you're not,' and everybody wanted to know where I'd been. They had come to try to kick me out and I wasn't even there. I missed the whole thing."

IT DOESN'T END WITH US

The *Wisconsin State Journal* described the situation:

> A chaos-as-usual atmosphere characterized the *Daily Cardinal* newsroom Wednesday despite the takeover attempt a day earlier by the *Badger Herald* publisher and his allies on the *Cardinal* board.
>
> Shortly after 1 p.m. Tuesday, *Badger Herald* officials arrived in an unsuccessful attempt to assume control ... David Atkins, president of the *Cardinal* board, and *Herald* editor Brian Beneker arrived at the *Cardinal* office with several other people to talk about the transition of control voted by the *Cardinal* board.
>
> "We said no, we don't recognize your authority," said business manager Tim Carroll, who was fired by the board along with Keefe. Both remained at their desks, and the takeover group left.

Keefe called the campus police and Ginsberg, who told the *Herald* staffers that until the issue was resolved, legally, they were to remain outside the *Cardinal*'s offices. The *Herald* staffers appealed to Associate Dean Roger Howard for support "in their efforts to implement the board's decisions," but Howard refused them.

The *Herald*'s accusations about financial malfeasance and editorial irrelevance were mostly unfounded. While the *Cardinal* did lend newsprint to worker strikes in rural areas and printed photo essays on poverty in Madison's sister city in Nicaragua, in 1987 it also heavily covered campus news. Editorials criticized the university for sexism and a lack of representation for minorities on campus. The paper was by no means the revolutionary underground organ of decades past, though the reputation stuck.

After the heavy losses of the 1970s, the *Cardinal*'s finances were on an upswing. Local advertising was up 25 percent. The *Herald*'s move to daily publication had not yet entirely taken hold. The *Cardinal* still, at that time, enjoyed an advantage in name recognition. Though many businesses advertised in both papers, few exclusively chose the *Herald* over the *Cardinal*.

"They didn't have near the circulation or the advertising of the *Cardinal*," Carroll said. "They had to go very low on their pricing to get people to advertise, but Ausman was determined to make it work, and if they had to take a loss to undercut us, that's what they would do. It was going to be trouble for us in the long run. At the time, however, people in Madison knew the *Cardinal*, they knew where the readership was, and we were doing all right."

At the time of the takeover attempt, the *Cardinal*'s board had four faculty members and five students, three of whom were now in service to the aims of

IT DOESN'T END WITH US

Ausman and Atkins. Since the 1976 strike, faculty board members were not permitted to vote on personnel decisions. The remaining student board members did not have enough votes, under the strictly democratic *Cardinal* system, to rescind the ouster of personnel.

Journalism Professor Robert Drechsel had joined the *Cardinal* board the year before. He liked the *Cardinal*'s independent spirit and respected the hard work the students put in to put a paper out each day. At an emergency board meeting called after the firings, Drechsel spoke up.

"This isn't right," he said. "You guys can't do this."

Atkins stared Drechsel down. "Well, we voted. It's done."

The *Cardinal* staff threatened to recall the *Herald*-affiliated board members and began gathering signatures on petitions for a special election. Keefe and Carroll hired a lawyer, determined to sue to get their jobs back.

Ausman went to the press, saying he had only the best interests of the *Cardinal* at heart. "Both papers will continue to hurt until one goes down," he told the *Wisconsin State Journal*.

At home, Drechsel called a friend of his, who was an attorney, and asked him to come over and help Drechsel review the *Cardinal*'s bylaws, to try to find some way to resolve the situation. Since the 1976 strike, the student board members, in an effort to gain more equality, had stripped the faculty of their power. Now a new generation of *Cardinal* staffers was at the mercy of the students, without the faculty to turn to.

Drechsel combed through the documents, looking for some way out. "If there was a 'eureka moment,'" he said, "it was an anti-eureka moment of realizing just how little power we had."

In fact, Drechsel discovered, the faculty had only reserved for themselves one single task: dissolution of the corporation. They could not change the *Cardinal*'s bylaws. They could not fire the new board members. They could not hire the old editors back. The only thing they could do was shut the paper down.

So that was what they did.

Drechsel and the other faculty, along with Keefe and Carroll, dissolved the paper under the terms of its old articles of incorporation. They then immediately reincorporated, with a new board of directors, none of whom were elected by the student body. A 95-year-old tradition had, by necessity, come to an end.

"It was an unfair advantage the *Herald* had had over the *Cardinal*," Drechsel said. "The *Cardinal*, via these student elections, was vulnerable to manipulation in a way the *Herald* never was. We removed that advantage."

The entire fight lasted less than two weeks. After Drechsel announced the shutdown plan to the board, Atkins realized he was beaten and resigned. McConville and Lawton followed, and Beneker returned to his job at the *Badger Herald*. Keefe said he felt sympathy, in retrospect, for the BKSOD devotees who had followed Ausman's lead.

"They were thrown onto this board with professors and people who really were devoted to the *Cardinal*," Keefe said. "They seemed like nice people, but they were there to do this guy's bidding and I don't think they realized what they were getting into. I don't think they knew we'd fight it as hard as we did."

There was no question they would fight it, he said.

"At no point did I ever think this was over," Keefe said. "It was never my feeling that we were done. I knew there was going to have to be some kind of process, and through that we would find a way to keep this from happening. And that's what we did. We just outmaneuvered them."

The iconic photograph, in the *Cardinal's* pages, is of Ausman, his head buried in his hands, staring at the top of the conference room table. His entire posture spoke defeat, and the *Badger Herald*'s editorials disavowed him:

> In the controversy surrounding Mr. Ausman's appointment [to the *Cardinal* board] we, the members of the Board of Directors of the *Badger Herald*, feel we should put forth our position.
>
> We have the greatest respect and affection for Mr. Ausman, but we must also emphasize the fact that his appointment to the *Cardinal* board of control was not instigated, promoted or in any way supported by the *Badger Herald* or any of its employees in any official capacity. To put it bluntly, the *Cardinal's* board is acting on its own — as it always has.
>
> The frosty relations between the *Badger Herald* and the *Daily Cardinal* are no secret. The Board of Directors of the *Badger Herald* are not fond of the *Cardinal*, but neither are we trying to acquire our rival newspaper. We have neither approved nor directed Mr. Ausman or any other member of the *Herald* to "take over" the *Cardinal*.

Ausman denied anyone at the *Badger Herald* had any knowledge of his scheme. "When I finally told them, the day before we did it, I thought they were going to faint," he said, chuckling at the memory. "This was not a *Herald* thing, this was not a political move because one paper was liberal and the other was conservative. This was business, and I did it alone."

He admitted without rancor that the *Cardinal* beat him fair and square.

"I wish it would have worked," he said. "I think the *Herald*, especially, would have come out of that time stronger and what we were trying to do would have been better if the two papers would be combined. But I don't have regrets in my life. It was a great learning experience."

Though it only lasted a week and a half, the takeover attempt established the *Herald* in the minds of *Cardinal* staffers as aggressors. With such a frontal assault, the *Herald* effectively cemented animosity between the staffs. Had Ausman approached the *Cardinal* more gently, as both papers moderated their pol-

IT DOESN'T END WITH US

itics in response to the times, there might have been support — on the papers' boards if not in their newsrooms — for a merger. As it was, the two rivals were now mortal enemies. Further merger offers were met with derision and rebuff.

"Should you run out of copies of the *Badger Herald*, we have some toilet paper you can use," read one mocking fax sent from the *Cardinal* offices to the *Herald*'s. The *Herald* continued to attack the *Cardinal* as dependent on the university, saying in ads that "It's okay, just put it on our tab."

The takeover also shifted the grounds for rivalry between the two papers. The *Herald* under Korten and Loniello was ideologically driven, a paper motivated by its editorial message, not unlike the *Cardinal*. Ausman's ruthless tactics turned the paper's mission to money. It was a critical distinction: For another decade, the *Cardinal* continued to fight battles over principles, while the *Herald* pulled in the cash.

Wisconsin's and the nation's larger newspapers often make light of the competition between the two papers. During the takeover attempt they ran articles full of equal parts amusement and condescension about those quirky children and their toy newspaper war. Forgetting, as they often do, that neither paper was pretend. The journalists involved, despite their years, worked as hard as any paid writer ever would, and cared about their papers as much — if not more — than most "professionals" can claim.

"This was a great institution for which we were wholly responsible," Keefe said. "And that's what they were up against. If it was just a paper, that would have been one thing. But it wasn't. It was a cause and a movement to us, a place where people felt they were making a difference. And having somebody out there who wants to destroy that really opens your eyes to what people can do with the legal system if they want you gone. We weren't going to let that happen, not on our watch."

In a strange way, Ausman got his wish. The competitive newspaper training Wisconsin's student papers now offer is unrivaled anywhere else in the country. For journalism students, those who really want to learn what newspapering is all about, there is no better way to learn what big city competition will feel like than to wake up for your early class and find out on the way that you have been scooped.

"It definitely made us stronger," said Abigail Goldman, former campus editor at the *Cardinal* who went on to earn a Pulitzer Prize at the *Los Angeles Times*. "We really had separate identities and we knew what we were about and what they were about. It gave you an idea of where you stood on campus, what paper you were with."

In recent years both papers have been more moderate politically, though the *Cardinal* is more loath to endorse Republican candidates for office and the *Herald* more likely. The *Cardinal*'s news coverage tends to be sober and focused, while the *Herald* glories in the UW-Madison's reputation as a party school and falls back on encouragement for the fraternity-sorority life that is still very much a part of campus.

IT DOESN'T END WITH US

"I never thought they'd both still be there," Ausman said. "I was proven wrong, very wrong, on that point."

---

[1] The *Badger Herald* staff, *About The Badger Herald*, http://www.badgerherald.com/about.

IT DOESN'T END WITH US

IT DOESN'T END WITH US

12.
Typographical Error

The Campus Publishing Company donated equipment and supplies worth $60,000 and $32,000 in cash to the University in 1956, which with inflation would now be worth $500,000 — more than four times our debt to the Type Lab. Also donated was the land on which Vilas Hall now stands — you're welcome.
— The Daily Cardinal, Aug. 28, 1989

ಜ

The idea developed slowly. In the early '20s, an unhappy *Cardinal* was publishing downtown, only slightly consoled by its profits from a few good years. Around 1925 a particular thought popped into the minds of such Wisconsin men as John B. Sanborn, Grant M. Hyde, Elmer W. Freytag, John L. Bergstresser and Porter Butts, to mention a few.

Why not buy a press and publish the *Cardinal* right there on campus?

The idea kicked around for two years. The *Cardinal* finally took a last, long peek at its trust agreements and decided to come in. The corporation was legally organized on March 31, 1927.

For a brief, hectic spell, the Cardinal Publishing Company, as it was first called, was little more than a name. It had an

IT DOESN'T END WITH US

idea, but no home. Machinery was finally tucked into a bed of concrete in the basement of the University YMCA. Editorial offices of the *Daily Cardinal* were set up in the Memorial Union, and from there it was only a stumble down several flights of stairs and next door to watch a newspaper roll off the press.

Such reads the official history of the Campus Publishing Company, renamed from the Cardinal Publishing Company in 1938 when the printing plant, organized as a collective owned by UW students, began taking on printing jobs for the university itself: athletic programs, letterheads, fraternity papers, invitations to events. By the time the company and its assets were given as a gift to the university in 1956, it was the third largest shop in Madison, with 30 employees and its own building.

The plant's main client remained the *Daily Cardinal*. Many of the directors of the company were current or former *Cardinal* staff members or advisers: Porter Butts, then director of the Wisconsin Union, had been a *Cardinal* editor; Grant Hyde was a faculty director on the *Cardinal's* board, as was Lester Hawkes. The company's fortunes were tied to those of the *Cardinal*: when the paper fell financially ill in 1953, it nearly took the printing plant down with it.

Following that near-miss, the press took on other major university clients, and began to become profitable. So profitable, in fact, that it had nearly $40,000 in cash reserves when its board approached the university about making the presses theirs.

After the press, the company, the corporation's savings and equipment and the building and land were all donated to the university, the Typography Laboratory was run by a director, usually a member of the UW Journalism School faculty, and its union pressmen. The *Cardinal* moved its offices into the lakefront-located Journalism Hall, and, while the liquidation was completed and the details of the lab's governance, rates and structure were worked out, rented the presses back from the UW for $800 per month.

In 1965 the university decided to demolish both Journalism Hall and the Campus Publishing Company's old building at 823 University Avenue. The Typography Laboratory purchased a new press, the first offset press in the state, then the finest and most modern printing money could buy. The new press and the *Cardinal* were situated in a building at 425 Henry Mall, west of their old location, while the new journalism building was completed on the Campus Publishing Company's former land.

The leftover proceeds from the company's liquidation were placed in a trust fund: $14,000 intended by the company's former directors to be used to maintain the lab and buy new equipment.

In 1972 the *Cardinal* and its offset press, as well as the Type Lab's employees, some of them old Campus Publishing Company hands, moved into the new Vilas Communication Hall at 821 University Avenue. The *Cardinal* was

IT DOESN'T END WITH US

granted space in a small room on the building's bottom floor. Down the hall was the Type Lab, its noisy, greasy presses taking up one side of a long and narrow hallway beside the university's theater department. For more than a decade, students learned the typographical trade, the practical method of getting a newspaper from idea to actuality, in that room.

Like the *Cardinal*, it was an institution. To the *Cardinal*, it seemed it would always be there.

Until the letter came.

> June 6, 1989
>
> Brannon Lambert
> Business Manager
> The *Daily Cardinal*
> Vilas Hall
>
> Dear Brannon,
>
> This is to notify you that the UW Typographical Laboratory will go out of existence July 14, 1989.
>
> As I indicated in previous conversations, the Type Lab faces two lethal problems, both owing to desktop typographic technology. One problem is that the instructional value of the Lab is essentially eliminated by the removal of [newspaper page] composition from the Lab to the *Cardinal* office and to School of Journalism laboratories. The other problem is that the loss of composition revenues prevents the Lab from balancing its budget ... However inevitable this seems, in light of advancing technology, it is still sad news for those of us who have enjoyed a long relationship. The Type Lab grew out of a bequest to the Regents of equipment from the Campus Printing Company, which had printed the *Cardinal* for many years. A good many students learned a great deal in the lab over those years.
>
> I know that you have already scouted other places where you could get printed, and we wish you well. You may have any standing ads in the lab's possession. And we are prepared to print the *Cardinal* through the week of July 10-14.
>
> I also remind you that the *Cardinal* owes the Type Lab more than $100,000 for services. We expect that to be paid off on the schedule provided in the report of the *Cardinal* to the

IT DOESN'T END WITH US

Cardinal Board dated May 19, 1989. This called for monthly payments until the debt is retired in May, 1991. Although the Lab will be closed, its books will remain open to receive payment.

Sincerely,

William B. Blankenburg
Professor and faculty director of the UW Typographical Laboratory

In the late 1980s, journalism production was changing. Desktop publishing had begun making the printing equipment the *Cardinal* relied on for its production obsolete. One-fourth of student newspapers had already moved to desktop publishing[1] and centralized computer systems by the time the *Cardinal* considered such a shift. The UW Journalism School was struggling to adapt to the changes in the industry.

There was more to Blankenburg's memo, however, than mere "times they are a-changin'" regret. The *timing* of the letter was key. The *Cardinal* reduced its printing schedule during the summer to once a week. Editors adopted a more leisurely schedule, seldom visiting the office every day. Blankenburg's missive could have sat in Lambert's inbox for days before the students noticed it.

Lambert had joined the paper two years prior, as an advertising representative hired during a period of resurgence at the *Cardinal*. His boss, Business Manager Jordan Kern, had taken an underperforming ad staff and put them on a strict quota system, adhering to clear rules about how much to sell and to whom.

Lambert, a business school student, liked the rigorous training Kern gave him and in when Kern left in January 1989, Lambert took over his job. After a successful semester, he was looking forward to the summer off.

"In the summer, everything was shutting down," Lambert remembered. "We'd hired an ad manager and some summer editors but everybody was done and going home."

After he read the letter, Lambert's first call was to Ivan Strmecki, who had been a copy editor at the paper and was now its summer editor.

Strmecki called a meeting with the UW's chancellor, then Donna Shalala, who would later become President Bill Clinton's secretary of health and human services. Shalala professed sympathy for the bind the *Cardinal* was in, but did not offer any hope of reversing the Journalism School's decision.

"She gave us a politico's answer," Lambert recalled. "She said, 'We'll look into it, see what we can do.' Well, we didn't have the luxury of waiting for her, so we started working on our own."

Strmecki, a dedicated journalist, started digging. The University of Wisconsin is a public institution and so nearly all of its boards and committees and

IT DOESN'T END WITH US

faculty organizations are subject to Freedom of Information Act standards. With the livelihood of his paper at stake, Strmecki filed requests seeking any and all journalism school memos relating to the closing of the Type Lab, the Lab's finances and the finances of the *Badger Herald* and the *Daily Cardinal*.

He got more than two file boxes full of information: rates charged to Typography Lab clients, lists of early contributors to the *Badger Herald* (filed publicly with the *Herald*'s faculty advisors), bills sent from the Lab to its newspapers, and more importantly letters: to and from deans, professors and printers detailing nearly every aspect of the lab's operation. Almost immediately, Blankenburg's story started to fall apart. Strmecki's first find was a memo from Blankenburg to another university official, dated March 17, 1989:

> I need to make some early — and quiet — preparations for the possible closing of the Laboratory. Could you give me some idea how close [the Lab's head printer] Phil Holen is to retirement and what sort of bumping rights or opportunities the printers might have? I'd appreciate it.

Strmecki and Lambert released the memo to the Madison press, along with another missive, dated May 1, from College of Letters and Science Assistant Dean David Dean, also a *Cardinal* alumnus. That memo read, in part, "After deliberation and based on projected income, we have decided to phase out the Type Lab."

Blankenburg responded by going on the attack in the Madison press.

The Type Lab had been allowing the *Cardinal* to pay its printing on credit since 1986, when rate increases forced the paper into a $19,000 debt to the Lab. By 1989, that debt had ballooned to more than $120,000, and the Lab had demanded a payment plan which the *Cardinal* board provided, to Blankenburg's apparent satisfaction, as he raised no protest at the time.

"We knew we owed money," Lambert said. "We'd been printing far more pages than we could afford, and Jordan and I had put a stop to that. We were doing better, and we thought we'd had it all worked out."

Blankenburg's original press release announcing the Lab's closure stated that the *Cardinal*'s debt "was not a contributing factor." However, after the staff began asking why they had not been told about the closing sooner, Blankenburg went to the *Badger Herald* and gave an interview blasting the *Cardinal*.

"You could argue that the lab, by tolerating the paper's debt, was subsidizing it," he said, also highlighting the *Cardinal*'s rent-free offices in Vilas Hall as evidence that the university was benevolent towards the paper. The *Herald* seized on Blankenburg's words as proof the *Cardinal* was lying about its "independent" status, and attacked the *Cardinal* as somehow under university control.

After that, Lambert and Strmecki drew battle lines. They felt their livelihood was at stake — and like *Cardinal* staffs of years past, they circled around their paper and fought outside attacks hard.

IT DOESN'T END WITH US

"We FOIA'd every chancellor's and professor's records, every record ever kept on the *Daily Cardinal*, every file in the journalism school, every file of every professor," Lambert said. "We thought it was purposeful, that the university was trying to force the *Cardinal* out of business. We found a document in someone else's file that shouldn't have been in the file."

In 1970, when the *Badger Herald* first became a client of the Typography Laboratory, the UW's regents had assured the nervous *Cardinal* staff that its competitor would be charged the same rates for the same work, thus ensuring a fair competition between the two papers.

Strmecki's searches led him to a series of memos that proved that this promised equity was a fiction. For years, the *Herald* had been charged drastically less than the *Cardinal*.

For example, in August 1985, Blankenburg issued memos to both the *Cardinal* and the *Herald* informing them of the lab's present printing rates. Because the *Herald* provided its pages to the presses already pasted-up and ready to go, its rates were lower.

However, even accounting for this difference and the difference in frequency of printing the *Herald* weekly and the *Cardinal* daily, there were striking disparities. For example, from September 1985 to May 1986 (when Ausman took the *Herald* off the university presses) the *Herald* paid the lab $40,453. For the same services, the *Cardinal* paid $56,636.

"It all provided a very strong argument that journalism professors were gunning for the *Cardinal*," Lambert said.

Armed now with numbers, he and Strmecki called in the lawyers. They hired a Madison attorney, Norma Briggs, to draft a letter to Shalala outlining their case and asking for an immediate halt to the lab's closing. She reminded university officials of what they seemed to have forgotten: The presses were a gift, not to be thrown away lightly.

"It is the position of the *Cardinal* that if the University no longer wants the gift made possible by the liquidation of the Campus Publishing Company's assets, or is no longer willing to abide by the conditions of that gift, that it may return it," she wrote.

"That is, the university may return the initial $100,000 with 33 years' worth of compound interest minus the outstanding operating deficit incurred by the Typography Laboratory."

The university responded by demanding payment in full of the *Cardinal's* debt, along with a legal opinion that the Type Lab owed the *Cardinal* nothing. The university's lawyers noted that the terms of the original gift, back in 1956, "*may* be used for the production of a student newspaper, now known as 'the *Daily Cardinal*'." *May* being a term of permission, *shall* being one of legal requirement. One word, they said, made all the difference.

"Well, that was when the shit hit the fan," Lambert said. "We looked at that and said 'You've got to be kidding me.' We were all pretty hot about it at the time."

IT DOESN'T END WITH US

Intense negotiations began. The *Cardinal* wrote more letters, stronger, asking for meetings and for Shalala to intervene on their behalf. Shalala agreed to a time and place, and then cancelled. Finally a group of *Cardinal* staffers piled into a car and drove to a board of regents meeting being held in Milwaukee. They enlisted the help of the student government president, James Sullivan, who told the regents they had violated the state's shared governance statute by bypassing any attempt to solicit student opinion on the lab's closing. The student body as a whole, since the time of the Campus Publishing Company's founding, was the legal owner of the facility.

"Our trust has been shattered," Sullivan told the regents, noting the "contempt" with which the faculty had treated the *Cardinal*. "We are through playing around."

The regents, to whom the *Cardinal*'s radical days were just a few short years ago, were unsympathetic. According to the *Cardinal*'s story of the meeting, one regent joked about the Type Lab closing. When Sullivan asked what he'd do if the *Cardinal* shut down, he replied, "I expect I'll get up in the morning, have my breakfast and go about my business," drawing laughter from his colleagues. The board told the *Cardinal* staff to resume negotiations with Shalala, who saw them at the meeting and realized how angry they were.

"She saw us coming and said, 'Okay, we'll sit down,'" Lambert said.

While the private negotiations went on, a public relations war played out. The *Cardinal*'s summer staff mounted a "Save the Presses" rally and got local politicians to sign on to support their cause. The *Cardinal*'s own board was horrified.

"The *Cardinal* was making its public argument from an incredibly weak position, which was that somehow the university was maliciously forcing this great institution to close," said Robert Drechsel, the journalism professor who had helped solve the *Cardinal-Herald* takeover incident. "I remember just being appalled by that, as a director, that these editors were taking this maverick action and arguing that the university owed it to them."

The Madison press concurred, calling the *Cardinal* staffers spoiled children and seizing on Blankenburg's narrative of debt. No one knew, at the time, about the overcharges, and few people read far enough into the *Cardinal*'s history to understand the magnitude of the original gift.

Capital Times columnist Patrice Wendling sniped that the *Cardinal*'s "lackluster" protests amounted to "squawking" and wrote sarcastically that the university was daring to "put the kibosh on the Mike Roykos of tomorrow." The *Badger Herald* was even less kind. Its editorials made no mention of its own past at the Type Lab, instead saying the *Cardinal* had "taken freedom of the press too literally."

Most of the work was falling on Strmecki and Lambert, who were spending every day and night in the office, the lab, on the phone with printers and lawyers, trying to think of ways to keep the lab open and find places to print the *Cardinal* if they couldn't do it.

IT DOESN'T END WITH US

The easiest question for the *Cardinal* to settle turned out to be the lack of a printer. The University of Wisconsin's Extension Printing Services, which printed university calendars and class schedules and other basic educational materials for the UW's various schools in the state, offered to buy the Type Lab's presses. Extension also offered to hire printers David Newman and Emery Pourier, who by this time had worked for the *Cardinal* and then the Lab for years.

The presses would move from Vilas Hall just a few blocks away to Extension's building on Murray Street, within walking distance of the *Cardinal*. *Cardinal* staffers could lay out their pages in the Type Lab's old space, with the help of Newman or Pourier, and then they'd make the short trip to the presses each night. The printers stayed employed, the *Cardinal* did not need to change formats or any kind of typesetting procedures, and the university got the money it was seeking for the presses.

Extension Printing Services Director John Schuon told the Madison press he'd initially been interested in adding the *Cardinal's* large press to Extension's current stable of 12 different presses, but was further motivated by the *Cardinal's* need.

"I really wanted to print the paper on campus," Schuon told the press at the time. "That's where it belongs."

Lambert and Strmecki, along with the rest of the staff, were ecstatic. "It was a sweet deal," Lambert said. "We could set our own printing deadlines, which was a godsend to the news staff, and now all that was left was to settle the debt."

And on that, the *Cardinal* was willing to deal. The staff met with Shalala, and struck a bargain. The university would cut the *Cardinal's* debt in half, allowing the sale of some of the printing equipment — which had been purchased with *Cardinal* profits — to offset the full amount. The *Cardinal* would occupy rent-free space in Vilas Hall — built on the foundations of the building Campus Publishing donated — in perpetuity. The *Cardinal* would pay off the remaining debt over the next ten years.

"All of Ivan's hard work really paid off in that meeting," Lambert said. "We went in there, said, 'This is what we want,' and Shalala said 'Okay.' We put up our best argument and they believed us."

The *Cardinal's* statement on the matter, issued in February 1989 when the final papers were signed, made no mention of Blankenburg's actions or the memos Strmecki had discovered, saying only that the *Herald* had been undercharged for services in the past.

The university said it relented because it did not want to force the *Cardinal* out of business.

"We didn't want to create a situation," Lambert said. "We wanted it to end and get back into business."

It had been a trying summer and an even more trying fall. Every day, Strmecki would walk into the office with another stack of papers, the results of

IT DOESN'T END WITH US

his tireless investigations, and sit down with Lambert and the rest of the summer staff, trying to puzzle the problem out. Lambert was working a night job as well as one at the *Cardinal*, and when classes started up again, the extra work of putting out a paper, going to school and running a legal investigatory operation had nearly crushed the students.

But they never, Lambert said, thought about giving up.

"We had just celebrated our 95th anniversary," Lambert said. "It was very powerful, the idea of all this history and then two years later we're being faced with the idea that we would be the first ones to shut it down. At that point, we just had to make sure it would continue.

"It was all economics to the university. It was something else entirely to us."

Blankenburg, now retired and living in California, denied any ill will toward the *Cardinal*. He maintained that any rate disparities between the *Cardinal* and *Herald* could be explained by differences in the type of work the two papers had done at the Lab.

"There was no personal vendetta," he said. "I was glad it was settled the way it was. I don't know if the university found some validity in their claims or if they just wanted to get away from a pissing match with a student newspaper, but if it provided some heart balm to the *Cardinal* that's just as well."

In 1992 the *Daily Cardinal* turned 100. A century of daily campus coverage was a milestone just a few other student papers could claim. Alumni from all over the country flocked back to Madison for a gala banquet. The celebration included office tours, venerable speakers and a local radio station dedicating a day of broadcasting to the paper.

It was a high point: the Great Hall of the university's Memorial Union, filled with journalism luminaries, all of them toasting the *Cardinal*.

Three years later the paper stopped publishing.

---

[1] Atkins, *College Daily in the United States*, 39.

IT DOESN'T END WITH US

IT DOESN'T END WITH US

13.

Shutdown

On Feb. 7, 1995, the paper's dwindling cash reserves finally ran out. The Cardinal couldn't afford to print the next day. To a staff kept largely in the dark about not only the events of the past few months, but those of the past few years as well, the shutdown came as a complete surprise. Initially, the shutdown was treated as a cash-flow problem. But as the first week wore on, staffers became more and more curious, and the Cardinal's skeleton board of directors launched an investigation. What they found, when all numbers were tallied, was a debt totaling $137,700, and $43.71 left in the Cardinal's checkbook.
– On Wisconsin magazine, May/June 1997

ଔ

There are few places more miserable than Madison, Wisconsin in February. All the area's natural beauty lies smothered under a shell of hard, graying snow; buildings' concrete facades drip with icicles. The last glow of the holidays is gone, but spring is still far away. Midterm exams loom. Flu and colds run rampant through the dormitories.

Inside the *Cardinal* office on Feb. 8, 1995, staffers sat around a large gray conference table, not writing, not calling, not working, not really doing very much at all. Now and then someone would try to start a conversation only to be met with stony silence, or inappropriate laughter, or withering glares.

It was very much like a wake.

On the table in front of them lay a copy of the *Badger Herald*. Its banner headline screamed "'*Daily Cardinal*' Ceases Publication."

IT DOESN'T END WITH US

Editor-in-Chief Kristen Komisarek had been up all night. She did three television interviews and threw up.

For the first time in 103 years, the *Daily Cardinal*'s staff had failed to do what even the most inept or unwise staffs in the past had been able to accomplish. For the first time in 103 years, the *Daily Cardinal* had not published a scheduled issue.

The headlines were like a nightmare. The Madison press was comprised of a good number of *Cardinal* alumni and UW graduates; most were familiar with the *Cardinal*'s struggles in the past two decades. While some of the news reporting of the *Cardinal*'s collapse was sympathetic, most had a distinct overtone of "I Told You So," a contempt for the students who had — to all outside observers — ruined a great newspaper and squandered its history.

"In the end, free market competition silenced the *Cardinal*," State Journal columnist and *Cardinal* alumnus Bill Wineke wrote. "Along with the [paper's] freedom from external control came a freedom to go for broke. Apparently, after 103 years, that's what happened."

To the public, the *Cardinal*'s shutdown would play out as the result of an unscrupulous business manager's failure to do his job, a morality tale of how one man brought down a journalism institution.

In truth, the *Cardinal* had been heading for disaster for years, its headlong rush to the cliff's edge fueled by arrogant editorial staffers, an apathetic board of directors and a university community changing faster than the paper serving it. The paper had faced financial and editorial obliteration before, but its dedicated staffs had always managed to keep the teetering train on the tracks. This time, it went off the rails.

In 1984, the *Cardinal* had more than $100,000 in savings and investments, a surplus built up after the lean years of the 1970s. Declining advertising, distribution woes and other money problems depleted that fund to $36,000 by 1992, and by the following year, the *Cardinal* was bleeding red ink. The weight of the Type Lab debt payments and insistence by editors that the paper make room for all copy — even if the amount of advertising couldn't support it — had eaten away the *Cardinal*'s savings slowly for more than a decade.

Staff members' bickering made more news in those years than the *Cardinal*'s reporting; one editor instituted a public "purge" of anyone deemed politically unsuitable for *Cardinal* editorship, and another was reported to have implied that straight white men were unwelcome on staff, leading to an exodus. The paper was becoming a parody of its former progressive self.

"The tone of the staff before my term was very, very ideological," said Kate Misurek, who became editor-in-chief in 1993. "I worked under the people who were very staunch and very radical ... Then the next generation of leaders emerged. And there was sort of a period of time where there was a tug of war between the new and the old."

Meanwhile, the *Badger Herald* was thriving. The *Herald* capitalized on Dick Ausman's achievements in partnering his paper with the Madison city dailies.

IT DOESN'T END WITH US

Madison's economy was changing in ways the *Cardinal* was too wrapped up in internal conflict to understand: Rising rents on State Street — the students' main shopping district — were driving out local businesses. National chain stores and restaurants quickly filled the vacant storefronts.

The national chains bought student newspaper ads through advertising agencies headquartered out of state. They had no ingrained loyalty to the *Cardinal* and merely wanted the most bang for their buck. The *Herald* bumped its circulation up to more than 17,000 copies, far more than the university's readership required, to make themselves more attractive to national advertisers than the lower-circulating *Cardinal*, and the money rolled in. Fat with ads, the *Herald* could spend more on marketing, raising its profile in the Madison community.

The university the *Cardinal* purported to cover also was remaking itself. The UW's leadership had begun to seek corporate partnerships for everything from drug research to building projects. The UW's Journalism School, moving to emphasize academic prestige over practical print journalism training, cut back its newsroom-style courses and in the early 1990s gave up its national accreditation.

The sense of history and tradition that had tied the *Cardinal* to its campus, the way the *Cardinal*'s apprenticeship model had mirrored the way university students were educated, those factors combined into nothing more than nostalgia, hardly a sound business strategy.

The Madison campus was becoming an unhealthy environment for an ideologically driven, idealistically run organization.

By the early 1990s the paper's board of directors had dwindled, in response to the varying degrees of hostility and neglect it had faced from the paper over the years. Stripping the board of its hiring and firing powers, stripping it of its fiscal responsibilities, the paper had left its academic members with the feeling they were figureheads, and they acted as such.

The student members were more often than not former *Cardinal* editors who wanted to continue managing the paper in some capacity. Some were conscientious, some were not.

By 1994 the board of directors consisted of just two faculty members, journalism professors Sheila Reaves and Raymond Anderson, and seven student members. The faculty members particularly took no hardline roles in enforcing fiscal discipline; presented with financial information they rarely questioned its veracity. They did not feel their duty was to the fiscal health of the *Cardinal*, nor did they hold themselves responsible if something went wrong.

"Professors were not supposed to interfere," said Anderson, a former Moscow bureau chief for the *New York Times*. "As I said a number of times at meetings, the students should run the newspaper, even if they run it into the ground."

Staff turnover decimated the paper's traditional system of training new editors. Where once editorial elections had been staggered, so that several experienced editors were always on duty when new leaders came aboard, now almost all new editors were chosen together. There was no guarantee of any institutional memory from one year to the next.

The paper had a brief reprieve in the fall of 1993. Experienced editors began to stabilize the paper. Editor-in-Chief Misurek was a four-year *Cardinal* veteran, and she and Business Manager Tom Bernthal worked closely together, in contrast to the business-editorial hostility that had allowed the paper to suffer in the past. They put a stop to much of the internal strife that plagued the *Cardinal*, and focused the paper's news staff on the campus, rather than on overseas news or national politics.

"We enjoyed a period, during my term of editor in chief, of a little bit of a financial boom," Misurek said, citing the Badger football team's run for the Rose Bowl as an economic opportunity that Bernthal skillfully exploited. "Every business wanted to place 'Congratulations Wisconsin Badgers' ads. Everybody wanted to get a piece of the pie ... to cash in on this great experience."

At the end of Bernthal's tenure the newspaper had $10,000 in its checkbook and another $35,000 in a certificate of deposit at a local bank, a large rainy-day fund for emergencies. The paper was in better fiscal health than it had been in almost a decade. During all this hard work, Misurek and Bernthal spent long hours discussing ways to improve the *Cardinal*.

"In the spring of 1994, we had a very conscientious team at the helm," Bernthal said. "We were bringing in many more times revenue than we had in previous years."

As the 1994 school year was ending, they initiated a debate within the paper's staff. Blaming the financial disparities between the *Cardinal* and the *Herald* on the paper's physical size, they proposed a radical change. The longtime-tabloid paper would become a broadsheet, the traditional metro newspaper format and the one utilized by the *Herald*. The *Cardinal* also would leave its printers of the past five years at UW Extension to print at Madison Newspapers, Inc., the same place the *Herald* and Madison's city dailies were printed.

The paper could also increase in circulation, until there was no measurable physical difference between the two papers. Then, they felt, the *Cardinal*'s superiority would shine through, bringing the advertising now going to the *Herald* back to the *Cardinal*.

The staff debated the change for hours. It would cost up to $7,500 to print for one week as a broadsheet at Madison Newspapers, more than three times the rate of its current printer.

In addition, the paper would have to significantly upgrade its production capabilities, replacing a computer system which had worked well for nearly a decade with more expensive desktop publishing equipment. Purchases like this would drain the paper's savings.

Moreover, there was a clause in the *Cardinal*'s contract with the UW Extension that made the move risky. Because Extension had taken on such significant improvements to secure the *Cardinal* a place to print, including buying

IT DOESN'T END WITH US

the paper's old tabloid press, their contract stated that if the *Cardinal* ever decided to leave the printer, it could never come back.

In the end, there were too many reasons not to make the change, balanced against a very slim and subjective chance the *Cardinal* could gain some advantage. The staff voted to stay a tabloid newspaper. Bernthal said he was relieved. "It was significantly cheaper," he said.

The year ended. *Cardinal* staff members, as was tradition, elected a skeleton staff to publish the paper weekly during the summer and Bernthal and Misurek hired a summer business manager to take the helm while they pursued internships out of state. They brought in a friend, someone they frequently drank with at the local bars, where *Cardinal* and *Herald* staffers mixed and mingled and occasionally hooked up in student journalism solidarity.

Joel Kaphingst grew up in Sun Prairie, Wisconsin, a prosperous Madison suburb. A political science major, he joined the *Badger Herald* in the early 1990s when the paper was at its competitive height. A talented reporter and charismatic leader, Kaphingst quickly rose through the ranks to become the *Herald*'s editor-in-chief.

After his *Herald* editorship ended in 1992, Kaphingst and other former *Herald* staffers founded a short-lived university sports publication. It was on the heels of that magazine's failure that he became involved with his former paper's competition.

"I never even thought about working for the *Cardinal* until its own staff members broached the idea, and even then it took a great deal of persuasion by them for me to agree," he remembered. "Although I still had some ties to the *Herald* at the time I decided to join the *Cardinal*, my substantive service with the *Herald* had ended."

During the summer Kaphingst determined that the "conscientious team's" instincts to change the *Cardinal's* format were correct. He went to Madison Newspapers, Inc. and negotiated a printing contract, and purchased computer equipment for the *Cardinal*. He cut off ties with UW Extension, and fired the paper's office manager, Cheryl Reddeman, who had worked at the paper for 24 years. She was responsible for billing and collections at the paper, keeping the money coming in while at the same time providing institutional memory for the students who worked there. She was one year away from retirement.

Kaphingst claimed he had both board and staff permission for everything he did.

"Members of the *Cardinal* staff themselves asked me to come aboard to help reorganize a business and advertising staff that was in disarray and had been for years," he said, adding that he had done large amounts of work in the summer to "improve the *Cardinal*, including delivering the paper during the summer months because no distribution staff had been retained from the previous spring."

Misurek and Bernthal both claim Kaphingst acted on his own, usurping power in their absence. They both claim he was hired only to be a summer care-

IT DOESN'T END WITH US

taker, and had no authority to take steps to change the paper's format or hire and fire staff.

I was the editor-in-chief in the fall of 1994, a 19-year-old sophomore with no desk experience, elected to the position directly from my job as an arts writer. I had gone home over the summer, to work in my father's pharmacy in Racine, Wis. and earn a little money for the coming year.

In mid-July, Kaphingst called my parents' house. He told me he, in consultation with Misurek and Bernthal, had decided to make the switch to a broadsheet paper. The summer board of directors, he said, had approved the change, and it was going forward, but he wanted my backing nonetheless.

I could plead inexperience to explain my compliance with their actions, but in truth I plead nothing. I agreed to the move, worried but certain in my ignorance that somehow, we would make things work. Kaphingst suggested I call the rest of my incoming editing staff and tell them the news, and I did so. Several expressed reservations, and some were enthusiastic and optimistic. As I trusted my predecessors, my staff trusted me.

The *Cardinal* published its first broadsheet issue Sept. 1, 1994. The paper was fat with advertising and copy, looked professionally designed, and showed no sign that its production had been fraught with problems that frustrated the editorial staff to the point of revolt.

To make the broadsheet switch, the computer system the *Cardinal* had used for eight years without major breakdowns was scrapped. The new system crashed, on average, once every evening, usually around deadline. Staffers who were trying to learn a new design system, new software, new methods of desktop publishing, found their efforts gone into the ether after a blip on the screen.

Some of the problems were due to the *Cardinal*'s new printers: Something as simple as the color on the paper's front page could not be regulated properly, so the paper's red accents appeared orange one day, scarlet the next. Photographs were most problematic because they were costly to process; mistakes cost the paper dearly. Late fees – $25 for every half-hour over deadline – piled up as the staff struggled to make things work.

All these problems occupied the editorial staff entirely during the first three months of broadsheet publication. In addition, the year began with bitterness.

At the end of the summer, Bernthal had returned from his summer internship and tried to reassert control of the *Cardinal*'s business operations, claiming Kaphingst had only been hired as a summer fill-in. A power struggle ensued and the paper's board of directors was called in to mediate.

The majority of the editorial staff, including myself, backed Kaphingst because he had been working with us during the first difficult weeks in our new format. He had made himself available to us at all hours, had spent days in the office teaching and cajoling and calming nerves, leading inexperienced people like the veteran he was.

We discounted Bernthal's experience.

It was a fatal mistake.

IT DOESN'T END WITH US

"There was a huge power play and political battle within the staff," Bernthal said. "There were several crucial board meetings where Kate [Misurek] and I went up against Joel to determine who should run the paper. The board largely supported us, but the staff largely supported them."

The board hammered out a compromise: Kaphingst would have responsibility for day-to-day business operations while Bernthal would oversee long-term planning in a publisher's position. Both men agreed, but Bernthal, about to graduate, spent less and less time at the *Cardinal*, not wanting to be where he was not wanted.

While the editorial staff scrapped and fought over mistakes in the early day of broadsheet publication, Kaphingst was becoming overwhelmed by the business operations of the paper.

When Reddeman was fired, Kaphingst bought an IBM computer at the recommendation of the paper's accountant and bought a billing program for it, to send out the bills automatically.

"They never really set it up and got all the files transferred so no bills were sent out," Bernthal said.

Kaphingst claimed he did not simply stop billing advertisers. Some bills did go out, but large university accounts, he said, required "specialized billing" that was difficult to arrange. He blamed poor record-keeping by Reddeman, an office manager of 24 years, for his resulting confusion and insisted he kept board members informed of the *Cardinal's* dire financial state.

"I asked for help many times," Kaphingst said. "I made others, including the board of directors, aware of [the university billing] problem several times over months beginning as early as September 1994 and was assured arrangements could be made to expedite those payments."

Anderson said Kaphingst never told the board he needed help. "There was no business report because we were told that the [software] materials were not ready yet [to produce a regular financial report]," he said. "It was informal like that. It wasn't like running the *New York Times*."

Money was going out, but none was coming in. By Oct. 9, 1994, a month after the *Cardinal* had begun publishing as a broadsheet, Madison Newspapers began to press Kaphingst for payment of the paper's printing bills.

Kaphingst accessed the only source of funds the *Cardinal* still had. He leveraged the *Cardinal's* $35,000 rainy-day CD, taking out a two-part loan using the CD as collateral. That money paid off MNI for a time, and in statements provided to the *Cardinal's* accounting firm, the loan appeared as advertising revenue.

No one dug any deeper into the *Cardinal's* finances to find out exactly where the money had come from.

When that money ran out, however, MNI told Kaphingst he would have to begin paying for publication in advance. Kaphingst did so, each week, beginning in mid-October. As editor-in-chief, I was unaware of the change, and the crisis that prompted it.

IT DOESN'T END WITH US

After an acrimonious semester, I resigned as the paper's editor, the stress of my own inexperience, numerous mistakes, and the paper's difficulties having burned me out. My staff was glad to see me go. In January of 1995, I reverted to a reporter, covering the occasional press conference and using my time to catch up on my studies. I had little contact with the paper's higher-ups.

On the night of Feb. 7, 1995, staffers were preparing the next day's stories when Kaphingst and Ward arrived for a board meeting, saying it was an emergency situation. While editors and reporters waited downstairs, unsure as to exactly what was happening, the board met in an upstairs Vilas Hall conference room.

When they came back down, Komisarek, who had been my managing editor and took over after I resigned, told reporters and editors to stop what they had been doing. The paper was not going to be printing the next day.

Vincent Filak was the paper's city editor, a junior-year journalism major from Milwaukee who had started out working at the *Badger* yearbook down the hall from the *Cardinal* offices. Madison was locked in a contentious mayoral primary and Filak had set himself the task of interviewing all nine candidates, even the ones considered by the city papers to be non-viable contenders.

That night, Komisarek approached him. "She said, 'We're not printing tomorrow,'" he remembered. "She said 'We don't know what's going on, and that's all I can tell you right now.' My college student experience stopped that day."

At the time, the board's plan was to tell the public little. Komisarek sent out a press release announcing suspension of publication, but stating the paper's intentions to return on April 4, the *Cardinal*'s anniversary. To the editors, the board members characterized the *Cardinal*'s financial situation as a "cash-flow problem," one in which several major advertisers had not paid. Once that money came in, they thought, outstanding bills could be paid and the paper could start again.

By the next morning that contention was revealed as a fiction. The *Wisconsin State Journal*, like the other city daily, the *Capital Times*, printed at MNI and executives fed details of the *Cardinal*'s printing debts to the "real" local press. The *State Journal*'s story revealed that MNI had refused to print the *Cardinal* because of outstanding debt.

The paper owed its printer $37,000.

The *Cardinal*'s board launched an investigation into unpaid bills and what they found shocked them. Money was owed to everyone from the phone company to the Associated Press, whose news feeds kept the *Cardinal* able to report on state and national stories. *Cardinal* staffers found bills in Kaphingst's desk that had never been opened, from as far back as October, as well as information about the loan.

The paper could not even use its own accounting firm to assess the damages, because it owed the company more than $3,000 for the previous year's tax preparation and financial statements.

IT DOESN'T END WITH US

When all the figures were totalled, the paper was looking at $137,700 in debt. It had only $43.71 in its checkbook.

The amounts were staggering. At first Kaphingst defended himself and his actions, telling his former colleagues at the *Badger Herald* that "anytime there is a person in a position of responsibility, I think the focus is going to be on that person ... It's important that people look at the big picture and realize that things don't happen because of one person."

By the following Monday, Feb. 13, Kaphingst had resigned. The *Cardinal* board began talking about bankruptcy declarations and changed the locks on the newspaper's offices. "What action can we take but bankruptcy?" Anderson asked at one board meeting.

The staff held caucuses, contentious gatherings that more often than not ended in shouting matches over who had done what months ago. I attended them and offered my help, but did little in the early days. Several *Cardinal* staffers left almost immediately to work at the *Badger Herald*. Others simply left, to return to their studies and whatever semblance of a college life they had left.

Every day the headlines were worse. "Board forces manager of *Cardinal* to resign," read the *Capital Times* on Feb. 14, 1995. The Associated Press predicted, "Student paper faces prospect of bankruptcy" on March 6. A week later *Wisconsin State Journal* columnist Phil McDade had begun to refer to the "*Cardinal's* long sleep." *Cardinal* staffers who went to classes found themselves stared at by fellow students; in one case a journalism professor used the paper's troubles as an example of journalistic irresponsibility while *Cardinal* editors were forced to sit and listen.

The *Badger Herald's* staff was enjoying its new role as the sole campus news outlet. They made the *Cardinal's* troubles front-page news for months, editorials professing regret at the *Cardinal's* demise but headlines saying otherwise, as every minute detail of the paper's maneuverings was covered in depth. *Herald* publisher Craig Cohen told McDade, "It sounds like their condition is fairly grim over there. I'd be surprised if they come back without the help of the university or some alumni."

The *Cardinal* board assembled a "recovery" team. Bernthal and Filak, as well as former Sports Editor Valerie Panou and former News Editors Chris Terry and Lauri Schumacher, put together a plan for the *Cardinal* to sort out its finances. Their aim was merely to pay off the paper's debt, settle its accounts honorably. No one expected the paper to return to publication.

At that point, they were worried that creditors could sue the board and take their personal assets.

Panou and Bernthal put together a list of creditors and Filak began working on billing advertisers. Terry researched legal options and other sources of funding, including university funds and grants. Everyone they could think of to ask for money, they did.

Bernthal took on the job of defending the paper in print, his optimistic quotes belying the harsh situation he faced behind closed doors. "Nobody wants to see this paper die," he told McDade. "A lot of people will do anything to keep it alive."

The *Cardinal*'s board and a number of outside observers in the Madison press suggested reaching out to the paper's alumni, but at that time the *Cardinal* had alienated them. The centennial celebration in 1992, meant to be a welcome-home party for the *Cardinal*'s graduates, left many dissatisfied. Staffers were too blunt about requesting fundraising help and donations; worse, those invited to speak were interrupted at the podium and their well-meant criticism of the paper rebuffed. The paper requested thousands of reminiscences from its graduates and promised that those would be turned into a book; no such volume was ever produced. A fundraising letter that later went out misspelled the name of *Cardinal* news legend Jim Rowen and generated little response.

One of the tasks the *Cardinal* staff undertook after the shutdown was to create a database of all presumably living alumni to use for future informational and fundraising efforts. Editors copied, by hand, staff lists in old archived papers from 1945 to 1995, pulling down bound volumes, writing down names and looking up addresses and numbers in phone books.

The *Cardinal* staff drafted letters to every known *Cardinal* advertiser: If you have already paid for your advertising, thank you. But if you have not, please pay. It was unheard of in business, but they didn't have a choice. Kaphingst had left them few business records to show what had been billed and what hadn't.

Former *Cardinal* ad designer Anthony Sansone, one of the few *Cardinal* staffers with any type of advanced technical experience, was working on recreating a billing program to track what was coming in and what was still outstanding.

"[Filak and Bernthal] asked me to come in and have a look at the situation, just to see what I could see," Sansone said. "They needed help with recovery, from a strategy point of view."

Sansone had been a summer graphics editor at the *Cardinal* and left in 1991 to work for the Wisconsin Students Association, then the Madison campus's student government. He followed that with a stint at the *Badger* yearbook, helping that organization recover from crippling debt not unlike the *Cardinal*'s.

"What I saw was that the *Cardinal* wasn't in that bad of shape, but there were definitely some things that needed to be done," he said.

Sansone contacted *Cardinal* alumnus Jim Burgess, the paper's business manager in the late 1950s, and asked for advice. He called in professors from the business school, helped rewrite the newspaper's bylaws and reform the board to provide more strict financial oversight.

"It was a lot of work, and there were times it just didn't seem worth all the work we were putting into it," he said. "But I felt I owed it to the *Cardinal*. The paper had given me a chance to do good work and meet people who would help me later in life, and it deserved the same chance to succeed."

The hours were more than long, they were unending, and the constant refrain from the public — everyone from news columnists to university professors

IT DOESN'T END WITH US

to the paper's own board — was that such efforts were sure to be futile. The people answering phone calls from reporters, reading their names in nasty news stories, were eighteen and nineteen and twenty years old. They were doing the jobs of news executives, business owners, public relations officers, private investigators, and accountants.

One night in March, Filak recalled, he was working at the *Cardinal* office putting bills together when Panou and Schumacher came to him in tears. They both confessed they could not keep up with the constant barrage of work. They were sleep-deprived, failing classes, losing weight. Filak sympathized.

"You're not sleeping. You're constantly worried. Sometimes I went to bed, and I didn't know if it was day or night," he said. "It really was something where I did every waking and sleeping moment in there. For so many weeks it was life or death, and we did not have a hope in hell of being able to figure our way out of this."

Panou and Schumacher asked for his keys. It's over, they told him. We can't do this anymore. We have to give up. They would give the keys to Anderson, who was still on the board, and close the paper down.

He gave them an old key that no longer worked, and when they left, he locked the office behind them and went back to work. He and I had become friends during my ill-fated editorship, and we talked on the phone late that night. He explained about Panou and Schumacher, and told me that honestly, he felt the same way.

"It's too hard, it's too much," he kept saying. "It's over, we're done. It's over."

During my editorship I had read a great deal about the *Cardinal*'s history. William Young on his horse, Richard Davis and the '38 strike, the women of World War II who kept the paper operating. I had heard of how the "Unorientation" issue was smuggled out under the regents' noses and the way Gail Bensinger stood up for her staffers when they were attacked as communists. Zuckerman and Schickel had refused to give up when they were nearly out of money.

Strmecki and Lambert had fought the entire university and won.

All of that, I thought, and we would be the ones to shut it down.

"It doesn't end with us," I told him. "I don't know how I know that, but I do. It ends somewhere else down the road, with some other bunch of kids. It just doesn't end with us."

It was easy for me to say, at the time; I was not the one in the office bearing the burdens. The next morning, however, I went into the office to help him measure classified ads, counting out words to determine the billing rate, using a ruler to guide me through the rows of tiny agate type.

Filak sent bills out, and with the money that came in, slowly started paying small debts.

It was punishing work. Advertisers who received those bills called up, angry, shouting that they had already paid or had expected the bill months ago, telling

IT DOESN'T END WITH US

Filak their entire year's worth of accounting had been screwed up and they could not balance their books.

Creditors were even angrier. The AP forgave the paper's debts, but revoked the *Cardinal's* newswire services.

The long-distance phone company wanted its money yesterday and was not interested in the paper's financial status: In the days before every student had a cell phone, staffers often called home from the office to save themselves some cash, and now those bills were coming due.

The largest debt the *Cardinal* owed was to its former printer, MNI. With the board's permission, Filak approached the printer's executive, Pam Wells, and offered her a deal. He explained that if the *Cardinal* was forced into bankruptcy, MNI would get nothing. He offered Wells an up-front payment of $5,500, which the recovery team had found in a forgotten savings account, and told her the *Cardinal* would pay the remaining debt off at a rate of 60 cents on the dollar.

"I waited for like two days," Filak said. He had been sleeping on the *Cardinal's* office couch to save time coming and going from his off-campus apartment. "At about 7 o'clock in the morning, the phone rings."

Wells accepted the deal.

"I just said, 'Okay, thank you very much.' It was like, 'Oh, my God, I cannot believe it actually worked.' We were just making this up as we went and I didn't expect her to take it."

Overjoyed, Filak left the Cardinal office and ran upstairs to the journalism faculty offices, looking for Anderson or another *Cardinal* board member, looking for anyone to whom to give the good news. He could not find a soul.

"I must have just looked like hell," he said. "After all, I hadn't been home in four days."

The staff kept quiet about recovery efforts, not wanting the Madison press to pry any more than it already had. With the printing debt settled and, for the most part, the billing completed, it began to appear that the *Cardinal* would be able to return to publication after all. Once the debts were settled, money that came in from advertisers could be used for the paper's expenses once again.

"Once we decided to revive the *Cardinal*, some staff members did heroic work," Anderson said. "With the help of everybody, we were overcoming the skeptics."

To print again there still was an immense amount of work yet to be done, most of it falling on Filak's and Sansone's shoulders.

A format for the newspaper had to be chosen, the newspaper had to be redesigned, old style and reporting guides re-written. The office needed to be cleaned out, old dead equipment disposed of, new equipment purchased, office staff hired, plans for recruiting writers made. Everything the *Cardinal* had taken for granted, every day-to-day underpinning of daily production, had to be reinvented, from scratch.

In May, the *Cardinal's* remaining editors, not really believing the paper would return, elected a staff for the fall semester anyway, just in case. When

IT DOESN'T END WITH US

summer came, many of those staffers took summer jobs or internships elsewhere. No one in any official capacity objected at the time. A skeleton crew remained to complete the recovery work, including copy editor Amy Eisenman.

A junior classics major from Racine, Wis., Eisenman had started working at the *Cardinal* shortly before the shutdown. During the summer, she became an integral part of the comeback effort, helping Sansone redesign the paper and write the official style guide, a book-length work that dictated every part of the newspaper's operations.

"We were doing all of this, and as we're doing it, people are telling us it's impossible," she said. "We had this terrible uncertainty. We kept asking ourselves, were we going to be doing all this for nothing?"

Her concerns were well-founded: by mid-July, even with all the advertising money that had come in, there still was not enough money to print in the fall.

MNI was insistent: Considering the *Cardinal*'s past debts, the paper would have to continue paying the printer in advance each week. The company simply did not trust the paper enough to give it a traditional long-term contract. Printing thirty days' worth of newspapers — which Filak estimated would be necessary to provide a buffer until the first advertising funds came in — would cost nearly $15,000, all of it needed in advance.

The *Cardinal* by July had slightly more than $11,000 in its bank account, but it faced a terrible choice. The office had few working computers, and none of them were kitted out with the necessary software to produce a daily newspaper: word processing, design, fax and e-mail capability. The lone printer was broken, so there was no way to print and proof pages. Newspapers across the country were starting web sites for the first time that year; the *Cardinal* had no plans for one nor anyone who knew the amount of programming necessary to put one together.

The *Cardinal* could either buy the equipment necessary to publish, or it could — almost — pay for printing. Not both.

The *Cardinal*'s last resort was any kind of funding associated with the university. Despite the *Herald*'s characterizations over the years, the *Cardinal* had never taken payments from the university, had never simply accepted money with no promise of a product or service in return.

Filak and I personally approached half a dozen local bank executives, floating them ideas from a loan — for which we could offer no collateral — to paid-in-advance advertising — an idea they found positively adorable in its absurdity. We swallowed our pride and walked into their offices, knowing they knew in minute detail from the press just how bad our financial situation was, and we asked them for help anyway.

Most people were sympathetic and kind, which only made what we were doing more humiliating. No one wanted to take a chance.

"The days just kept ticking off the calendar and we're not getting there," Filak said, remembering. "The pressure was just immense. I was sick all the damn time because I was just like how the hell are we going to pull this off."

IT DOESN'T END WITH US

In the *Cardinal*'s initial recovery plan, Terry and Bernthal had raised the idea of approaching the student government and asking them for a loan.

The Associated Students of Madison was swimming in money, the recipients of hundreds of thousands of dollars in fees from all university students, and unlike a bank, they would be willing to take the risk that offering a loan to the *Cardinal* meant. And while the funds could not be used for operating expenses like printing, they would free up the paper's existing bankroll for that purpose.

The paper's leadership approached the Student Services Finance Committee, which doled out student fees to various campus organizations, and asked for a loan. With about $13,000, the *Cardinal* could buy enough second-hand equipment to run a newsroom, leaving the money it already had in its bank account to pay for printing.

Before the SSFC could grant such a request, the *Cardinal* had to state its case in front of their committee, in an open meeting. All the work staffers had been keeping private for fear of negative press now would be out in the open.

"At the meeting ... we're kind of naked to the world," Filak remembered. "Sometimes you have to do things you normally wouldn't do if the circumstances were better."

The meeting was held Aug. 9, 1995. Filak and Sansone argued for the loan by demonstrating the paper's capabilities to return to publication successfully. They showed the committee members mock-ups of what the resurrected *Cardinal* would look like, demonstrated the new billing system, and explained the new board of directors' understanding of how to enforce fiscal discipline. They outlined all the work that had been done over the past six months.

At the other end of the conference table, across from Filak and Sansone and the rest of the *Cardinal* staff, sat Joel Kaphingst.

"He was there because if we tried to pin the blame on him, he wanted it recorded," Filak said. "I'll never forget that as long as I live. I knew that if I looked at him, I'd just snap."

Throughout the meeting Kaphingst needled the people who had been repairing the damage done to the *Cardinal*. "What makes you think?" Kaphingst asked at one point, "that you know how to fix the *Cardinal's* problems?"

Kaphingst later apologized for his attendance at that meeting. At the time, he said, he was fighting the *Cardinal* over money they owed him for the time he had served as business manager, and he was still embittered at what he characterized as "mudslinging" by his former colleagues.

He said he went to the meeting "because I wanted to make sure the whole episode wasn't laid at my feet, and because I was still engaged in battle over the stopped payment and was still angry at some individuals associated with the *Cardinal*. Attending that meeting is the only action I took after the shutdown that I regret – that was lashing out at the wrong people."

Despite Kaphingst's arguments, the SSFC later granted the *Cardinal's* request. Kaphingst, who would go on to a respected career in Wisconsin journalism, never contacted the *Cardinal* again.

IT DOESN'T END WITH US

There was one final hurdle. The last, and toughest, constituency of *Cardinal* doubters was the paper's own board of directors. By the end of July, the board was facing a final decision: To print or not to print. Anderson insisted the paper should exist solely as a web site, which would eliminate printing costs. He was convinced newsprint would be dead within a year. Filak countered that a web site would not generate enough revenue to pay off the *Cardinal*'s scheduled debt settlement payments nor the SSFC loan. Despite all the work that had been done, the board — newly instilled with a sense of fiscal discipline and fiduciary responsibility — was reluctant to believe. They demanded Filak live up to his prediction of thirty days' printing in the bank and refused to allow the *Cardinal* to even consider returning without it.

Printing 10,000 copies of an eight-page paper, at the tabloid size we had settled on with Madison Newspapers, would cost $476.10 per day. For 30 days' advance payment, we would need $14,283 on hand at the beginning of September. The *Cardinal* didn't have it; its account was $2,500 short. We could not think where to get it. Any alumni we could approach for funds had already turned us down. Our SSFC loan could only be used for equipment purchases. There was no more money out there to collect.

The night before the board meeting, we were facing the idea that $2,500 would be the amount that finally broke us.

The meeting had already started in a conference room four floors above us, and Sansone was upstairs stalling for time. Filak was sitting at the paper's one working computer, running the numbers. I was, as had become my habit over the summer, cleaning the office. There were stacks of scraps of paper everywhere: notes we had scribbled down, plans that never made it to fruition, old desk calendars, trash. I was trying to sort it all out and make room for someone to at least put a cup of coffee down.

I remember how Filak looked up at me, like he was almost afraid of the idea in his head. He called to me across the office, "Allison, thought process. Do we need thirty days or do we need a month?"

The *Daily Cardinal*, despite its name, only publishes Monday through Friday. In all our calculating, we never considered that we did not print on weekends.

We tore apart that office looking for a calendar for September. Factoring in Saturdays and Sundays and the Labor Day holiday, the *Cardinal* would only print nineteen issues that month. Even with extra costs figured in for color photos and special issues — plus estimated late fees for missing deadline, a chronic problem with new editors — the numbers worked.

"I punch nineteen into the computer and it comes out as $11,000," Filak recalled. "We're already late for this meeting."

We tore up the Vilas Hall staircase toward the board meeting. I shouted out figures and he scribbled them onto his notes as we ran. We burst into the conference room, flushed and out of breath, oblivious to the skepticism on the faces in front of us.

IT DOESN'T END WITH US

The board listened to our numbers, our arguments, and then they closed the meeting to discuss the paper's future in executive session. Three hours later, they opened the conference room doors, all smiles.

"We had been doing all this work, and we had never been sure," Eisenman said. "Try to imagine it. We were kids. Kids on Gilligan's Island, trying to build a Geiger counter with a coconut. It was such an incredible leap to take, not knowing.

"In a lot of ways I still can't believe it worked."

Editors returned from their summer vacations and on Aug. 31 were gathered in the *Cardinal* office to put the final touches on their registration issue. The night was chaotic, plagued with complications. Not all the new computers worked, inexperienced designers mixed up copy, and night editors pasted pages up backwards.

After seven months, the *Cardinal* newsroom sounded like a newsroom again: full of shouts and ringing phones and the tap of keyboards, overlaid with cursing and requests for more copy pens. After seven months, the *Cardinal* newsroom looked like a newsroom again: crumpled bits of paper flying everywhere, books stacked and teetering precariously on the edges of desks, empty coffee mugs and hamburger wrappers underfoot, and newsprint tacked to bulletin boards on the walls. After seven months, people worked with hope, not fear.

The *Cardinal* staff worked without high-fives, congratulations, or noisy celebrations that night. It was almost as if we did not want to jinx it. So much had gone wrong. The enormity of it would not hit us until the next morning, when we all stumbled out of the International House of Pancakes on University Avenue, four blocks east of the *Cardinal* offices. Stuffed to the gills with onion rings, jittery from coffee, we parted ways to go home and get what little sleep we could before the paper was delivered.

It had been the hottest summer any of us could ever remember. We had been up for days now, without showers, without changing clothes; we looked and smelled like refugees.

A thick haze hung over the state capitol dome, its marble façade glowing pink and orange in the sunrise. It was just before 6 a.m.

Eisenman and I looked at one another, and looked up at the sky and then back down again. We took off down the street, jumping and skipping and turning cartwheels and screaming out loud to passing cars, "We're printing, we're printing!" We must have looked mad. We could not have cared less. We ran the four blocks back to Vilas, and collapsed on the building's stone steps, laughing and crying.

We're printing. We're printing.

In 1972, there were 2,500 student newspapers in America.[1] By 1995, those ranks had thinned by a third.[2] The ranks of independent papers, papers not officially published, managed or sanctioned by their institutions, were even thinner. While student publications often die out and return under new management with the help of enthusiastic editors and interested faculty, no in-

IT DOESN'T END WITH US

dependent student newspaper has overcome a debt as formidable as the *Cardinal's*, with as little official outside support.

The very freedom that the *Cardinal* had always prized, the freedom that got the paper into the trouble that had led it to the shutdown, was the same freedom that instilled in its staff a sense that they had the power to repair the damage done. That the *Cardinal's* demise was not, as so many in the Madison press had said, inevitable, and that they were the ones who could stop it from happening.

In the *Cardinal* office that afternoon, staffers milled and waited for the distribution manager to come back with the papers. They had worked for months, and last night's joy had been heady, but the *Cardinal's* comeback would not be real until they held the papers in their hands.

When the truck finally rolled in with a stack of *Cardinals*, the deliveryman watched in bemusement as disheveled college kids practically tore them from his grasp, cut open the twine binding the papers, and clutched them to their chests. They hugged and kissed and jumped up and down. Someone had turned on the radio and people were dancing. Someone had popped champagne and we toasted with it in our coffee mugs.

A fiery bird — half-cardinal, half-phoenix — swooped across the paper's red ground, beneath a headline reading "Start the Presses!" The front page was devoted entirely to the story of the *Cardinal's* comeback.

Editors had debated late into the night about the story itself: would it seem narcissistic, to devote so much valuable news space to the paper's own story? Was it really the most important story on campus? Would anyone even care?

In the end, they decided to tell their own tale. The Madison press had spent months ripping the *Cardinal* apart; if it was not important, why had other news outlets devoted so much time to the paper's inner turmoil? *Cardinal* staffers had — for too long — heard others telling a story they alone knew best. The *Daily Cardinal* deserved a chance to speak on its own behalf:

> The board wanted to close the *Cardinal's* doors for good. Some Madison papers declared the *Cardinal* dead. But into this seemingly hopeless situation came a small group of editors and other dedicated staff members who said, "Give us a chance." Having little or no business experience, they dedicated themselves to bringing back the student voice that had been on the campus for over a century.

That night, staffers gathered at the home of now-Editor-in-Chief Valerie Panou and toasted the *Cardinal's* return with beer in plastic cups. They look, in photographs, like ordinary college kids: underfed and overtired, in clothes that have seen better days. They look like the eighteen and nineteen and twenty-year-olds they were.

"It was a defining moment," Eisenman said. "It was just a huge confluence of factors — the right people, the right place, the willingness to go through all

IT DOESN'T END WITH US

of that – all surrounding this little student newspaper. I think it'll be there fifty years from now. I think there will be some other bunch of kids in that newsroom laying out the paper in 2050, debating newspaper ethics, and hopefully not screwing it up too badly."

Just as the paper's freedom had brought about its lowest moments, it instilled in the shutdown staff the value of the *Cardinal* itself, that this was a place worth fighting for, caring about and working for, and that a death sentence was unacceptable.

Eisenman, who had been majoring in classics before her *Cardinal* work began, became a newspaper copy editor. Sansone parlayed the technical expertise he gained at the paper into work managing corporate computer systems. Filak went on to teach at the University of Missouri-Columbia and Ball State University, and author a news reporting textbook.

In 1998, Sansone founded the Daily Cardinal Alumni Association, a 750-member organization dedicated to furthering communication between the paper's graduates and its staff.

The alienation that had followed the 1992 centennial, the disaffection of prominent alumni toward the paper that had given them their start, Sansone took it upon himself to rectify.

"We couldn't ask them to give back to the *Cardinal* without first giving them something to believe in, without giving them something back first," he said. "Otherwise there's no point."

Above Filak's desk in his university office hangs a relic of his *Cardinal* days. When he settled the *Cardinal's* printing debt with MNI, the company sent him a letter outlining the terms of the deal.

"My diplomas are in a box under my bed with some football cards, but that letter ... it's framed in my office and I look at it every day," he said. "I don't think it would be too much to say that that was the most important thing I've ever done."

Since the shutdown the paper has had small ups, small downs. Its first year was an immense financial struggle, with staffers at times unsure if they would print the next week, publication hinging on the arrival of one or two checks in the mail.

The generosity of the paper's alumni, spurred by Sansone's efforts, paid off, and two years to the day after the shutdown, Filak stood in the *Cardinal* office, burning a copy of the *Cardinal's* debt settlement with MNI. An alumni fundraising drive had brought in enough money to pay off the paper's printing debt, and with this mortgage-burning ceremony, the most difficult chapter in the *Cardinal's* long history was finally, finally over.

Flames licked the pages. Staffers cheered.

---

[1] Ingelhart, *College and University Campus Student Press.* 61.
[2] Associated Collegiate Press.

IT DOESN'T END WITH US

14.

Cardinal Journalism

In publishing this study, the Cardinal has no delusions of ridding the University of reactionary businessmen or of sparking a political upheaval in the state. We realize fully well that this is only a slice of the cheese, and that Wisconsin is only a microcosm of a much more frightening national picture. Our primary purpose, moreover, is to lay bare some of the ugly facts of life in the love affair between corporations, financial elites, state and federal governments and the University. This series only touches on the personal gains made by individuals holding key posts in this relationship, but nevertheless the possibilities are clear.
— Daily Cardinal editorial, 1969: Profit Motive 101

଼

Through the years the *Daily Cardinal* has often played host to journalists who would go on to do nationally and internationally honored work in their field. But what is truly remarkable about the newspaper is that those journalists often did that kind of work — public service projects, national breaking stories, investigations worthy of the largest city daily — while they were still at the *Cardinal*.

The newspaper was renowned on campus and read statewide because its journalism contributed to real change at the university. Without a hard-line school advisor or the constraints of a journalism-class atmosphere, *Cardinal* editors pursued the stories they wanted to pursue, and the results of their investigations often were shocking.

IT DOESN'T END WITH US

Miriam Ottenberg won her Pulitzer Prize at the *Washington Evening Star* in 1960, for a series of investigative reports on deceptive practices among used car dealers in the nation's capital. She got arrested at the *Cardinal*, for stealing ballots from the student elections.

In the spring of 1934, student government officials at the University of Wisconsin, stung by accusations that past elections had been tampered with, bragged that their new security procedures could not be surmounted. Elections would be free of interference, they claimed.

Ottenberg thought she should test that theory.

A native of Washington, DC, Ottenberg was the daughter of a suffragette mother and a lawyer father, well-versed from childhood in the tradition of challenging the powerful. At the *Cardinal* she was one of a very few reporters to have front-page bylines, at that time a rarity reserved only for the most accomplished writers. Her campus editor put her on the election-security story, and she threw herself into it with the kind of vigor that would later earn her a place among the nation's finest journalists.

The night of the voting, she walked into the *Cardinal* office, notebook in hand and cat-that-ate-a-canary grin on her face. Out of her pocket she pulled five ballots — swiped from under poll-watchers' noses, she said, to prove how easily it could be done.

The following day, March 8, 1934, the *Cardinal* carried this story:

ELECTION LAXITY STARTLES POLITICIANS

> Unwatched, Unpadlocked Ballot Boxes Tempt Bosses
> Five Ballots Gypped to Show With What Ease Boxes Could Be Stuffed

BY MIRIAM OTTENBERG

> In an election the laxity of which startled campus vote-swappers, 12 candidates came into office Wednesday.

> Unwatched, unpadlocked ballot boxes, placed near enough to the exit to make ballot-stuffing a definite temptation, roused observers to protest the carelessness of the election management.

> Five ballots were brought into the *Cardinal* office during the election to show the ease with which the boxes could be stuffed. Three of these ballots had been obtained at the scene of the voting and two were taken from the Cardinal Publishing Company office.

IT DOESN'T END WITH US

Because there were neither observers nor directions to tell the voters where to go it was perfectly possible to take the ballots obtained at the election tables and give them unmarked to political bosses away from the scene of the voting.

Ballots Secured Thus:
The three ballots obtained in Bascom [Hall, the campus's main building] and brought to the *Cardinal* office were secured in this manner:

One student secured two ballots from the Cardinal Publishing Company merely by stating that she was on the elections committee.

Observers criticized particularly the general organization and confusion at the scene of the voting. No cases of ballot-stuffing were reported to Kenneth J. Wheeler '34, elections chairman. Much of the ballot checking was done at the middle tables [in the polling places] where frank comparisons of the candidates was carried on.

Boss Checks List:
One of the most flagrant abuses noted was that of a politician who calmly went down the list at the freshman election table, checking off his cohorts to see who had voted. When last seen he was dashing off to urge those who had not voted to get their choice in before the boxes closed.

Another infringement of the election rules were the cars that carried voters up the hill and left them practically on the spot.

Ottenberg's story was not without consequences. The day the story ran she was arrested by Madison police for stealing university property. The *Cardinal's* board, saying they could not employ a law-breaker, fired Ottenberg from the staff.

The board underestimated her *Cardinal* colleagues, who refused to work another day on the paper unless she was reinstated. "She was a pistol," said Austin Wehrwein, whose tenure at the *Cardinal* followed Ottenberg's. "People talked about her for years after she left. She was a legend."

The *Cardinal's* achievements weren't limited to its news pages. Sports coverage has always been one of the paper's greatest strengths. Bob Teague came to the *Cardinal* office straight from the football field. And he came with stories to tell.

IT DOESN'T END WITH US

Wisconsin's football coach in 1948 was Harry Stuhldreher, the legendary Notre Dame quarterback. From 1922 to 1924 he led a backfield so fierce, so feared, that famed sportswriter Grantland Rice once wrote, "Outlined against a blue-gray October sky, the Four Horsemen rode again. In dramatic lore, they are known as famine, pestilence, destruction and death. These are only aliases. Their real names are Stuhldreher, Miller, Crowley and Layden."

Stuhldreher came to Wisconsin in 1935 as head football coach and was later named athletic director. He arrived on a campus that treated football not just as a pleasant Saturday outing but as a matter of personal pride. He had, in his first year, six starters who had won national awards for their play.

However, Stuhldreher's legend wore thin as, year after year, his teams failed to finish in the top five of their division, never once winning a championship.

In 1948 Teague, a Badger fullback from Milwaukee, approached the *Cardinal* with an offer to expose what he said was Stuhldreher's incompetence, which was doing a disservice to talented players who worked hard for their university. Over the next two months, he wrote numerous pieces about life behind the scenes on the Badger football team, from the antics after games to the second jobs players had to take to work their way through school.

The stories humanized the players and threw an unflattering light on the coach. By November 1948 the fans were up in arms, holding up signs at a game against Yale that read "Goodbye Harry." Some students began to petition the board of regents to have the coach replaced.

In the face of all this opposition Stuhldreher maintained that the team was on his side. His supporters cited a wallet the players had bought their coach as a symbol of their loyalty to him. Teague, his reporter's instincts as sharp as his game day play, thought the wallet story rang false. After all, he was on the team, and he had not heard word one about it. The story he published on Dec. 11, 1948 was the final blow to the embattled coach.

> Coach Lanphear Admits He Bought Stuhldreher Gift
>
> Freshman football coach George Lanphear admitted yesterday that he bought the inscribed wallet given Stuhldreher by "the '48 squad" after the Yale incident — without previously consulting anyone.
>
> Referring to his action Lanphear said, "I have no apologies to make whatsoever. I am not ashamed."
>
> He said he "felt thoroughly disgusted after the Yale incident" and thought it was a terrible blow to the morale of the squad and the coaching staff. The incident had shaken the confidence of some players, he stated.

IT DOESN'T END WITH US

Because of this, Lanphear said he bought the wallet as a psychological morale booster. "I felt it was needed," he said. After ordering the wallet, which was inscribed, "We're all behind you Harry — The '48 Squad," Lanphear said he talked with five or six players among whom were Bendrick, Dreyer and Embach. They thought the idea was good, he said.

In further explanation the freshman football coach declared that the gesture had to be made "right away" and that there wasn't time enough to contact anyone before ordering the wallet.

In discussing recent *Cardinal* articles on the issue, Lanphear asked the writer and another *Cardinal* staff member who was present whether positive opinions had been brought to the writer's attention.

The writer reaffirmed that he had been unable to find any favorable opinions — in spite of the fact that he had talked with players whom Lanphear named as having expressed opinions which were pro-Stuhldreher.

When the interview opened, Lanphear asked the writer for definite statements as to what he thought about Coach Stuhldreher, his methods, his policies, and his character.

There has been a disproportionate amount of criticism printed against Harry and very little has been said favorably, Lanphear asserted.

The writer answered that his articles were not a personal attack against Harry. But that since several players had expressed critical opinions and since these players had been misrepresented in the wallet presentation, he felt they had a right to be heard.

When questioned, Lanphear declared emphatically that none of the criticisms made against Harry were "valid."

After stating that the offensive system was not obsolete, Lanphear said, regarding the criticism leveled at the type of practice session held, "I think even Mr. Stuhldreher would admit that some of those practice sessions near the end of the season were not run the way they should be."

IT DOESN'T END WITH US

The coaching staff was aware of this unsatisfactory situation; they discussed the problem and are planning to correct it, Lanphear added.

They did not get the chance. Campus opposition to Stuhldreher was mounting, student petitions forcing a referendum on the issue of his retention. The day Teague's story appeared — laying out for all to see how the team simply didn't back the coach anymore, and that a member of Stuhldreher's staff had to create a fake morale-booster for him — Stuhldreher resigned.

Teague, who would go on to work for 28 years in television news, winning Emmy and Peabody awards for his work, said at the time that he took no personal satisfaction in Stuhldreher's ouster. "It was too bad that a man like Harry had to serve as a whipping boy for something not entirely his fault, but I am glad he didn't have to face the referendum and instead made his own choice."

The *Cardinal* struck a similar tone in its editorial:

> It is the *Cardinal*'s responsibility to report the news that students want. Our news policy must keep faith with our readers. During the weeks prior to the Stuhldreher resignation the student body wanted news about referendum petitions, how the team felt about Harry, what lay behind the loyalty gifts and the rest — the *Cardinal* dug out the facts and presented them.

Challenging the powerful on campus was the *Cardinal*'s most important journalistic tradition, and those challenges often made headlines far outside Wisconsin. Anna Gould's little brother led her to the biggest story of her college career, that would land her in the pages of the *San Francisco Chronicle* and on CNN.

The *Cardinal* reporter's younger sibling showed her a recruitment brochure he'd received for the 2001-2002 undergraduate term.

Its cover featured a crowd of UW students at a football game, cheering on the Badgers. Gould took the brochure to her campus editor, Kevin Warnke, and said, "Look at the guy in the corner."

One of the faces in the crowd, that of a young black man, was visible smiling, the sunlight bright on his face. The others in the crowd, Gould said, looked like they were half in shadow.

Something was wrong.

> Doctoring Diversity
> Admissions officials alter photo to include minority
> By Anna Gould and Kevin Warnke
>
> The cover photo for UW-Madison's 2001-'02 Undergraduate application features a picture that has been retouched to

IT DOESN'T END WITH US

include a reversed image of an African-American student without letting the student know.

Both original photos, one taken during the 1993 Rose Bowl and the other during 1994 Wisconsin Welcome Week, are available at the University Communication's Web site, www.news.wisc.edu/ucomm.

UW-Madison Undergraduate Admissions Director Robert Seltzer and University Publications Director Albert Friedman said they regretted inserting the student, whom the *Daily Cardinal* was able to identify as UW-Madison senior Diallo Shabazz.

"We were looking for a great cover picture, we came up with that picture without Diallo's picture on it and it just looked like it was not representative because it was all white and that's not our undergraduate population," Seltzer said. "I approved the decision to add the picture."

Seltzer added that Undergraduate Admissions staff considered alternate photos — none of which invoked the "spirit" for which he was looking. Friedman said University Publications provided Seltzer with the original cover photo and, at Seltzer's request, doctored the image.

"We said, 'What about if we just add a photo there that ... would be more representative of our actual campus climate?'" Seltzer said. "We really should have said 'No, let's not do that. Let's get more pictures, let's stop, rethink this.'"

Shabazz, who was a freshman when the picture was taken, said he knew the picture was doctored because he had "never been to a Rose Bowl or to a Badger game."

"They inserted my picture without my knowledge or consent," he said. "I don't mind being used on university publications, but I think that there's more effective and efficient ways of using any students of color to represent the small amount of diversity that exists on this campus."

UW-Madison Media Specialist Jeff Miller, who is credited for both original photos as well as the retouched one, said the alteration of the photo took place without his consent and undermined his credibility as a photographer.

IT DOESN'T END WITH US

"In this particular incident, I do not have any knowledge or awareness of this happening," Miller said. "We [University Communications] do not alter the content of our photos."

Seltzer said when he allowed the picture to be retouched, he did not concern himself with the ethics involved in presenting an altered image.

"I didn't spend a lot of time agonizing over [the decision] — we were running out of time to get the cover done and we wanted the cover to be more representative of the campus and so we just said, 'OK, let's do it,'" Seltzer said.

According to Seltzer, the Undergraduate Admissions office wants to feature diversity on the cover, but altering images to achieve that diversity was and is a mistake.

"Our intention was to do what I thought and still think is the right thing to do. We didn't do it the right way. We made a mistake and we will apologize to the student for that," Seltzer said.

Seltzer said he realized a mistake was made after he became aware that Shabazz, who still attends the university, discovered his inserted image.

"As soon as we heard that ... everything became kind of clear, and [we] said 'Oh, geez, that really wasn't the right thing to do,'" Seltzer said. "In retrospect, it was clearly the wrong thing to do."

Shabazz said this incident is part of a larger issue in which diversity is not being properly addressed at UW-Madison.

"It's the same kind of thing that can happen next week, it can happen tomorrow, it can happen every single day of the year," he said. "Just because it happens doesn't mean that you need to address that immediate situation because it happens in the context of a much larger problem."

Shabazz and Seltzer said they were trying to involve students in the decision-making process as to how future photos will be chosen in university publications.

IT DOESN'T END WITH US

Associate Dean Roger Howard said he thought the altered image was a "mistake."

"We've got tens of thousands of photographs. It seems to be that we don't have to doctor a photograph," Howard said. "I would not do it and I would not permit it in any of our publications.

"The images we present to [prospective students] ought to be absolutely accurate," he said.

Shabazz said his altered image simply confirmed his belief about how diversity is treated on this campus.

"I think if I say that I was shocked by this, then that would make me very naive," he said.

Vice Chancellor of Student Affairs Paul Barrows, who oversees the Undergraduate Admissions Office, could not be reached for comment.

The story caused national outcry and sparked a campus-wide debate about how best to increase the number of minority students on campus. Shabazz became a campus spokesperson for diversity efforts, and the *Cardinal*'s story was picked up by newspapers from Chicago to New York.

In an editorial accompanying Gould and Warnke's story, signed by the entire *Cardinal* staff, the paper noted that "a disembodied head of an African-American edited into a picture behind a bunch of cheering white students is an apt symbol of the kind of pressure that minorities face on this campus."

If there was one story that defined the *Daily Cardinal*, that typified both the paper's crusading spirit and the power of its voice, that story was Profit Motive 101.

Jim Rowen's 1969 series on money, power and conflicts of interest within the University of Wisconsin administration was unparalleled among *Cardinal* projects in its scope and effect. Over the course of six months Rowen, armed with secret university documents, outlined a web of covert deals through which the university's regents profited both from their UW status and their private-sector contacts.

The stories he wrote would end up legend at the *Cardinal*; thirty years later *Cardinal* staffers were regaled with spy-movie tales of Rowen "breaking into people's offices in the middle of the night and stealing things," tales Rowen insisted were completely false.

"I never had to do anything like that," he said, laughing. "Everything I got, I got through the Freedom of Information act."

IT DOESN'T END WITH US

Rowen, who later became chief of staff to the mayor of Milwaukee and wrote for dozens of national publications, began working at the *Cardinal* in 1967, during his first year of UW graduate study. He was 22, attracted by the passion of the *Cardinal's* left-wing staffers and intoxicated by the chance to put his name in print.

"Think about it: It's a huge ego thing," he said with a self-deprecating laugh. "You're in college, all this stuff's going on around you, here's your chance to make your mark. And thousands of people will see it."

Covering one of his first stories, the board of regents' deliberations over disciplining student radicals following the violent Dow Chemical protests in the fall of 1967, Rowen was transfixed by the university leaders' decision to expel one accused student without any opportunity for the student to speak in his own defense.

"I didn't think much of the guy," Rowen said, referring to the student in question, "but I was appalled at the abuse of power it represented. And I remember thinking, 'What they are doing is wrong.'"

He set out to learn all he could about the regents. He researched their positions in government and civic life, how they came to be in power at the UW, and what they did with that power.

Dozens of open records requests and hundreds of hours of reading and interviewing later, he walked into the *Cardinal* office with a sheaf of typewritten pages and handed the stack to editor Rena Steinzor. Then he sat silently as she read, hoping she would find something in those paragraphs that was publishable.

"Holy shit," was all she said.

Rowen had laid out, in excruciating detail, a case against a number of regents who had systematically used their position as the governors of the state's higher educational system to reap their own rewards. Heavily based on state-mandated financial disclosure documents, Profit Motive 101 deconstructed the ways in which directors of the state's largest bank holding company, First Wisconsin Bankshares Corporation, exerted significant influence over the university through partnerships and friendships with the UW's leaders.

According to his story, regents routinely voted to take out loans on behalf of the university through banks which they governed, setting up in one case a special committee to sell university-owned land in small parcels through a realtor partnered with those banks. They also invested university funds in those banks.

Regent Walter Renk, for example, had channeled almost $200,000 in public money through a bank he helped to oversee as a director. A dummy corporation was set up to run the hugely profitable Hilldale Shopping Center. That corporation was staffed by people with close ties to the regents.

Rowen detailed certain corporations that, through relationships with the regents and a special "business school advisory committee," were able to gain special access to the university's business school and influence its development, as well as direct talented students to particular employers.

IT DOESN'T END WITH US

The portion of the series that would garner most of the attention on a campus roiled by opposition to the Vietnam War was Rowen's discovery that Wisconsin's Army Math Research Center, established in 1955 through alumni donations, secretly was being used for weapons research.

WARF Builds Army Math Center

"One of the activities of Fiscal Year 1968 (reported in section V.A.) illustrates how this works. The effective employment of rockets and missiles requires stochastic optimization and control techniques, since an actual missile flight will be subject to random influences. In the case of interception of enemy missiles, complete dynamical information will not be available, so the operation will have to be carried out in such a way as to maximize the probability of success ... Three non-permanent members, Case, Danskin and Lukes were appointed for the fiscal year 1968 to work particularly in this area.

"This reflects a policy of MRC, that it should not merely wait until approached by the Army for advice and assistance with respect to the solution of mathematical problems. In addition, it should attempt to anticipate the needs of the Army, and when it is able to develop or learn of new techniques to meet these needs, it should forthwith call these to the Army's attention and help it find areas in which these techniques can be used."
— MRC Summary Report, July 1, 1967 – June 30, 1968

Wisconsin Bankshares officials have a predominant influence over two major University Alumni foundations, the Wisconsin Alumni Research Foundation and the University of Wisconsin Foundation.

The WARF and UWF grants to the University have been enormous and politically significant – one grant from WARF funded the establishment of a U.S. Army research center on the Madison campus.

WARF was established in 1925 by a group of University alumni who wished to exploit, for the University's benefit, the patents Prof. Harry Steenbock had just been awarded for his processes of irradiating Vitamin D.

IT DOESN'T END WITH US

Cooperating with Prof. Steenbock, whose discoveries helped rid the nation of rickets, these alumni established a foundation which would receive royalties from this discovery and others like it.

Money which the Wisconsin Alumni Research Foundation thus took in was invested, and investment profits were granted to the University regents as WARF donations beginning in 1938.

Since that time, according to the February 1968 Wisconsin Alumnus magazine, over $45 million, primarily for natural science research, has been donated to the University.

Two major sources of money which WARF has obtained for investment have been royalties from Prof. Steenbock's Vitamin D discoveries, and the anti-coagulants invented in the laboratories of Prof. Karl Paul Link. WARF markets several of these, primarily Warfarin, as rat poisons, which kill rats by causing them to internally bleed to death.

Little is known about the specific investments WARF has made which provide their annual grants to the University. It was reported in the Wall Street Journal, Feb. 1961, however, that WARF owned $50 million worth of stock invested for them by a New York brokerage firm, the Smith, Barney Co.

This same firm is an investment counselor for the University Board of Regents and the money they manage. With Bankshares bankers holding four of the eight officer positions on the 15-member WARF board of trustees, it is interesting to speculate if the repetitive pattern of Bankshares' investments is present somewhere in WARF's enormous portfolio. Consider the current interlocks:

Walter Frautschi, WARF president and Vilas Estate Trustee, is a director of the First National Bank of Madison.

Bernard Martz, WARF vice president and assistant secretary, is a director of the First National Bank of Madison.

Edwin Rosten, WARF finance director, is a director of the First National Bank of Madison, (also business school advisory committee member).

IT DOESN'T END WITH US

Donald C. Eichner, WARF vice president and assistant treasurer, is a Vilas Trustee, and a director of Bankshares Corp., and a business school advisory committee member.

These interlocks support the thesis of this series that Bankshares has a large and varied influence over the University, and University-related finances, and legitimizes the suspicion that WARF trustees may be presiding over a large Bankshares investment as are the Regents and Vilas Trustees.

An important measure of the Bankshares elites' influence over so many aspects of University affairs is an examination of the purposes of WARF grants. Of the $15 million granted to the University for building and equipment purchases since 1938, $12 million has gone to the natural sciences, $2.7 million for University faculty housing, and $400,000 to the Elvehjem Art Center.

Clearly, the orientation of the grants is nearly exclusively towards the natural sciences. For example, WARF funded the construction of the U.S. Army Mathematics Research Center in Sterling Hall, with a $1.2 million grant in 1955.

While the Center was dedicated in 1959, the accompanying University press release had this to say about the WARF-built facility, all of whose activities benefit the U.S. Army:

"In explaining the purposes of the Center, Prof. Langer points out that in its day to day operations, the Army leans upon mathematics as a necessary tool for the design of weapons and structures, for the compilation of maps and tables, for the organization and analysis of systems of communication, transportation, and logistics.

"Naturally, therefore, the continued perfection of mathematical methods," he adds, "and the rounding out of applicable theories, may open avenues to improvement of efficiency, to better procedures, designs, and organizations, and to more dependable bases of prediction about mechanical systems."

MRC personnel make frequent trips to military bases and facilities to give advice on the solution of Army problems. Prof. Karreman's tour of three Air Defense bases is an illustration.

IT DOESN'T END WITH US

Another was his recent visit to the Army Edgewood Arsenal, Maryland, on March 20, 21, 1969.

According to Prof. Karreman, he discussed with Edgewood Arsenal officials "the most effective and economical" methods for the Army to procure its needed munitions, a problem which arose due to the destruction by fire of an arms plant in Louisiana. The discussion then turned to the Army's future munitions requirements for the next "10 to 15 years."

The types of munitions discussed, Karreman said, were only small arms and artillery, mainstays of the Army's actions in Vietnam.

Thus the power of these bankers is not merely limited to financial and educational manipulation of the University. It extends to aiding the military-industrial complex's growing usage of universities for development of new and more sophisticated weaponry, and systems which are being used in Vietnam and around the world to protect the interests of America's industrialists and bankers.

The University of Wisconsin Foundation, established in 1945, is currently managed by men with strong ties to Bankshares, the Vilas Estate, the Hilldale dummy corporations, and the Board of Regents. Having contributed $18 million to the University since its founding, the Foundation is another structure dominated by the financial elite of the city and state.

The following relationships point up the continuing concentration of influence possessed by a few individuals and corporations in all facets of University affairs:

Harlan Nichols, treasurer, UWF; director, Hilldale Inc.; VP of Bank which financed center; director, First National Bank of Madison.

Robert Rennebohm, executive director, UWF; director, Hilldale Inc.; trustee, Vilas Estate.

Gordon Walker, executive vice president, UWF; regent, UW; director, Bankshares.

IT DOESN'T END WITH US

Ray Stroud, secretary and counsel, UWF; trustee, Vilas Estate; Clients: Hilldale, UWF, Vilas Estate, NW Mutual.

In summation, the total number of director ties Bankshares has with the board of regents, their investment counselors, the business school advisory committee, the Vilas Trustees, WARF, UWF, and the Hilldale dummy corporation is 17. The total number of interlocks between all of these managing boards is 15.

Rowen detailed how UW faculty tested drugs for the Army, measuring how animals responded to LSD and other drugs, some of them only identified as "classified drug A" or "classified drug B," that might be used as weapons. Professors attended briefings and visited missile ranges. Army personnel were granted what were called "research residencies" to allow them to stay at the university for extended periods while consulting with scientists at the center.

The reaction to Profit Motive 101 was as violently polarized as the country was becoming at that time. Rowen's stories were picked up by the *Capital Times*, which paid him $100 to re-run the pieces. Anti-war student organization leaders read the portions that dealt with the AMRC at rallies. Faculty would come up to him after class and, while congratulating him on the scholarship that clearly went into them, tell him his pieces were fueling anti-American sentiment.

A university committee was appointed to investigate Rowen's claims, particularly those about the Army Math Research Center. It issued a report stating that no classified work was done; a report Rowen, his colleagues, and his readers dismissed.

"Those articles had a huge impact on me," said Walt Bogdanich, a reporter who worked with Rowen at the *Cardinal* and is now investigative editor at the *New York Times*.

"That series just amazed me, that a student could cover that and that a student paper would print it. It gave me the chance to see, for the first time, the kind of serious journalism that newspapers could do."

Part of the reason Rowen's words were so shocking was that they struck at the heart of the University of Wisconsin's image of itself. From the time of its founding, the UW thought of itself as a place where the children of factory workers and factory owners could study side by side, where both farmers and physicists could learn together, as equals.

Rowen's stories, illustrating as they did the ways in which the rich and powerful were manipulating the university to their own benefit, stripped away that illusion. Profit Motive 101 revealed what Rowen saw and still sees as a cancer on public education, the lucky few gaming a system designed to benefit many.

Though the stories were later used as an example of the *Cardinal* rabble-rousing for the anti-war movement, Rowen said he didn't think his work was responsible for the bombings and arsons that occurred later.

IT DOESN'T END WITH US

"I don't think anybody really knows what those guys were thinking about," he said, referring to the Sterling Hall bombers.

"I'm still proud of those stories. People deserved to know what their tax dollars were being used for, and they deserved to know how they were being manipulated by people who had an obligation to the university and to the people of this state. It was important. It still is."

IT DOESN'T END WITH US

15.
Distinguished Graduates

At first, my Cardinal work was for free – the only ones on the newspaper staff to receive pay were the publisher and the editor – but even later, after I was promoted and allowed to share in the profits, the pay was never really enough for all the hours we put in. The money, however, was not the point. The real reason that I put in so much time on the job was simply that I liked the work. I found that I was quite good at the art of persuasion, and that I greatly enjoyed doing it.
– Irwin Maier, chairman, Milwaukee Journal Company, in "A Career in Newspapers and Broadcasting"

೦ಜ

Anthony Shadid's voice crackled over the speakerphone as more than 100 *Cardinal* alumni and staff listened, spellbound. The Pulitzer Prize-winning *Washington Post* reporter had only just returned from Baghdad, where he was covering the American war against Iraq.

Just two years before, Shadid had been in Ramallah covering the Palestinian uprising for the *Boston Globe* when he was caught in the crossfire and badly wounded.

It wasn't those heroics he was speaking of to his fellow *Cardinal* veterans on April 29, 2005. It was his days as a campus editor at the *Daily Cardinal* in 1989.

"The work I did at the *Cardinal*," he said, "was some of the bravest I've ever done."

Of all the things the *Daily Cardinal* has been to all its staffers and readers, to its university and to the larger community, it has remained first and fore-

IT DOESN'T END WITH US

most what William Wesley Young intended it to be. When he returned for the 50th anniversary of his creation, he described it a "a living school of journalism." And that school has produced some of the most notable American journalists in the history of the craft.

Nine Pulitzer winners — with eleven prizes among them — began their careers at the *Cardinal*, and every major newspaper in the country has had at least one *Cardinal* alumnus in its pages. Emmy and Peabody awards grace the desks of those alumni whose news sense led them into television.

Edwin Newman of NBC News wrote articles for the *Cardinal*. As did CBS reporter Rita Braver, *Washington Post* scribes Shadid and Len Shapiro, *New York Times* foreign correspondent Rosanne Klass and late journalism professor and author Scott Cutlip, called the father of modern public relations.

Leaders of our country's discourse took the lessons they learned at the *Cardinal* — about newswriting, news judgement, news coverage — and translated them on the national stage.

If there is a way in which the *Cardinal* truly has affected the world outside its coverage area, it is the influence its lessons have had on the brightest stars in the world of journalism.

Klass's career included **international aid work, ballet, and reporting from the Middle East and Asia, but one of her greatest scoops came during her years as *Cardinal* arts and drama writer. In a 1992 letter to the *Cardinal*, she recounted the story of Kirsten Flagstad:**

> When World War II broke out, Flagstad, the greatest Wagnerian soprano of the 20th Century, went home to Norway where her husband was an official of the Quisling Nazi regime, and during the war she sang for Hitler & Co. When she attempted to resume her career after the war, she was denounced, blackballed, picketed, booed and hissed everywhere — London, Paris, Bayreuth, New York. There was a near-riot when she tried to perform at Carnegie Hall. The scandal made headlines around the world; she was forced to retire and refused to see the press under any circumstances.
>
> In the fall of 1949 I discovered Flagstad was in Madison, visiting her daughter and son-in-law, who were graduate students living in Badger Village, a jerry-built housing area the university had taken over for the married veterans after the war. Her visit was completely private; even the fact that she was in this country had been kept secret. (Her daughter's identity was known only to a few people in Madison.)
>
> I don't recall how I talked her into an interview, but the rules were: any reference to the scandal was absolutely verboten,

IT DOESN'T END WITH US

while of course her pre-war career was old stuff not worth rehashing. That didn't leave me much room to maneuver.

When I arrived, the door was opened by a rather dowdy middle-aged Norwegian hausfrau in a cotton housedress who was, of course, the once great and glamorous Flagstad herself. She was very nervous. I couldn't get anything out of her — until I asked about the composer Richard Strauss (another Nazi collaborator!) who had died three weeks before. For years it had been received wisdom that Strauss had lost his touch around 1915 and wrote nothing important in the last 40 years of his life — what did she think?

Suddenly the great Flagstad emerged and came to life. She emphatically did not agree! Strauss had been a genius to the end, and in fact shortly before his death he had written four magnificent songs which he had dedicated to her! She started opening up, talking music. I had my story.

I broke the news of Richard Strauss' unknown last four songs, which are now considered to be among the greatest *lieder* ever composed (and the competition includes Schubert and Beethoven). And I broke the story in the *Cardinal*.

Austin Wehrwein would not have won his Pulitzer Prize without the *Cardinal*. The Minnesota native was passed over for a *Cardinal* editorship in 1937, and instead of heading the paper, he headed for the Madison bureau of the *Milwaukee Journal*.

"I wasn't that strong of a candidate, though of course I thought I was much stronger than anyone else there at the time," Wehrwein said. "For a long time I looked at the job at the *Journal* as my consolation prize."

A consolation prize that turned into the 1953 Pulitzer for International Reporting, after Wehrwein wrote a series of stories about Canada. More than 50 years later, he credited his college newspaper.

"I dropped out of the journalism school," Wehrwein said. "I got all the stuff I needed from the *Cardinal*. I learned about make-up, about how to put the paper to bed, about lots and lots of stuff that is absolutely obsolete now, but which I greatly enjoyed at the time. It became a campus career, overtaking everything else I did."

Los Angeles Times reporter Abigail Goldman won a Pulitzer Prize in 2005 for her investigation into the effect of Wal-Mart on the global economy. In the lead story in the series she contrasted two stories: that of a bargain-hunter shopping for cheap eats for her family, and a grocery clerk put out of work when competition from a Wal-Mart closed her store.

185

IT DOESN'T END WITH US

The company has prospered by elevating one goal above all others: cutting prices relentlessly. U.S. economists say its tightfistedness has not only boosted its own bottom line, but also helped hold down the inflation rate for the entire country. Consumers reap the benefits every time they push a cart through Wal-Mart's checkout lines.

Yet Wal-Mart's astonishing success exacts a heavy price.

By squeezing suppliers to cut wholesale costs, the company has hastened the flight of U.S. manufacturing jobs overseas. By scouring the globe for the cheapest goods, it has driven factory jobs from one poor nation to another.

Wal-Mart's penny-pinching extends to its own 1.2 million U.S. employees, none of them unionized. By the company's own admission, a full-time worker might not be able to support a family on a Wal-Mart paycheck.[1]

Throughout the series she and her fellow reporters avoided the easy characterizations favored by both the company and its opponents. They examined every assumption about Wal-Mart and its influence on America and the developing nations that supply the store with its products, and were cited by the Pulitzer jurors for an "engrossing account."

Goldman said the same skepticism that informed her work on the Wal-Mart series led her to request the University of Wisconsin chancellor's phone records while she was a student.

"That's the way I approach stories today," she said. "I still take a highly skeptical approach to conventional wisdom and not take hook line and sinker what I'm told. I learned that at the *Cardinal*. I learned that any good journalist at the *Cardinal* was one who questioned everything."

She requested the phone records, she said, thinking she'd call all the numbers and see with whom the chancellor regularly spoke. "It annoyed her, and I liked being annoying."

Goldman said she still looks back on the *Cardinal* as the beginning of a love affair with the kind of life lived by the people she worked with, "smart people who were kind of scary, but who loved being there, who wanted to be there all the time, who really loved what they did all day long."

Walt Bogdanich, now investigative editor of the *New York Times*, won two Pulitzer Prizes. The first was **1988 for his articles in the *Wall Street Journal* on substandard medical laboratories.**

The second came in 2005 after his *Times* series, "Death on the Tracks."

He started reporting because he wanted to attend an anti-war conference in Cleveland 1970 but he couldn't afford the travel expenses. His brother

IT DOESN'T END WITH US

George, already a *Cardinal* reporter, told Bogdanich the *Cardinal* would pay his way if he wrote a story about it.

"I read newspapers but I had no idea how to write stories for newspapers," he said. "It was a crazy plan, but I called the paper and they said 'Sure,' and that's how I became a journalist."

He brought in that first story and watched as an editor covered it — positively drowned it — in red editing marks. He was "horribly embarrassed," but the editor kept reassuring him that it was wonderful and asked him to do more work for the *Cardinal*.

"That helped me get over my humiliation at the lousy job I had done," he said. "I came back for more torture."

He dove into covering campus news, then a beat consisting mostly of protest, drug busts at the dorms, and student politics. Eventually the *Cardinal* sent him on assignment again, to cover the shooting of demonstrators at Jackson State University in Mississippi.

"It was quite an experience for a young reporter to go down into a situation like that," Bogdanich said. "The National Guard was still there, in their tanks and armored vehicles, in battle gear. It was a black university and so it was one of the student shootings that didn't get the kind of attention that Kent State did. It was nice that the *Daily Cardinal* had the resources to go down there and report on that when it wasn't — in my view — a topic that was covered aggressively."

That freedom to report inspired Bogdanich in his later career, which took him from newspapers in Cleveland to CBS News to the *Wall Street Journal* and finally the *Times*.

"What happened to me wouldn't have happened on other campuses, at other papers," he said. "At other places you have to work for the journalism school or be a major and take classes, and the papers are usually run under the auspices of the journalism department. This one wasn't. That was the reason I was able to walk in off the street without any discernable training whatsoever and learn among fellow students. I was one fortunate fellow."

Nancy Bobrowitz, former vice president of Reuters USA, walked into the *Cardinal* offices in 1975 and looked up. There, on a shelf, were bright red hard hats with the letters "PRESS" emblazoned in white. "During the not-then-distant days of student protest against the Vietnam War, *Cardinal* reporters wore those hard hats for protection when riots broke out on campus."

Her *Cardinal* taught her to handle a deadline, she said, and as she progressed from general assignment reporting to night editing, she made more and more friends, and had more and more fun.

"When you were putting the paper to bed and [printer] Norm emerged from the backshop to shout 'OK kids, stop monkey-farting around!', you knew it was time to close up the front page and hand it over," she remembered.

Immediately following her *Cardinal* experience Bobrowitz took jobs at the *Wisconsin State Journal*, *Chicago Tribune*, and Reuters news service bureaus in New York and London. She now teaches at Columbia University.

IT DOESN'T END WITH US

Milwaukee newspaper legend Irwin Maier, chairman of the company which published the *Milwaukee Journal*, devoted a chapter in his autobiography to his days at the *Cardinal*. As a young advertising salesman in 1918, Maier recalled being too shy to approach businessmen and ask them to spend their cash in the *Cardinal*'s pages:

> ... I had to walk around the square twice before I could get up the courage to make my first call. Finally, I stopped in front of Simpson's Apparel Shop, swallowed hard, walked into the store and asked for the manager. A tall young man came onto the floor and asked what I wanted to see him about. I told him I was from the *Daily Cardinal*, and before I could say more, he said, "Just a minute," and went back to his office. He reappeared with a layout for a three by ten advertisement — a substantial sale. My confidence considerably bolstered, I thanked him, and proceeded to make the rest of my calls with some success.
>
> I stuck with the advertising job at the *Daily Cardinal*, and soon my work there almost took precedence over my work for college classes.[2]

Neal Ulevich recognized the inherent humor in his situation even as he described it: a world-renowned photographer, famous for his Pulitzer Prize-winning photos of a violent uprising in Asia, so inept in the darkroom that he set the photo engraving machine on fire.

"It wasn't that spectacular," he protested. "You could beat it out with a towel pretty easily."

Ulevich started out at the *Cardinal* in 1964, wandering into the building and asking to do any task that needed doing. Which that night turned out to be sweeping the floor.

"It was dirty," he said with a chuckle. "I walked into this great institution and I was prepared to do whatever I had to do in order to get in the door. I wasn't trying to start at the top."

Photography had been a hobby since high school, but Ulevich was a reporter and copy editor before he became a photographer. There was so much talent on the photography staff at the time, he said, there was barely room for him.

"There were certain tradecraft things I learned in that environment," he recalled. "Deadline copy editing, deadline writing, writing a story while the night editor's standing over you because it has to be done right now, all these wonderful, visceral skills, like learning to put aside everything else and just do what needs to be done. It was my first journalism job, and it made a life out of journalism for me."

IT DOESN'T END WITH US

Dwight Pelkin parlayed his *Cardinal* experience into a career that spanned four decades, becoming a civic institution in Sheboygan, Wisconsin. Fresh out of college just before Pearl Harbor, Pelkin knew he wanted to be a journalist, and the only place that would have him was a telephone company in Green Bay, Wisconsin. He inventoried transformers. For $12 a week he signed on as a headline writer for the Green Bay *Press-Gazette*, so when the *Sheboygan Press* offered him $15 a week to replace a sportswriter who'd quit, he jumped.

At the *Cardinal*, he said later, he'd learned to forgo money for the joy of newspapering. "$25 a week when I became sports editor. The hours? Oh, anywhere from 50 to 80 or so. Who cared? You just worked as long as it took to get the job done."

He'd fallen in love with the connection with the community that comes with service to a small newspaper.

Shadid had tried to join his college newspaper at the University of Oklahoma, but found the hoops he had to jump through — tryouts, tests, qualification requirements — too complicated. When he transferred to Wisconsin, he strolled into the *Cardinal* and got himself assigned to writing campus news.

"I knew I wanted to be a journalist," he said, "and when I walked into the *Cardinal*, I knew I was home."

The paper's only criterion for staff membership was that he be willing to work, and Shadid, a native of Oklahoma City with a lifelong interest in newspapers, would have done anything to be part of that environment.

"More than what I wrote about, I just wanted to be at the paper all the time," he said. "It was so much fun. It was a place where a group of like-minded students was working toward the same thing. They had a vision for what journalism should be, and they really believed in that."

Shadid's *Cardinal* endorsed an approach called, then and now, "advocacy journalism." Every staff defined advocacy differently, but most took the philosophy to mean seeking out stories uncovered by Madison's daily press or local TV stations, eschewing local celebrity interviews for examinations of social issues, for example.

"The debates we had — the ideological debates — were healthy," Shadid said. "We should have more of that kind of debate at 'professional' newspapers, have everything out in the open and be aggressive about our views. Ideology doesn't hurt anyone."

Shadid's stories then were examinations of student government wrongdoing, accounts of efforts by university faculty to secure funding for scientific research, a group of students living overseas who got "lost in Colombia," he recalled.

More than the stories themselves, his fellow editors taught Shadid what kind of journalist he wanted to be, and when he left the *Cardinal*, it was as a product of his environment.

"What I've taken away from the *Cardinal* is a critical eye, a skepticism, a certain distrust of people in power and what they will do to maintain that power,"

IT DOESN'T END WITH US

he said. "I took away the idea that I should do stories other people aren't going to do, stories that aren't dictated by authority. The *Cardinal* taught me that journalism had — and has — a social responsibility."

Shadid's work at the *Washington Post* reflected that philosophy, as he told the tales of ordinary Iraqis caught up in the destruction of their country:

> Abdel-Jabbar was in his workshop, putting together cardboard boxes. The blast collapsed the shop's entrance, showering the store with bricks and cinderblocks. He said the shock waves tossed cars and people several feet. One of them was Sattar, a 22-year-old friend repairing his car in the street. Sattar survived, Abdel-Jabbar said, but his legs were severed.
>
> "Does he carry weapons of mass destruction?" Abdel-Jabbar shouted, as the sirens of ambulances, police cars and civil defense vehicles tried, in vain, to navigate traffic that had come to a standstill in the wrecked street. "Do his wife and children carry weapons of mass destruction?"
>
> Next door, two workers had been scurrying around the Dulaimi Restaurant, preparing for lunchtime. Both were killed in an instant. The restaurant's red and blue tiles lay splintered on the sidewalk, plastic white tables and chairs were turned upside down, wires hung from the ceiling like a spider's web and its sign dangled overhead, giving perch to a bird.
>
> Within moments, the second blast struck the other side of the street. Qais Sabah and his family of eight were sitting down to a breakfast of falafel, boiled eggs and bread. They jumped at the first explosion, then were thrown to the ground by the second.
>
> Hours later, the 35-year-old day laborer looked out over the detritus of his house. A cracked porcelain plate that read "God" hung askew on the wall. On the sidewalk outside was the severed hand of Samad Rabai, 17, the owner of an appliance store.[3]

The details are those others might consider unimportant, useless decoration. The *Cardinal* trained Shadid's eye for the ordinary turned extraordinary, the telling moment others might overlook.

"The philosophy I've carried over into journalism is one of keeping my ear close to the ground and focusing on how greater forces affect people at the

IT DOESN'T END WITH US

ground level," Shadid said. "The *Cardinal* taught me that institutions, especially journalism institutions, had to stand for something."

---

[1] Nancy Cleeland and Abigail Goldman, "An Empire Built on Bargains Remakes the Working World," Los Angeles Times (Nov. 23, 2003): 1.
[2] Irwin Maier, *A Career in Newspapers and Broadcasting*, (Milwaukee: The Journal Company, 1981), 9-10.
[3] Anthony Shadid, "In a Moment, Lives Get Blown Apart" The Washington Post (March 27, 2003): 1.

IT DOESN'T END WITH US

IT DOESN'T END WITH US

16.

Life Lessons

Oh, my, try to remember those days! The smell of the linotype, the closet darkroom in the basement with plumbing that usually worked, and temperature control for solutions difficult at best! Oh, we can't forget those many nights when staff would have to read the page proofs and retreat next door to Roy McCormick's Paisan's [Restaurant] and enjoy a cold beer and a hot pizza as the candlelight played over the proofs. Romantic as hell, wasn't it? The assignment list posted for review by staffers looking for their own scheduling. The fantastic up to date typewriters that never needed repair or ribbons. And the joy and relief when the Cardinal was put to bed and everybody went home – usually to their own beds!
– Duane Hopp, Cardinal Photo Editor 1954, letter to the Cardinal

☙

The influence of the *Daily Cardinal* stretched well beyond its boundaries as a teaching institution, which anyone might expect to influence the lives of its graduates. Over the past 115 years it has been more than a newspaper. It has also been a gathering place for friends, a staging area for politics and protest, and the backdrop for dozens of great love stories.

Those who lived within its walls during their college years found themselves learning more, far more, than just how to set headline type and write captions. The lessons they took from the *Cardinal* influenced them in a careers and lives that often had little to do with newspapers.

Jack Geiger arrived at the University of Wisconsin in 1941 a prodigy; at fifteen years old, he was the youngest student admitted under a special program for the gifted. The New York native had spent summers working as a copy boy for *the New York Times*, a position made possible because the older employees were being drafted in great numbers. So one of the first places he went on campus was the *Daily Cardinal*.

"My ambition was to be a journalist, and here was a real live daily newspaper that was open to anybody interested in journalism," he said.

Today, Geiger is a doctor. More than that, he is one of the most highly honored physicians in America, a professor emeritus at the City University of New York Medical School, recipient of the National Institute of Medicine's Gustav O. Lienhard Award for advancement of personal health services.

Throughout his medical career, he has focused on how to get health care to the poor, the desperate, to minority communities and developing nations. His work, which included establishing a network of community health centers across the country to bring medical care closer to the homes of those who need it.

His days at the *Cardinal*, Geiger said, pointed him in the direction of these issues: fairness, equality, protection for all American citizens, especially the weakest and most helpless.

"In 1941 it was perfectly legal for university-approved housing to refuse any minorities as well as Jews and Catholics," Geiger said. "When I first started as a reporter at the *Cardinal* I ran into an Asian student who couldn't find anywhere to live. And we decided to take a look at what the whole situation was with Asian-American and African-American students, and the hardships they faced. It was a considerable campaign on our part and it attracted a lot of attention."

The university would go on to ban discrimination in any housing it approved for students, something Geiger recalled as "a great victory."

"It created a discussion about something everyone knew was there, but nobody wanted to talk about," he said. "It was a way of showing people that the larger structure, the larger issues of society really did affect their little community. And that has stayed with me to this day."

Former Madison Mayor Paul Soglin began his political career and his *Cardinal* one at roughly the same time. During the late 1960s Soglin wrote columns for the paper on the intersections of academic research and corporate dollars, issues, he noted, that are still relevant to the university today.

"We were really focused at that time on how the private sector drove the UW agenda," he said. "I picked something innocuous to make the point in one of my columns: a grant from a farming company to develop a bigger and better potato. And my point is that when you're getting a grant to research potatoes, you're going to do that rather than research green beans or broccoli. It opened up a whole series of questions about how the research agenda is decided, because while one day it's potatoes, the next day it's anthrax."

Involvement in discussion over those kinds of questions served Soglin well when he joined the contentious Madison City Council as an alderman representing the student wards, and later, when he became the city's mayor.

IT DOESN'T END WITH US

"The big political meetings, with their endless hours of discussion, were invaluable," he said. "It was a version of the Socratic process, bringing up ideas and challenging one another to defend our opinions."

Allen Swerdlowe works for Design Seven Associates in New York City and is one of the architects working to reconstruct the former World Trade Center site. His journalism experience was limited to the *Cardinal* from 1967 to 1969, but in those three years, he said, he gained a lifetime's experience of people, how they made decisions and responded to a crisis.

"I was the night editor and 10 p.m. was our drop-dead deadline. The printers were employed by the university and without the permission of the regents or someone, we couldn't get them to hold the presses," Swerdlowe said. "So when we got the call one night that Martin Luther King had been shot, we had to try to get the story and we needed a lot of troops jumped up in order to do that. The editor was on the phone trying to wake somebody up and we were pulling the story together, and I set the headline with my own hands."

"The power of that experience has never left me."

Newsrooms are notoriously romantic set-pieces. Directors and authors have littered their amorous tales with caricatures of the ink-stained and the overworked, the idealistic and the adrenaline-addicted. Those stories are not rooted entirely in fantasy: poll a group of married journalists. More of them than not will have met their spouses over typewriters or keyboards. Sleepless nights, bad food, an emotionally charged story, one drink too many, of these things newsroom love is made.

Braden Smith and Rachel Kappelman met in the *Cardinal* darkroom in 1999. He was a lowly copy editor and she was the photo chief. Their first date was at a construction site.

"Second semester of my freshman year I was commissioned to write an opinion article about urban sprawl and I wanted pictures of these huge houses in Middleton," Braden said. Rachel accompanied him to the prosperous Madison suburb and watched as he took photos of homes being built.

"I think she thought I was a large dork," he said.

Their next encounter came when she assigned him to take photos of a meeting of the student government. Associated Students of Madison meetings were notoriously uneventful that year, and were thought suitable for new photographers as easy assignments. Rachel had been to dozens of the meetings, and was sick of them.

Smith arrived expecting to photograph junior bureaucrats sitting at a table and talking to one another. Instead, he found a fistfight.

"The ASM chair had just burst out the door followed by the head of the College Republicans," he said. "They were shouting at each other and shoving each other and I just stood there trying to take pictures of this. The ASM chair tried to grab my camera. The cops showed up, it was a mess."

He rushed back to the office, calling out to Rachel, "This is the best thing that has ever happened!"

IT DOESN'T END WITH US

They were inseparable after that.

Jerrold and Leona Schecter, now celebrated co-authors of volumes on Russian and Near-East history, learned how to write together at the *Cardinal*, but their romance wasn't love at first byline.

"I can't say either of us looked at each other and said 'This is for me,'" Leona said. "But we worked together and we moved along together and we learned about each other, and as life moved along, we just ... stayed together."

"I tried to boss her around," Jerrold said. "I wasn't very successful."

"After 51 years of marriage," she answered, "nothing's really changed."

He was the paper's managing editor in 1953; she edited the *Cardinal*'s weekly magazine section, a job that had her dealing with abstract ideas while he handled day-in, day-out operations.

Leona's magazine gave space to both liberal voices and nascent conservative ones like a young William F. Buckley, then a recent graduate of Yale, who wrote a long essay opposing the cherished Wisconsin principle of academic freedom.

After several months' side by side labor, Leona asked Jerrold out.

"She said 'Do you want to go to the movies?'" he recalled. "I said, 'Sure, do you have any money?' She's been making me pay it back ever since."

"We still fight over our books," she said. "When you work together the way we did, you find each person has very different talents. He from the beginning was a real reporter. He can find anything he wants to know about. I'm more of a 'putting things together and questioning the philosophy' person. I ask 'Who wrote that history?' because I long ago came to the conclusion that history is whoever wrote it. But we find that if you allow each person to follow his own talents, as at the *Cardinal*, everything comes together."

Alan Higbie and Andrea Schwartz met just prior to the 1976 *Cardinal* staff strike. As a sophomore, Andrea had gone to cover a meeting and came back to the office. "I started writing out a story in longhand with a pencil and this editor said, 'What are you doing?'" she remembered. "He said, 'You don't write it out longhand, you type it.' He sat down next to me and showed me how to write a story, how to set it up, put the important facts first."

He cared about her learning and doing well, she said. Being together during such a charged time brought them close quickly.

"It was a magic time, it was the best years of my life," Andrea said. "There was such a sense of purpose, because we all shared a lot of the same political beliefs and goals. We spent so many summers in that basement, and I'd go down in the morning and come up just before the sun went down, and I'd be pasty white all summer long.

"You stay up all those nights and you feel a little buzzed. It was a weird, good feeling, even in the midst of a long, awful fight."

Working together taught Alan and Andrea to admire each other's strengths and take advice from one another.

"He was a great editor," she said. "He really was the backbone of the strike newspaper and he kept us all together. I learned things from him that I never

IT DOESN'T END WITH US

would have learned in journalism school, where you're learning in a pure academic forum."

Douglas Gomery came to the *Cardinal* not for news, but for film. In the late 1960s, long before home video and DVD made watching movies a more solitary experience, film societies were springing up all over the Wisconsin campus. Students gathered in darkened classrooms in Madison's commerce and social sciences buildings, screening efforts from the likes of Igmar Bergman and Don Siegel; John Ford and Jean Luc Godard.

Every screening began with a plea for the Bail Fund, a pot of money used to get student protesters out of jail, Gomery recalled. And after the films, he would return to the *Cardinal* office to talk with his fellow student scholars and write about what he'd just seen.

His fellow film reviewers and writers included such future luminaries of the field as Michael Wilmington, now film critic with the *Chicago Tribune*, Joe McBride, who became a critic and screenwriter, and Lawrence D. Cohen, who wrote the films *Carrie* and *Ghost Story*.

"Mike Wilmington called it the best staff of film reviewers ever assembled, and I think he was right," Gomery said. "It was a group of people who loved movies and were passionate about them, and who wanted to talk about film and culture and politics and the way they all intersected."

The *Cardinal* was more than a newspaper where reporters worked, he remembered. It was a campus information spot, where anybody with anything important going on naturally went to make his or her voice heard.

"It was the center of campus culture," he said. "It was where you went to find out about the next rally, the next protest meeting, the next film. By working there you were immersed in everything important that was going on on campus. The hardest thing about it was leaving."

Gomery himself went on to author ten books about the mass media in the United States. He has written more than 600 articles, appearing in such publications as the *Village Voice* and the *Baltimore Sun* and is quoted by the *Washington Post* and *New York Times* as an authority on film. He recently retired from the University of Maryland's Philip Merrill College of Journalism.

It was the *Cardinal*, Gomery said, that gave him the freedom to develop his skills, nurture his love of movies, and find validation for his interests with other like-minded students. He could grow there, he said, because there was no one to tell him not to.

"I was stunned that there was no professor looking over my shoulder telling me what to write," Gomery said. "Instead it was a hierarchy of students teaching one another. That system produced a lot of very good journalists but more than that, it produced a lot of very interesting people.

"If I had to date when I became an adult, it was in college, but it wasn't during academic programs. It was at the *Daily Cardinal*."

Such a place, with such opportunities, engendered fierce loyalty among its graduates, strong memories for those who made them. *Cardinal* staff members

IT DOESN'T END WITH US

can recall, with crystal clarity, stories they wrote, arguments they had, mistakes they made, even if those incidents happened decades in the past.

Jack Zeldes, while a *Cardinal* editor, had sought endorsements for the University of Wisconsin on the occasion of its birthday in 1948. Zeldes wanted to print one from each American university president, including the then-president of Columbia University, Dwight David Eisenhower.

Eisenhower had an aide, Zeldes recalled, an officious little man who continued to reply to Zeldes' inquiries with the flat statement, "The General doesn't do endorsements." Finally Zeldes, in a fit of frustration, cabled Ike directly. This isn't soap flakes or cereal, he implored the future U.S. president. This is the University of Wisconsin and it deserves your consideration. The next day, he got a telegram.

The telegram was lost, somewhere in a box or drawer emptied sometime thereafter, a precious historical memento thrown away. But Jack Zeldes, age 82, knew it word for word after 50 years.

"'Your persistence has been rewarded,'" he quoted it with a laugh. "'Here is my message.'"

Carl Adam's allegiance to the *Cardinal* was such that not even a U-Boat could sink it.

A top reporter for the paper in December 1941, Adam was assigned a story about the American Field Service visiting the campus, seeking ambulance drivers to go overseas. He wrote the first half of his story and then, inspired by patriotism and a thirst for what he later called adventure, filled out an application himself.

On April 23, 1942 he sailed from Philadelphia, bound for Cairo aboard the Swedish freighter AS Agra with another *Cardinal* alumnus, reporter James Atkins, in tow. "There was no anti-submarine protection along the U.S. eastern seaboard then and the U-boats wreaked havoc on coastal shipping," Adam recalled.

"About 3 p.m. the second day out, my partner Peter Brooks and I were told to stand down after one hour of a two-hour stint on the bridge, looking for the telltale 'feather' of a submarine periscope. We were supposedly far enough east ... to be relatively safe."

No sooner did Adam relax and agree to a game of chess with Brooks than a torpedo slammed the ship on its port side. The young man watched, horrified, as "an orange-red wall of flame fingered its way a hundred feet up a curtain of blue sky."

Fifteen hours of floating in rough waters in a lifeboat followed, Adam thinking of his camera and typewriter, now left behind on the ocean floor. Picked up by a Norwegian freighter, he and 26 other sailors were taken to Bermuda, where they were kept for five days before being flown to New York.

When he got off the plane, tired, frightened and cold, Adam placed a phone call.

To the *Daily Cardinal*.

IT DOESN'T END WITH US

UW TRIO IS SAFE IN NEW YORK - EXTRA!

(Note: The following message was telephoned directly to the *Daily Cardinal* late last night by Carl Adam, former *Cardinal* reporter, upon arrival to New York after being torpedoed en route to Egypt with the American Field services.)

Seven American Field service men, including James Atkins, Jacob Volrath, and myself (all former university students) were rescued from a torpedoed steamer by a freighter after the steamer had been sunk by an Italian submarine recently.

The captain and several men of the steamer's crew were lost.

We drifted in an open life boat which was towing a life raft with other survivors for 15 hours in high seas, rain, squalls and a cruel wind.

The ship burned as it sank and the three of us were slightly singed, but not hurt.

All our belongings were lost when the ship went down, including my camera. It will probably be necessary for us to return to Madison and be re-outfitted.

The freighter took us to Hamilton, Bermuda where we joined other torpedo victims. From Bermuda we were flown to New York by Clipper.

We're all broke, haven't a cent, and hope to be in town soon.

Adam resumed his journey overseas that June, eventually becoming editor of the American Service's magazine. He referred to his dispatch as the end of the story he'd started to write about the search for ambulance drivers, five months ago. "It may be," he said, "the longest press-collect account the *Cardinal* copy desk ever edited."

To some, the *Cardinal* came to symbolize idealism and naiveté best considered through the lens of nostalgia, an almost imaginary place where they allowed themselves to redefine the possible instead of resigning themselves to the achievable.

Cardinal columnist Leon Lynn wrote back to his old paper after taking a job at a small rural daily. In his letter, he recounted that his new employers made a choice that would have been unthinkable at the *Cardinal*: ordering him to quote a particular advertiser in a story.

IT DOESN'T END WITH US

It may sound like a small thing. And of course history wasn't changed much by the addition of two meaningless paragraphs to an already innocuous story about satellite dishes in Iowa. But the incident left its mark on me.

Before I went to Iowa, I had worked at the *Cardinal* for almost five years and had written more than 400 articles. Many of them made people angry ... And not once did anyone ever change a word of what I'd written because it might displease an advertiser or a reader ...

It may have cost the paper some money from time to time, but the result was a measure of press freedom not often available to journalists these days. Especially for students writing their first published articles ...

I sometimes wish I'd stood my ground and refused to change the article, which of course would have meant being fired immediately. It didn't seem to be worth it, not over a lousy story on satellite dishes, anyway.

A little piece of my idealism died that day, I guess. But at least I've seen a different way of doing things. Hopefully that will sustain me as the attacks become more frequent, and more important.

For those who took the *Cardinal*'s lessons to heart, who lived those principles so well-learned and well-loved and refused to give in to disillusionment, the paper was just the start of their extraordinary lives.

Mary Jo Kochakian, neé Ross, who would go on to work as a columnist for the *Hartford Courant*, looked back on her days at the *Cardinal* during the '76 strike and said it taught her how deeply it is possible to care about your work, about politics, about things many people allow to become part of the background noise of their lives.

"Passion, that's what stands out for me," she said. "Passion that is so particular to that time and that place. I don't think it could have happened at any other place. Never."

IT DOESN'T END WITH US

17.

The Cost

"I don't understand the game. I just don't understand this game we're playing. Here are my keys. My desk is cleaned out. So is my film locker. Find yourself another managing editor. I hope that he is able to eat more shit than I was."
— From the Daily Cardinal archives, resignation letter, April 1975

ଔ

Jim Gunderson was the first one in and the last one out of the *Cardinal* office every day from 1953 to 1955. He organized the paper's sports department, creating a beat system, coordinating coverage with other Big Ten schools, inventing procedures to divvy up sports photo assignments that photographers otherwise fought and scrapped over.

At the end of his term he checked into a hospital and had a kidney removed.

The *Daily Cardinal* is not an easy place to work.

Cardinal staffers who credit the paper for their success often speak of its realistic deadlines, its do-or-die-trying attitude, the way it integrated their education and social lives until their days were the *Daily Cardinal* from beginning to end. It was their work, their home, their family, every day for four years or more. It became, in many cases, their lives, and in some cases it remains so.

And such all-consuming passion, such force of will in pursuit of one goal, exacts a high price.

Through the years arguments over editorial policies have escalated into shouting matches, shoving matches, in some cases even fistfights. Senators castigated student editors on the statehouse steps. Protesters burned student editors —19-year-old kids — in effigy and picketed their houses.

The work hours alone, up to five days straight without sleep in more than one editor's recollection, can drive staffers to the breaking point. *Cardinal* editors work with only the vaguest of schedules: printers' deadlines dictated when the day would end, true, but not when it would have to begin and begin again. Part-time jobs, classes, things that require commitments at specific times and in specific places, become impossible, subsumed by breaking news or office disputes. Cash-strapped students who try to work while working at the *Cardinal* often find themselves with little or no time to study, choosing between food and sleep, because the *Cardinal* is the last thing they sacrifice.

Spending so much time with the same people, day after day, in intense political situations and close quarters, only heightens the stress. Relationships are broken when partners don't understand the schedule. Opportunities for other pursuits are abandoned and nineteen-, twenty- and twenty-one-year-olds go broke, crack up, flunk out and drop out, just to put out the paper.

It happens fast, this change from a normal college student into an ink-stained, caffeine-addicted, hopped-up night owl who cannot get enough of talking about the board of regents' meeting. Jean Matheson began the fall of 1952 on the Dean's List. She took on an editing job at the *Cardinal* and ended the academic year on probation.

"I spent so much time down there I almost didn't graduate," she said. "I'm not sure I would have regretted it."

Fights at the *Cardinal* are not just arguments between fellow students. They are bitter, life-and-death battles that color how people see the world for the rest of their lives. When someone has called you a fascist pig and screamed curses in your face in a conference room, that is not the sort of thing that just goes away.

In the world of print, mistakes last forever. Editors will meet after 50 years and renew arguments over typos now nearly turned to dust. Former editor Zeldes is still angry at whoever turned his 1951 headline about "The Cost of a Football Coach" into "The Cast of a Football Cooch."

On the day Saigon fell, April 30, 1975, the *Cardinal* trumpeted the event with a huge headline reading "VICTORY!!!!!" To the students running the paper at the time, the United States' war had been an act of aggression and they welcomed its failure and end. David Newman, the *Cardinal's* former editor-in-chief and then its printer, can only see the way the staff used green ink for the letters.

"I told them," he said, "that that would look like crap."

It is the responsibility that often weighs heaviest on *Cardinal* staffers' shoulders. Other extracurricular activities, supervised by paid adults, have safeguards against catastrophic failure, built-in structures to avoid institutions and those who attend them from self-destruction. The *Cardinal*, for most of its existence, had none. No one came to tell Brannon Lambert and Ivan Strmecki that they did not have to fight the entire University of Wisconsin on their own.

IT DOESN'T END WITH US

No one ever relieved Arlene Bahr of the responsibility of selling the only advertising the *Cardinal* had during the lean years of World War II. No one, save Stan Zuckerman, had the burden of figuring out how to keep the paper printing while its bills were piling up.

The students who work in the *Cardinal* office work alone. If they don't do their jobs, no one will. For many, it is the first time they are responsible for something, the first time they are in charge of someone. For that something to be a paper of 100 years' history, for that someone to be a classmate, turns what is under the best of circumstances a stressful job into death march of paper and pen.

Amy Eisenman, the *Cardinal* copy chief during the paper's 1995 return from its seven-month shutdown, had the job of shepherding the *Cardinal's* major return issue through publication.

" I had no idea what I was getting myself into," she remembered. "I showed up that afternoon, armed with the AP Style guide, and I had it in my head that that paper was going to be perfect. It had to be perfect."

Her workday began at 2 p.m. By 10 p.m., most of the paper's pages were laid out, end to end, odd-numbered pages on one side and even-numbered on the other as dictated by the printers. The paper's graphics editor, Jason Heiser, walked over and looked at the stack of camera-ready sheets, each with waxed stories and photos glued on them, being placed into a box to be taken to the presses.

"And I'll never forget," Eisenman said. "He yelled out 'Oh, my God, they're backwards.' We had put the even-numbered pages and the odd-numbered pages on the wrong sides of the paper. We had to rip them all up [from their boards] and start again."

Her first night as copy chief turned into her first morning. She went home at 6 a.m., changed clothes, and came back to the office, where she started sweeping the floor.

Inside-the-office stress aside, outside is a student body, a large portion of it politically astute and articulate, prepared to argue every turn of phrase in every word a *Cardinal* sports columnist like Arlie Schardt wrote. Schardt's picture appeared next to everything he put in the *Cardinal*.

Which made it that much easier for dorm waiters who disagreed with him to dump breakfast in his lap.

"I was a student waiter and we each got a meal at the end of our shift, so I was sitting there eating," he said. "And this other waiter, I think he was a Republican from Illinois somewhere, came up to me and said everybody at the *Cardinal* was a bunch of communists, and then he poured a whole pitcher of milk over my head."

Such reactions didn't always come from strangers. Matheson's own father stopped talking to her for two months because of her editorial policy that university athletics were overemphasized and should be curtailed.

"He was a big Wisconsin booster and he was very angry with me for saying that," she said. The castigation extended cross-country. "There was a column in the *New York Herald Tribune*, that great newspaper, about how dumb and naive I was."

The numbers of *Cardinal* staffers who thrived on such pressure and flourished in the hothouse do not far eclipse those who simply burned up, and out. The *Cardinal* keeps a thick file of resignation letters in its archives. They range from short handwritten missives from editors leaving to take on new jobs or move out of state, to four-page *cris de couer* from frustrated staffers pushed past their limits, like this one from the late 1980s:

> It may as well be said quickly. After listening to the speeches that were intended to communicate and encourage new people to the paper — give them some reason for coming down except for the beer — I was shocked. A tirade of negative, get-down, we're-not-that-good-but-why-don't-you-work-for-us (so what if the pay is poor) speeches cannot inspire anyone to work. It was depressing ...
>
> It's the irony of the *Cardinal* that people can give their lives for the paper, that they can surrender the stuff that makes life anything but misery to see a creative effort on the streets five days a week. And then to slap that experience to the floor is unfortunately the reality of the *Cardinal*.
>
> It's a reality that I no longer feel the need to deal with. I have seen flashes of talent and togetherness which have — so seldom — jelled at the *Cardinal*. These times have been few and far between.
>
> I wish I saw purposefulness at the paper and some positive motivation for staying there, besides "experience." I can no longer justify the "experience" of the paper.
>
> For these reasons, I can no longer, and cannot be persuaded, to work at the paper again. Hard decisions are never easy to make but this one has been made, in finality.

Eisenman found her health deteriorating under the pressures of being the *Cardinal's* last line of defense from mistakes. During her tenure the *Cardinal* had a practice of reviewing each week's papers at its regular Friday staff meeting. As staffers flipped through pages and pointed out errors, she began to feel that they were pointing out problems that were her fault.

"It was pretty awful in there," she said. "Almost every night, I was the only copy editor there, and I just became obsessed with that paper. I was very glad when I went home for Christmas that year."

IT DOESN'T END WITH US

The paper, only recently returned from shutdown, wasn't doing well financially, putting added stress on its editors. The *Cardinal* had to pay its printers in advance, $1,500 per week for the next week's printing, due every Friday at Madison Newspapers, Inc. One Wednesday night, the paper's editors sat down and faced the inevitable. They had to deliver a check in two days, and their bank account was $1,000 short. Unless enough advertising money came in in the next day and a half, they were sunk.

Eisenman will never forget what happened next.

Many poor college students donated plasma for money at the local blood bank. You could donate up to two pints per day, each day, and the blood bank would pay $17 per pint. Nearly everyone around the table in the office had done it at least once, for beer or pizza money. They counted, and the numbers worked out: Fifteen editors, two pints each, two days, equaled $1,020.

"There was an element of real gravity to it," Eisenman said. "We were ready to do it. We'd given so much up for the paper already that blood would be the easy part. We'd just troop down there, all together, and then we'd have the money to keep it going."

Disaster was averted. Enough money came in the mail the next two days to make opening a vein for the paper unnecessary. The willingness to do so, Eisenman said, demonstrated how far *Cardinal* loyalists were willing to go — all for their student newspaper.

Eisenman went farther than that. Feeling that every error someone pointed out in the newspaper was an error she had failed to prevent, she quit sleeping, spending every spare minute in the office, bent over the circular copy desk. At the end of her spring semester she was physically and emotionally exhausted.

"I just felt horrible all the time," she said. "I was supposed to be this bastion of stability, this person who knew what to do, who could tell other people how to do it, and I was clueless, just as clueless as the rest of them."

Most *Cardinal* staffers do not alert their fellow students, no matter how close they have become, to their frustrated state until they have neared the breaking point. Fear of disapproval, of everyone else working just as hard but handling it better, fear of letting your fellow staffers down, runs through every "I quit" letter in the *Cardinal's* file, even the most vitriolic ones.

"I've been pulled into a million little pieces," one editor wrote, " Please don't hate me; this decision was tough enough, I don't want to walk away with a bunch of enemies."

When your world shrinks to the size of a small room full of typewriters and scrap paper, minor incidents assume an importance and intensity they would never otherwise attain. Editor Gilliam Kerley came into the office one day to find a typed and photocopied complaint against him being distributed to the staff. It listed 13 faults, among them that he was derelict in his filing duties, and was often late returning from meals.

Even as *Cardinal* alumni who treasure their experiences rejoice in near-perfect recall of days and nights in the office, others are haunted by the same.

IT DOESN'T END WITH US

"In some ways it's like we're all post-traumatic," Eisenman said. "It took me a long time to forgive myself for what I saw as my own culpability in the paper's failures. It's all such a blur at the time, so that it's only later that you realize everyone is fallible and we really were just kids."

Richard Davis had far more serious regrets. During correspondence in which he laid out the facts surrounding the strike that ousted him from his editorship in 1938, he described facing people he thought were his friends as they denounced him and his faith. Eventually, he broke off writing, saying:

> Trying to help you has brought back memories long buried — and has not been a happy thing for me ... I am not happy to have this particular past replayed for me now. It might have been better if, when you first called, I had simply declined to help.

Sixty-two years after his ordeal ended, he was unable to speak of it without pain.

In the editorial announcing Jim Gunderson's departure, *Cardinal* editor Lee Feldman noted,

> Last semester there was hardly a time of day when one would walk into the *Cardinal* office and not see former sports editor Jim Gunderson working feverishly at his desk. The sound of his typewriter zipping along at breakneck speed is familiar to all *Cardinal* staffers.
>
> Seldom have we seen such a hard-working, conscientious student so devoted to his work.
>
> Unfortunately, the loss of sleep and irregular meals took their toll and has finally resulted in a breakdown in Jim's health.
>
> Jim is going to the hospital this morning and will undergo major surgery tomorrow.
>
> The entire *Cardinal* staff conveys its sincerest appreciation to him for a job well done and wishes him a very speedy recovery.

Gunderson's son Tom said his father spoke throughout his life about his time at the *Cardinal* and how much he enjoyed working there. "It wasn't just a job, it was a passion to him," Tom Gunderson said. "Not a lot of people have that. He loved it and he wasn't going to let the opportunity to spend one minute there pass him by, no matter what the cost."

IT DOESN'T END WITH US

Gunderson's recovery was indeed speedy. Three weeks after his operation, he was on his feet.

And back at his desk at the *Cardinal*.

IT DOESN'T END WITH US

IT DOESN'T END WITH US

18.

What's Next

Wisconsin's daily paper has a history to be envied by any college publication. Those students who next year are to take up the work will add another roll to its history. The Cardinal will go steadily ahead under their guidance, keeping alive old policies and the spirit of Wisconsin.
– Daily Cardinal editorial, June 2, 1919

ଔ

The past ten years have been, for the *Daily Cardinal*, those of ordinary struggle and extraordinary achievement, precarious finances and precocious journalism. In 2000, the paper received national acclaim for its coverage of the presidential elections, coverage that included sending staffers on the road with the campaigns. It was the first time in decades that the paper had undertaken such an ambitious project, or garnered such recognition.

Though the paper's competitor, the *Badger Herald*, out-sizes and out-earns it, the *Cardinal* continues to out-fight its opponents, making up with effort what money might provide.

In 2006, the Society of Professional Journalists named the *Daily Cardinal* the best all-around student newspaper in the Midwest. It beat out the *Minnesota Daily*, which has a circulation of 24,000 to the *Cardinal's* 10,000. Its annual budget of $3 million, including university funding, is almost 20 times the *Cardinal's* costs.

On the walls of the *Cardinal* office hang front pages from the paper's past: the '76 strike paper, the Pearl Harbor issue, and the very first proof copy of the

IT DOESN'T END WITH US

Cardinal, signed by William Wesley Young. Below it hangs a photograph of one of the first *Cardinal* staffs: six men and two women who worked there in 1895, now looking out into rooms where their ideals are lived each day.

"Are we twelve pages for tomorrow?" Campus Editor Emily Winter shouted across the room to Editor-in-Chief Evan Rytlewski.

"We're eight for Monday, twelve for Tuesday," he called back, tearing into a Big Mac. "We're sixteen for Thursday."

"Don't tell me about Thursday till Wednesday," she laughed. "I'll never remember."

"We have this story about inmates escaping using a toilet paper tube as a gun," News Editor Maureen Backman announced.

Rytlewski yawned. "It's interesting," he said with world-weary confidence, "but it's not that interesting."

At Backman's glance, he repeated the page count and said, "I don't want to smush too much in."

"Is that the technical term," she asked, "smush?"

Winter looked at her watch, then at Backman. The entire newspaper was done. It was after 11 p.m., and Managing Editor Danielle Sulczewski was gently heckling copy editors who tried to fit too many words in too small a space. Winter was waiting on one more reporter, one more story.

"If he's the reason I'm here past midnight again ..." she said, letting the threat hang in the air.

The *Daily Cardinal* as it is today could have ended in 1926, when state legislators wanted the paper's anti-Prohibition stances curbed by UW faculty. It could have shuttered in 1938, after the first divisive strike, or in 1953, when money problems struck.

It could have closed its doors in the 1960s as a result of anti-communist pressures, or disappeared in the wake of the bombing of Sterling Hall.

The *Badger Herald* could have swallowed it in 1986; the university, in closing its press in 1989, could have destroyed it.

Its staff could have accepted the shutdown of 1995 as the end, packed up their notebooks, and gone home.

Instead, for 115 years, the *Daily Cardinal* has fought on. Its editors, reporters, managers, photographers, artists and copy editors and delivery boys and readers passed on that fight to the next generation of students. Each refused, in his or her own time, to submit to outside influence, university control, government censure.

Each refused to surrender to the inevitable, to take no for an answer, to be satisfied with the status quo. Each created journalism that changed the community it covered. Each produced journalists that influenced the national discourse. Each inspired lives that reflected the lessons learned at the *Cardinal*.

They echo one another, across decades, across generations when asked about the days when, in the face of overwhelming adversity, they refused to give up on their paper and on each other.

IT DOESN'T END WITH US

Richard Schickel, when asked why he and Stan Zuckerman did not abandon the *Cardinal* in 1953 when its finances were in a state of collapse and the two of them were carrying the daily operations of the paper on their backs: "We said 'By hook or by crook, we're gonna keep this thing going.' We really had a sense of tradition and we understood that it had been there a long time. We were not going to be the guys who shut it down, no matter what. It would have to be somebody else."

In 1987, Tim Carroll, when asked why the staff did not abandon its offices in the face of what looked like an inevitable *Herald* takeover and dissolution: "What weighed heavily on me and everybody is that you think about the tradition of the *Cardinal*. It's been there a hundred years. I just felt like, 'Oh, my God, I'm not gonna be the one that wrecked it. I'm not gonna let that happen.'"

In 1995, the shutdown staff, when asked how they ever thought they would pull this off: It doesn't end with us. It ends somewhere down the road, with some other bunch of kids. Not with us.

"It's a proving ground," said Jean Sue Johnson Libkind, *Cardinal* managing editor in 1964. "It's a student newspaper but it's more than that. To the people who worked there, it's life. It's the first time and sometimes it's the last time you get to do anything and everything you can do. The only limits you have are your own."

The results of that limitlessness, to write and to publish, to succeed and to fail, are in the University of Wisconsin's Journalism School, the pages of the *Washington Post*, and the vivid memories of every *Cardinal* staffer.

"Most of the people I knew there had their lives completely changed by the *Cardinal*," said Karl Meyer, who edited the paper in its postwar prosperity and went on to the editorial board of the *New York Times*. "One of the most important lessons I took from the *Cardinal* was about the dangers of timidity, that if someone tries to talk you out of publishing something, you've got to make your own judgments and not be swayed by outside influences. That was a lesson I learned firsthand and it served me very well."

Perhaps what is truly remarkable about the *Cardinal* is not all the changes it has gone through, but all the ways in which it has not changed. Within its walls, be they in the *Madison Democrat*'s offices in 1892 or the dark and smoky Campus Publishing building in 1953 or the fluorescent-lit basement of Vilas Hall in 1999, the staff of the *Daily Cardinal* is still hard at work, doing exactly what William Wesley Young envisioned: Telling the students' stories.

Sulczewski danced in the back corner of the office as she looked over the projections for the following week's paper. It would be fat with advertising, giving her writers and editors room to do what they did best, and that, the simple fact of a job done well, made her dance.

Backman determined that her writer had to make one more phone call to make his story complete. She handed him a university professor's home number on an index card and leaned over his shoulder.

IT DOESN'T END WITH US

"Tell him this," she said matter of factly when the reporter hesitated. "Just say you're sorry to bother him at home, don't be overly apologetic, but say you have to ask him some questions.

"Tell him who you are, and tell him you're with the *Daily Cardinal*."

The copy editors sat beside her, arguing over a synonym for clean, "meaning not corrupt." They went back and forth. Pure. Honest. Aboveboard.

Sulczewski looked up from her advertising layouts and saw that a new kid, one who'd wandered in that night and been handed a pen for his first copyediting shift, was gathering up his coat and preparing to leave.

She took his arm and pulled him back to the table. "We're almost ready to put the paper to bed," she said with a wide grin, as if this was the most exciting thing she could imagine.

"Stay. Pull up a chair. I want you to watch."

Afterword: Print is Dead

When I was a student editor at the *Daily Cardinal* in 1995, the newspaper was shut down. The office was empty, the presses were silent, and though I would never admit it out loud, it seemed there was no real way the paper could ever publish again. It's hard to imagine now, and harder still to explain: the quiet, in this place that was always noisy; the hopelessness, in this place that was always about hope.

In that discouraging environment a few people still worked, and one of them was our campus editor, Amy Zarlenga. Cleaning the office one day, she found an old and cracked newspaper in a broken wooden frame, shoved behind a filing cabinet. It was the copy of the very first proof copy of the *Daily Cardinal*, the one William Wesley Young pulled off the presses with his bare hands.

Trite it may have been, reductive it certainly was, but we needed a symbol in those long hot days of work with no reward, and this became it, became the story of the *Cardinal* writ tabloid: History disregarded, ruined, and now rescued.

Amy took that paper to a Madison frame shop and had it painstakingly restored, mounted on archival paper and sealed behind protective glass. She had it framed in gilt and had the university install special hooks, so that it was bolted, one day in that very long summer, to the *Cardinal* office wall.

It hangs there today.

This history is by no means meant to be a recounting of every story ever told by the *Cardinal*, or a biography of every now-famous person who ever worked there. It's not an excuse, and if it is an apology, it's only my own, for not appreciating what a gift I had when it was, briefly, in my hands. This history is a story of the struggle of a great journalism institution to make its surroundings better, to teach people at the point in their lives when they most needed instruction, and to challenge the status quo, both outside its walls and within them.

That struggle could not be more relevant now. In the 10 years since I started formally researching this book, journalism has undergone seismic change that shows no signs of stopping.

Corporate ownership continues to starve newspapers for profits, making demands for money on what should be regarded as a public service. For all that they blame readers' changing tastes for declines in subscriptions and sales, newspaper company CEOs reward themselves with bonuses and shareholders with returns while telling their reporters there's no money for journalism. Marketing and distribution suffer under the budget-cutter's knife as well, so that communities no longer know which is "their" paper, nor why they should care about it.

As ever, new media challenge the established press. Ten years ago, newspapers gloomily predicted the death of print within the decade; now, they repeat their erroneous predictions and attempt to ape the Internet instead of using it as the reporting tool it can be. Frantic attempts to follow every online entertainment trend diminish newspapers' still-relevant strengths in foreign report-

AFTERWORD

ing and especially community journalism, the sorts of cops-courts-schools coverage that connects a paper to its readers. Like a crow to a shiny object on the sidewalk, editors and "newsroom managers" flock to the next big thing, and what has worked for decades is discarded without thought.

The student press is not immune from these difficulties. Last year, the Gannett Newspaper Company began buying student papers, including the *Central Florida Future* at the University of Central Florida. Should the corporate ownership model overtake the independent student press, the journalism students currently learning the trade could find themselves suffering the same demands for profits as their "professional" counterparts — and paying the same price.

Those who seek answers to these crises in media are quick to look everywhere but at the beginning. Good journalism begins with good journalists, and good journalists begin with good training.

Journalism needs people who will stand up for the integrity of what they do from their first day at their first job because they know how hard it is to do it, and how important that it be done. It needs people who spent their earliest professional years not submitting to but fighting off suffocating economics, daily competition, and deadline anxiety. It needs people who were studying practicalities the pressroom, as well as hypotheticals in the classroom.

Journalism needs reporters and editors and photographers and artists and copy editors and salespeople and publishers who do not see themselves as part of the established order, who do not feel beholden to reputations, who are not cowed by power because as kids of nineteen and twenty they stood up to the powerful. It needs people who know that before being favored and being famous comes being fair, and being honest.

Journalism needs the *Daily Cardinal* right now, and the precious few other student papers like it. Journalism needs an example of a newspaper that takes its meager profits and puts them back into the newsroom, that teaches that words like truth and idealism are only ridiculous when you mock them from the sidewalk instead of living them in the street. Journalism needs a place where people are trained in healthy skepticism, not blanket cynicism.

Every year, young people leave the *Cardinal* having celebrated a real victory, mourned a real failure, made a lasting enemy, found a lifelong love, made someone laugh, made someone think, stretched farther, worked harder and believed more deeply than they ever have before that they can, in fact, change some small part of the world they live in for the better. They know this is possible because they saw it happen.

They made it happen, and the power of that never fades away, and nothing can take it from them.

There are a vanishingly small number of places left where you learn not just to read and write but to think and argue and care, by doing, by trying and failing and succeeding. The *Daily Cardinal* is one of them, and those who care about it must value that and support it, if they care about and value the future of the trade in which they work.

AFTERWORD

One of the difficulties of addressing the challenges of the student press is that there is little established scholarship on the topic. What student newspaper histories do exist, newspaper staffs have written most themselves, and have published them privately. Papers and surveys are tucked away in master's program theses, scattered in university libraries across the country (to which my interlibrary loan fees can attest). If the independent student press is to escape the travails that have befallen its grown-up counterpart, it will need the collective efforts of those thinkers and critics who aim to study journalism's future brought to bear on the very places where that future is birthed.

Great institutions like the *Cardinal* cannot be left to the mercy of market forces, or allowed to succumb to the attrition of time and be dismissed with a shrug and a fond regret. Not when solutions of every kind abound, from university foundations to generous alumni to non-profit institutions making of the vague desire to improve media actual fact each day. Not when money can be spent in the millions on every other facet of the newspaper trade.

Not when the *Cardinal* has so much to teach, and an endless supply of people eager to learn, and has not begun, in its second century, to even approach outliving its usefulness.

Newspapers continue to pronounce their own deaths and be reborn almost every day. After so many years of study of the *Daily Cardinal*'s history, I can only say I fervently hope that the paper's spirit of defying the expected and accepted continues to apply to itself as well.

I hope that those who learned never to give up at the *Cardinal* will never give up on the *Cardinal*, no matter what the market might say.

– *Allison Hantschel*
May 2007

Appendix: Notable Alumni

During its 110th anniversary in 2002, the *Daily Cardinal* honored what are widely considered to be its 110 most notable alumni, whether for their professional advancements or their contributions to the *Cardinal*. They were:

Eileen Alt Powell
Edited first Associated Press Style Guide

Michael Arndt
Chicago Tribune business editor

Arlene Bahr Chandler
First female Business Manager

Ed Bark
Syndicated TV critic

Cliff Behnke
2nd Cardinal Board Alumni Director; editor of Wisconsin State Journal

Gail Bensinger
International editor, San Francisco Chronicle

Lowell Bergman
Former producer, 60 Minutes

Tom Bernthal
Kept Cardinal board from closing Cardinal

Robert Besteman
Started Walldebig & Besteman

Willard J. Bleyer
Founder, UW Journalism School

APPENDIX

Nancy Bobrowitz
Former Senior Vice President of Corporate Communications for Reuters US

Walt Bogdanich
New York Times Pulitzer Prize winner 1988; 2004

Filip Bondy
Sports columnist, New York Daily News

Nathan Brackett
Senior Editor, Rolling Stone

Rita Braver
Former Chief White House Correspondent; CBS News reporter

Jane Brody
New York Times reporter and columnist

Dorothy Browne Haines
First female Cardinal Editor in chief

James Burgess
Former Publisher, Wisconsin State Journal

Avram Butensky
Former president, TV Bureau of Advertising

Porter Butts
First director of the Wisconsin Union

Tim Carroll
Business manager 1986-87; helped work through Herald takeover attempt

Jeff Cesario
4-time ACE winner; 2-time Emmy winner

APPENDIX

James Cohen
Senior Coordinating Producer, ESPN Sportscenter

Ted Crabb
Second director of the Wisconsin Union

Randy Curwen
Travel Editor, Chicago Tribune

John Darnton
Author, Pulitzer Prize winner 1986

Richard Davis
Editor of 1938 Strike Cardinal

Susan Davis
CEO, Susan Davis International

Tricia Deering
Ran Cardinal Centennial Celebration

Nancy Dickerson
NBC TV correspondent

Robert Drechsel
UW Journalism professor, Daily Cardinal board member; thwarted Herald takeover attempt

Gary Dretzka
Former Los Angeles correspondent, Chicago Tribune

John Eugster
Business manager of 1976 Strike Cardinal

Vincent F. Filak
Fixed Cardinal's finances to recover from 1995 shutdown

APPENDIX

Belle Fliegelman
Started Cardinal Women's Page in 1911

Ellen Foley
Editor-in-chief, Wisconsin State Journal

Peter Fox
Secretary of Employee Relations, State of Wisconsin

Samuel Freedman
Professor of Journalism, Columbia University

Steve Geiger
Business manager of Centennial Cardinal

Mark Giaimo
Editorial cartoonist and artist

Abigail Goldman
Los Angeles Times reporter, Pulitzer Prize winner 1993; 2004

Gregory Graze
Editor in chief, 1967-68; dealt with first fallout of 1960s

Peter Greenberg
Author, travel editor for NBC

Jeff Greenfield
2-time Emmy winner; CBS Political Correspondent

John Gruber
1965 managing editor; fought McCarthyism

Bessie Haggerty
Cardinal's first female staff member and first female reporter, 1892

APPENDIX

Phil Haslanger
Managing Editor, The Capital Times

Peter Heise
President and publisher, The Onion

Mahlon Hinkson
Longtime Daily Cardinal printer; manager of Campus Publishing Company

Daniel W. Hoan
Former mayor of Milwaukee

Hazel Holden Stauffacher
First female president, Daily Cardinal Board

Phil Holen
20-year Cardinal printer

Dirk Johnson
Chicago bureau chief, Newsweek

Jules Joseph
Started major Milwaukee public relations firm

Peter Kafka
Writer, Forbes magazine

Andy Katz
Chief of Correspondents, ESPN

John Keefe
Editor-in-chief 1987, led Cardinal during Herald takeover attempt

Steve Kerch
Former real estate editor, Chicago Tribune

APPENDIX

Adam Kolton
Advertising manager 1989, helped Cardinal during Type Lab shutdown

John Kovalic
Syndicated cartoonist, Wild Life

Brannon Lambert
Business manager 1989, helped resolve Typography Lab shutdown

Rocco Landesman
Theater critic

Greg Larson
Editor-in-chief during Cardinal Centennial

Orv Larson
20-year Cardinal printer

Adam Lasker
One of only three print photographers allowed into School Choice hearings before the Wisconsin Supreme Court; Editor in chief 1999-2000

Richard Leonard
Former Editor in chief, Milwaukee Journal

Morton Levine
Publisher, chain of California newspapers

Robert Lewis
Editor-in-chief 1941; led Cardinal through early days of World War II

Irwin Maier
Business manager 1918, former chairman of the Journal Co.

Eileen Martinson Levine
Helped lead Cardinal's all-female World War II staff

APPENDIX

Helen Matheson Rupp
Staff member, Wisconsin State Journal

Karl Meyer
Former Editorial Board member, The New York Times

Alice Munro Haagensen
Oldest living Daily Cardinal alumna (103)

Eric Newhouse
Pulitzer Prize winner 2000

Dave Newman
20-year Cardinal printer

Edwin Newman
Former NBC News anchor

Miriam Ottenberg
Washington Evening Star reporter, Pulitzer Prize winner, 1960

John Patrick Hunter
Former Editorial Page editor, The Capital Times

Keenan Peck
Organized 95th reunion; started work on first Alumni Association

Roger Rathke
Starter major Rockford public relations firm

Cheryl Reddeman
Cardinal office manager, 24 years

Steven Reiner
Producer, CBS News

APPENDIX

Dyann Rivkin
TV writer

Jim Rowen
Writer, Profit Motive 101 series, exposed university corruption

Anthony Sansone
Founder, Daily Cardinal Alumni Association

Maureen Santini
Former White House correspondent, Associated Press

William Saucerman
First Cardinal business manager

Jerrold Schechter
Former Moscow bureau chief, Time Magazine

Leona Schechter
Author and reporter

Richard Schickel
Film critic, Time Magazine; author of 29 books

Clarence Schoenfeld
Author of books about University of Wisconsin

Dan Schwartz
Helped fund Cardinal's 1995 return from shutdown

Anthony Shadid
Baghdad correspondent, Washington Post, Pulitzer Prize Winner 2003

Marilyn Shuman
First female managing editor; founder of Cardinal scholarship fund

APPENDIX

Jeff Smoller
First Cardinal Board Alumni Director

Paul Soglin
Former Mayor of Madison, attorney, and author

Rena Steinzor
Editor-in-chief, 1970; editorial policies resulted in lasting "radical" reputation for the Cardinal

Ivan Strmecki
Managing editor 1989, led Cardinal during Typography Lab shutdown

James Sturm
Artist and cartoonist, Down and Out Dawg

Bill Swislow
Editor-in-chief of 1976 Strike Cardinal

Robert Taylor
UW Journalism professor, assistant to UW chancellor, 36-year Cardinal board member

Robert Teague
Peabody, Emmy Award winner

Chris Terry
Helped restore Cardinal after 1995 shutdown

Carol Toussaint
PR executive; University of Wisconsin Foundation board member

Neal Ulevich
Photographer, Pulitzer Prize winner 1977

Mark Wegner
Editor-in-chief 1996-97, following Cardinal comeback

APPENDIX

Patricia Wells
Food critic and author, International Herald Tribune

William Wesley Young
Founder of the Cardinal

Mike Wilmington
Film critic, Chicago Tribune

Jonathan Wolman
Former editor-in-chief, Associated Press

ABOUT THE AUTHOR

Allison Hantschel graduated from the University of Wisconsin in 1996, and the *Daily Cardinal* in 1997. She is a ten-year veteran of newspaper journalism and the editor of the anthology, *Special Plans: The Blogs on Douglas Feith and the Faulty Intelligence that Led to War*. Her work has appeared in the *Chicago Sun-Times*, the *Daily Southtown, On Wisconsin, Sirens* magazine and *Alternet*. She blogs at First-Draft.com.

www.ingramcontent.com/pod-product-compliance
Lightning Source LLC
Chambersburg PA
CBHW060118170426
43198CB00010B/935